The Seven Summers of the Apocalypse
A New Journey Through the Book of Revelation

T. Mark Cossette

WESTBOW
PRESS®
A DIVISION OF THOMAS NELSON
& ZONDERVAN

WestBow Press
A Division of Thomas Nelson & Zondervan
1663 Liberty Drive
Bloomington, IN 47403
www.westbowpress.com
1 (866) 928-1240

ISBN: 978-1-5127-5771-2 (sc)
ISBN: 978-1-5127-5772-9 (hc)
ISBN: 978-1-5127-5770-5 (e)

Library of Congress Control Number: 2016916194

Print information available on the last page.

WestBow Press rev. date: 11/22/2016

To my dear wife Rachel and our two boys Stephen and David

PREFACE

Paradox: n. statement that seems absurd but may be true.

Throughout the history of the Church, the book of Revelation has been viewed as the written word of God—and a collection of enigmatic statements and images that none can fully understand.

As far back as Roman times, some of the Faithful regarded the book's very name a cruel euphemism since it is so steeped in cryptic imagery its revealing truth eludes its myriad of readers.[1] Nevertheless the Revelation remains the concluding book of the Christian Bible and through the ages a never-ending mystery for all who read it. To the present day, the book of Revelation has been the focus of educated speculation and colorful imagination by cleric, scholar, laity, and Hollywood. The result of such centuries-old attraction to the Revelation is the largest compilation of topical literature than any other book in the Bible.[2] Today, on the subject of Biblical eschatology (study of the End-Times), the Church has three primary views with their marked emphasis on the Revelation.

Futurism has the present attention of the Christian pop culture. As it is named, this view espouses the prophecies of the Revelation as future events.[3] Generally, Futurism offers the scenario of a Satan-empowered despot ruling a global anti-Christian dystopia for seven years prior to a literal Second Coming of Jesus Christ.[4] During this dark interval, the Faithful are supernaturally transported into the Heavenly realm; popularly called "the Rapture."

Recently, Preterism has been on the rise, but like Futurism, its basic tenets go far back into Church history. In strict classical terms, Preterism offers the Revelation as primarily fulfilled in the destruction of Jerusalem and the Temple by the Romans in A.D. 70, which is tagged as the 'judgment-coming' of Christ.[5]

Though having waned lately but still not without advocates, Historicism was an interpretative pillar of the Protestant Reformation. Indeed, such names belonging to Historicism were Martin Luther, William Tyndale, Ulrich Zwingli, John Knox, and John Calvin. Briefly, Historicism claims that Revelation's fulfillment span from the Apostolic Period (A.D. 33–70), across the entire Church Age, and to be concluded with a literal Second Coming of Christ.[6] Further, one of the more controversial points of Historicism is the assertion that the Roman Catholic Church is the Whore of Revelation 17, with the Papacy as the Beast whom the Whore rides (Rev. 17:2–6).[7]

All three eschatology schools base their arguments on the authority of Scripture. Partisans of each view insist they're right, while claiming the other two are sincerely, if not heretically, wrong. The primary cause for such a range of opinion is that the book of Revelation is typically approached with a flawed premise: the book is never allowed to speak for itself. Moreover, such a premise is engaged at the very beginning of the Revelation.

In the opening verses, the author states that the book's foretold events are to be fulfilled contemporary to the writing of the book itself:

> "The Revelation of Jesus Christ, which God gave unto
> him, to show unto his servants things which must *shortly
> come to pass*; and he sent and signified it by his angel unto
> his servant John. Who bare record of the word of God,
> and of the testimony of Jesus Christ, and of all things that
> he saw. Blessed is he that readeth, and they that hear the
> words of this prophecy, and keep those things which are
> written therein: *for the time is at hand.*[8]

In essence, this short-term temporal theme, found at the beginning of the book, and near its end (Rev. 22:6 and 10), serves as the gate keepers and bouncers to the book of Revelation. Because of this, when one reads through the book of Revelation, the reader enters and leaves the book with text-given knowledge that the foretold events of the book will "shortly come to pass". Whenever these verses are disregarded, one forfeits to understand the book's true message, and is left to wander the dark alleys of theory, guess work, and imagination. Nevertheless, rationalizing attempts have been made within the Church to do just that.

To the reference "shortly come to pass", the Futurist camp will insist that the fulfillment of the Revelation will not happen in the temporal *when*, but in the methodical *how*. So "shortly" is to mean 'suddenly', 'quickly', or 'rapidly' once the foretold events begin to happen. However, this assertion flies in the face of one English version of the Bible after another that clearly translates Revelation 1:1 in the time-orientated "shortly" or "soon".[9] The second short-term temporal aspect, "the time is at hand" (Rev. 1:3), Futurists assert that "time" is not based man's conception of time, but on God's. To shore up this point, Futurists cite II Peter 3:8, which states "one day is with the Lord as a thousand years, and a thousand years as one day". Therefore, according to Futurism, "the time is at hand" does not mean 'near' or "at hand" in the conventional clock and calendar sense of time, but in some ethereal other worldly notion.

However, when reading Revelation 20:2–7 regarding the Second Coming with the *thousand-year* reign of Christ, while through the lens of II Peter 3:8, does this mean said events will happen for only one day? The likely Futurist response would be 'of course not'. Why? Because Futurists allow Revelation 20:2–7 to speak on its own whereas they don't give Revelation 1:1–3 that same exegetic luxury, hence a conflicted premise when approaching the book.

The Preterism, on the other hand, does acknowledge Revelation 1:1–3 as "soon" and "near" in the natural sense. However, to the Second Coming of Christ as viewed in Revelation 19:11–16 and 20:2–7, Preterism makes the same premise mistake in preventing the book to speak. Instead of an incarnate return of the Risen Christ, traditional Preterists take said passages as a 'judgment-coming' of Christ in the A.D. 70 Destruction. What follows is the Gospel preached and eventually accepted throughout the world, which symbolizes the New Heaven and New Earth of Revelation 21–22. Such is classic Preterism's end-game, despite the highly obvious fact that the manifest glory and presence of the Father remains absent from the world while death, sorrow, and suffering remain (Rev. 21:3–4, 23; 22:5).[10]

Historicism makes the claim that Revelation's fulfillment spans from the generation that saw the First Coming of Jesus Christ to the generation that will witness his Second Coming. However, Historicism's interpretive gravity is centered on the events of 1500s to 1700s Europe and with much anti-Papal sentiment along the way. That time period in mind, and the Papacy not becoming an ecclesiastical monolith until generations after the Apostolic Period, such hardly constitutes "shortly come to pass" and "the time is at hand".

Though the three main views read the book in an inconsistent manner, they do share one common truth in that the Revelation speaks of historical persons, places, and events. In principal, for the Revelation to be properly understood, the three main views correctly depend on the unfolding of human history.[11]

So what is the correct way to approach the book of Revelation and read it? With the Revelation's prophetic message due to "shortly come to pass" (Rev. 1:1–3), with a literal Second Coming of Jesus Christ (Rev. 19–20:6), the reader is faced by what is known as a *paradox*: "a statement that seems absurd but maybe true". Probably, many throughout Church history have noticed this paradox in the Revelation. However, rather than trying to understand and resolve it, the paradox is either ignored or the short-term temporal references of Revelation 1:1–3 and 22:6, 10 are to mean something they are not. By not allowing the Revelation to speak on its own, and refusing to address the paradox, such has been an age-old stumbling block for any who reads the book and fails to understand it. To confront, learn, and resolve the paradox of the Revelation, one must allow the book to speak for itself.

When entering the book of Revelation, the first step is to realize that the book is the *Revelation of Jesus Christ*, not the Apostle John as incorrectly tagged in some Bible versions. It is Jesus Christ who receives the Revelation from God the Father and shows it to John (John 15:15). This is the same Jesus who spoke with paradoxical expression more than once during his ministry. Such includes the parable of the mustard seed (Mark 4:30–32)[12]; "The first shall be last and the last first." (Mark 10:31)[13]; "And whosoever of you will be the chiefest, shall be servant of all." (Matt. 20:26; Mark 10:44); "Except a Man be born again, he cannot see the kingdom of God." (John 3:3); and "Destroy this temple, and in three days I will raise it up." (John 2:19).

In order to resolve the paradox of the Revelation, one must go back to the days when Jesus of Nazareth walked the Earth; back to Passion Week in Jerusalem just days before his crucifixion. Back to that moment when the Nazarene delivered the most scathing indictment to his enemies, and shared the most wonderful yet frightening message with those whom he loved.

PART I

Preparing for the Journey

CHAPTER 1

Palms, Olives, and Stones

Several days after his Palm Sunday entry into the city, and two days before his crucifixion, Jesus of Nazareth defiantly stood across from the Scribes and Pharisees in the courts of the Jerusalem Temple.

There, his disciples watching, the Nazarene verbally scourged those religious leaders of Israel for keeping Torah (the Law of Moses) in a superficial manner of misguided priorities.[14] From such conduct, neglecting the spirit of Torah for external performance, ceremony, and the burdens of tradition, Jesus denounced their faith worthy of only the grave. Like their ancestors in the days of the Prophets, Jesus forewarned that these leaders would lethally reject those Jesus would subsequently send to them. Such action would make these leaders of Israel accessory-heirs to the murdered Faithful of Scripture, from Abel to Zechariah, to which such would occur contemporary with those present.[15]

Next, Jesus addressed all of Israel through Jerusalem, capitol of the Jewish nation and heart of its ancient and weather-resistant faith. Jesus lamented on how the Nation killed the Prophets and others whom God had sent to them. How he wanted to bring the Nation under his protection, but they refused.[16] Jesus then prophesied two visuals. First, because they rejected him, the Jewish nation will *see* their house, the Jerusalem Temple, abandoned for destruction. Second, the Nation would no longer *see* the Nazarene, *until* they welcome him back in the spirit of Psalms 118:26 (Matt. 23:38–39; Luke 13:35).

After addressing the Jewish nation, Jesus turned and departed the Temple complex, making this his last public appearance there. Leaving the hallowed precincts via the Treasury, one of Jesus' disciples commented on the Temple's

1

beautiful stonework and architecture. Architecture such as the colonnade courts, gates, ritual chambers, and the very Sanctuary itself. Within that sacred house was the Holy Place, where the duty Priests performed their appointed functions at the altar of incense and the table of shewbread. Both performed in the radiant glow of the seven-branch menorah. These representing the presence of the One True and Invisible God among Israel. Beyond, and pass the great veil, was to the inner chamber of the Holiest Place, where the Covenant-Presence of God dwelt in the darkness.

Still walking and in reply, Jesus gave another visual: Not one stone from the Sanctuary or any of adjoining buildings will be left upon another. One day, Jesus declared, the Temple and all its' functioning buildings will be ruined to its foundations.[17]

Though astonished at these horrid forecasts, the disciples were not unfamiliar with them.

Just days earlier, Jesus made his colt-borne entry into Jerusalem in fulfillment of Zechariah 9:9. Just prior to that entry, as they crested the Mount of Olives from Bethphage, Jesus and his disciples took in their first view of Jerusalem, the holy city of David. As they did, looking at the city and Temple, Jesus began tearing. Descending the mount and drawing near to Jerusalem, Jesus heavily mourned, saying that the city would one day be leveled to the ground, "...not one stone upon another". He added that such would be divine judgment upon the Nation, "because thou knewest not the time of thy visitation". Further still, Jesus said this coming destruction will be witnessed by that same generation of Israel, and their children, that saw his entry into Jerusalem (Luke 19:41–44).[18] As he rode through the city gates on the colt, his disciples and public waved palms and hailed him the Messiah, and the restoration of the kingdom of David (Matt. 21:1–11; Mark 11:1–11; Luke 19:28–44; John 12:12–16).

Now, exiting the Temple, the disciples again heard their Master foretell the destruction of the Temple as Daniel (9:26–27) and Zechariah (11:1–13) did. Yet, there was something else the disciples could not but wonder. What about the other part of the Master's prophecy: the Jewish nation never seeing him again, until they welcome him back in accordance to Psalms 118:26?

Outside the Temple, Jesus and the disciples crossed the Kidron Valley and to the nearby Mount of Olives. With its' namesake olive trees and grand vista, the great hill was an ideal place to find rest, yet remain close to the holy city. Once settled on the mount, four of the disciples, two pair of brothers, Simon Peter and Andrew b. Jonah, with James and John b. Zebedee, approached Jesus.

> "And as he sat upon the Mount of Olives over against the temple, Peter and James and John and Andrew asked him privately. Tell us, when shall these things be? And what shall be the sign when all these things shall be fulfilled? Mark 13:3–4

With Jerusalem and the Temple in panoramic view before these five Galilean Jews, Jesus answered his disciples by giving them a series of signs that will herald the coming destruction, and more.

He begins by telling them to not be deceived:

> "For many shall come in my name, saying, I am Christ; and shall deceive many. And ye shall hear of wars and rumors of wars: see that ye be not troubled: for all these things must come to pass, but the end is not yet. For nation shall rise against nation, and kingdom against kingdom: and there shall be famines, and pestilences, and earthquakes, in divers places. All these are the beginning of sorrows. Matthew 24:5–8

By themselves, the general signs Jesus gave to the Apostles could apply to nearly any period in history, including their own time. In fact, the coinciding of false messiahs, plus wars/rumors of wars, famines, plagues, and earthquakes during the Apostolic Period have been documented by contemporary and semi-contemporary sources:

False Messiahs: the Samaritan on Mount Gerizim, ca. A.D. 36[19]; Theudas at the Jordan, ca. A.D. 45[20]; the Egyptian on the Mount of Olives, ca. A.D. 55[21]; Menahem b. Judas in the Temple, A.D. 66[22]; Vespasian Caesar, A.D. 69[23].

Wars/rumors of wars: Herod Antipas' conflict with Aretas of Arabia, ca. A.D. 36[24]; planned Roman invasion of Arabia, A.D. 36–37[25]; Caligula

Caesar's intended invasion of Judea, A.D. 40[26]; the Roman conquest of Mauretania, ca. A.D.42[27]; Herod Agrippa's suspected revolt against Rome, A.D. 43[28]; the Roman invasion of Britain, A.D. 43[29]; Parthian attempts to annex Armenia, followed by a Roman military response A.D. 35–63[30]; revolt of Boudicca in Britain, A.D. 60–61[31].

Famines: World famines from mid-40s to the 50s[32]; an engineered famine on Rome, A.D. 69[33]; engineered famine on Jerusalem, A.D.70[34].

Plagues: Babylonia, A.D.40[35]; Armenia, A.D.51[36]; Rome, A.D.65.[37]

Earthquakes: Jerusalem, ca. A.D. 34[38]; Rome A.D. 51[39]; Apamea, A.D. 53[40]; Philippi, ca. A.D. 53[41]; Laodicea, A.D. 60[42]; Pompeii, A.D. 62[43]; Jerusalem, A.D. 66[44]; eastern Italy, A.D. 68[45]; Rome, A.D. 68.[46]

After disclosing these general signs, Jesus then gave information of a more specific and direct nature. Truly, with the four listening to Jesus' every word, the next series of signs will bring the time of "the End" far closer to home.

> "Then shall they deliver you up to be afflicted, and shall kill you: and ye shall be hated of all nations for my name's sake. And then shall many be offended, and shall betray one another, and shall hate one another. And many false prophets shall rise, and shall deceive many. And because iniquity shall abound, the love of many shall wax cold. Matthew 24:9–12.[47]

Almost from its' beginning, a climate of resentment and hostility against Apostolic Church reached a point of fatality. Such was the case in the stoning of Stephen in ca. A.D. 35, and soon followed by the aggressive hunt for Christians by Saul of Tarsus (Acts 6:9–8:3). Next was the death of James b. Zebedee by Herod Agrippa in A.D.44 (Acts 12:1–2). On the eve of Passover of A.D. 62, the Sadducean-led Sanhedrin in Jerusalem carried out a summary execution on James the Just.[48] Finally, beginning in A.D. 64, and as a bloody climax to the Apostolic Age, the sadistic persecution of Nero saw the death of a vast number of Christians in Rome.[49] With news of persecution reverberating throughout the Greco-Roman East, an unfavorable demeanor was expressed towards any who proclaimed Jesus of Nazareth as Lord and Savior.[50]

During this same general time, violence, villainy, and false prophets, rummaged throughout the land of Israel. In the early 50s, the *Sicarii*, one of the first politically orientated terrorist organizations, emerged in Judea. Their specialty: assassination, which included the Jewish high priest Jonathan b. Annas, and followed by the murder of many others. By A.D. 65, with the thought of national revolt on many of minds, a great fear, suspicion, and distrust grew among the general public.[51] Moreover, whole families were divided in whether to support the revolt against Rome: the younger generation wanting armed conflict while the older refused to take part.[52]

While Jesus told the Apostles they would face persecution, the rise of violence and immorality, he also assured they would receive help. Help in a very particular way.

> "But when they shall lead you, and deliver you up, take no thought beforehand what ye shall speak, neither do ye premeditate: but whatsoever shall be given in that hour, that speak ye: for it is not ye that speak, but the Holy Ghost. Mark 13:11.

On the pilgrim-feast of *Shavuot* (Pentecost, A.D. 33), and in fulfillment of Joel 2:28–32, the Holy Spirit descended on the Apostles and fellow Faithful, thereby commencing the work of the Church to announce the Gospel to Israel and the World (Acts 2:1–40). Despite the newborn Church facing deadly persecution, by the guiding assistance of the Holy Spirit, the Faithful will bring the Gospel message out from Jerusalem to Judea, Samaria, and "to the uttermost part of the earth" (Acts 1:8).

> "And this gospel of the kingdom shall be preached in all the world for a witness unto all nations; and then shall the end come. Matthew 24:14

Unlike the Greek *cosmos* (κοσμος), which owns a global/universal designation (Matt. 24:21, 25:34; Mark 14:9; John 3:16), "world" in Matthew 24:14 is *oikoumene* (οικουμενη). This term speaks more to the immediate realm of civilization: the Roman Empire.[53] After the Pentecost outpouring of the Spirit in Jerusalem, churches in Judea, Galilee, and Samaria soon followed. Next, a gathering of Christian faithful was found in Damascus. So notable were the Christians of Damascus, Saul of Tarsus was commissioned by the High Priest in Jerusalem to journey to that ancient city to make arrests. A journey that proved well interrupted (Acts 9:11–19).

Under divine instruction, the Apostle Peter set the precedent in presenting the Gospel directly to Gentiles in the baptism of the Cornelius family in Caesarea (Acts 10:1-11:18). By A.D. 45, a robust Antioch congregation of Jewish and Gentile believers flourished in Syria. Moreover, a remote outpost of Christian fellowship was found even in Rome.[54] Soon, a Gentile mission, carried out by Paul (formerly Saul of Tarsus) and Barnabas, and sanctioned by the Apostles and Jerusalem church, began (Acts 15:1–35; Gal. 2:1–9). The Gospel message had traveled from Judea to Antioch, Cyprus, Galatia, Asia, Macedonia, and Athens, with newborn churches in the wake. Further, such an evangelical task was achieved inside a twenty-five year period, which in historical terms was of considerable speed.[55] By the early 60s, a Christian foothold was firmly and widely planted in the Roman world. Once this beachhead of Christian evangelism was accomplished, so the Gospel may further proceed to the entire globe, the time of "the End" began.

After giving the Apostles the general signs, followed by more specific signs, Jesus began to disclose the *one* sign that will herald the coming of God's judgment and wrath. As Jesus spoke to the Apostles, back across the Kidron Valley toward the city, a lone column of smoke rose from the Temple. Inside the Court of the Priest, and in the sacerdotal service of said personnel, the daily sacrifices burned on the great altar as stipulated by Torah.[56] As the fire took the offering, the billowing smoke rose from the altar and went heaven-ward.

> "When ye therefore shall see the abomination of desolation spoken by Daniel the prophet, stand in the holy place (whose readeth, let him understand,) Then let them which be in Judea flee into the mountains; Let him which is on the housetop not come down to take anything out of his house. Neither let him which is in the field return back to take his clothes. Matthew 24:15–18

After the Gospel message was initially introduced to Israel and the Roman world, a desecration would occur inside the Temple. Specifically, a defilement of the Sanctuary as foretold by Daniel to prelude its' destruction (Dan 9:26–27). Furthermore, by citing Daniel to be read and understood, Jesus indicated to the Apostles that the otherwise sealed book of Daniel was now opened.[57]

Once the Faithful of Jerusalem and Judea witness this initial act of sacrilege in the Temple, they are to depart from Jerusalem and not return. For the many the Torah-observant Jewish Christians of Judea however, to leave the city and not return would be very difficult. To depart and remain away from Jerusalem would mean to disregard the Torah in observance to the pilgrim-feasts of Israel. Since the Sanctuary was at Jerusalem, all men of Israel were to stand "before the Lord" in the Temple during the three pilgrim-feasts: Passover/Unleavened Bread, Pentecost, and Tabernacles.[58] Because of this situation, many Jewish Christians might have allowed exceptional pilgrimages to Jerusalem and the Temple to comply with the feasts.

However, Jesus provided a second and final warning-sign to all to leave Jerusalem and *never* return. This second sign offered definitive proof that God's judgment on Israel was set and approaching.

> "And when ye shall see Jerusalem compassed with armies,
> then know that desolation thereof is nigh. Then let them
> which are in Judea flee to the mountains, and let them
> which are in the midst of it depart out, and let not them
> that are in the countries enter thereinto. Luke 21:20–21

Soon after the Temple is profaned, armies will surround Jerusalem, making this the final warning to leave and remain away from the city. Once such a military display is seen around the city, the Jewish Christians are to leave Jerusalem; immediately and unconditionally.

Following the departure of the Jewish Christians from the city, a horrific period of divine retribution begins:

> "For these be the days of vengeance, that all things which
> are written may be fulfilled. But woe unto them that

are with child and to them that give suck, in those days, for there shall be great distress in the land, and wrath upon this people. And they shall fall by the edge of the sword, and shall be led away captive into all nations; and Jerusalem shall be trodden down of the Gentiles, until times of the Gentiles be fulfilled. Luke 21:22–24

While Matthew terms it as "great tribulation" (Matt. 24:21), and Mark describes it was "affliction" (Mark 13:19), Luke calls this dire period as "the days of vengeance". It is a time of violence, death, destruction and terror. A time that not even expectant mothers and newborns will be safe. A time when "all things which are written may be fulfilled", and will reach zenith in the bloody destruction of Jerusalem and the Temple. It is a time when Jerusalem will be cast in ruins and the land of Israel is under foreign rule, to which Jesus called the "times of the Gentiles".

"Then shall be great tribulation, such as was not since the beginning of the world to this time, no, nor ever shall be. And except those days should be shortened, there should no flesh be saved: but for the elect's sake those days shall be shortened. Matthew 24:21– 22

Even though the coming Tribulation will have much horror and bloodshed, Jesus assures that genocide shall not be the finale for the Jewish nation. Though the Tribulation will be sure and severe judgments from God, it is God's will that Israel survives, endures, and prevails over it. Therefore, for the sake of the "elect", God will confine the Tribulation to a set period of time (Matt. 24:22; Mark 13:20).

Next, Jesus offers to the Apostles a parting but cryptic snapshot of the Tribulation:

"For wheresoever the carcass is, there will be the eagles be gathered together. Matthew 24:28

Immediately after giving the visual of fowl upon carrion, and with imagery found in the Old Testament, Jesus states that the sun, the moon, and the stars will go dark (Is. 13:10; Joel 2:10, 31; 3:15). Following this darkness, Jesus continues:

> "And then shall they see the Son of Man coming in the
> clouds with great power and glory. Mark 13:26

A clear citation of Daniel 7:13–14, the one called "the Son of Man", and coming in the clouds of Heaven, appears before and is seated with the One whom Daniel calls "the Ancient of Days": i.e. God. Next, seated with God, the Son of Man is given "dominion, and glory, and a kingdom, that all people, nations, and languages should serve him." Not only did Jesus indicate Daniel 7:13–14 as the moment when the Jewish nation will see him again, but see him as the Divine King coming in the clouds of Heaven and glory to rule forever.

Jesus continued:

> "Then shall he send his angels, and shall gather together
> his elect from the four winds, from the uttermost part of
> the earth to the uttermost part of heaven. Mark 13:27

Along with the Jewish nation, and with the Gospel message going out to the Roman world, the proverbial staging area for global evangelism, his "elect" shall be from all nations. The "four winds" representing the four directions of the map to where the Holy Spirit will travel, all who declare and live Jesus Christ as their Savior and Lord will witness his glorious return. For this to happen, he will gather all who are in Christ, Jew and Gentile, near and far, living and dead, to witness and welcome his Second Coming as the glorious King-Messiah.

Next, Jesus makes his summation: the parable of the fig tree. Like all fruit trees, when the branches get tender and bud, such indicates the soon arrival of summer. So in the same manner, when they see all the disclosed warning signs come to pass, they were to recognize his return as near; at the very doors.[59]

Finally, to close his summation, Jesus gives the most focused statement in the Olivet Discourse:

"Verily I say unto you, this generation shall not pass away, till all these things take place. Heaven and Earth will pass away but my words will never pass away.[60]

After this point, the synoptic Gospels depart in form but not in underlying theme. In Matthew, Jesus compares the general time of his return to the days of Noah. But of the exact day and hour, God the Father only knows. Next, he follows up with a series of parables (the Two Servants, the Ten Virgins, and the Talents), and a description of Judgment Day (Matt.24:36–25:46). By Mark's account, Jesus emphasizes to be watchful, for his return is unknown and ends with the parable of the Long Journey (Mark 13:32–37). According to Luke, Jesus cautions his listeners to not go unaware, but remain prayerfully vigil so to escape what is to come, and be worthy to stand before him at his return (Luke 17:22–30).

Two days later, Jesus hung dead on a Roman cross. A crown of thorns on his head, a spear thrust to his side, and the veil to the Temple's Holiest Place ripped in two for Eternity.

Because of the similarities between the Olivet Discourse and the Revelation, the Discourse has been given the pseudonym "little Apocalypse".[61] So notable are the similarities, a consensus is held that the Olivet Discourse of Matthew 24, Mark 13, and Luke 21 was the prophetic base for the book of Revelation.[62] However, when determining a time-frame of fulfillment for both the Discourse and the Revelation, the two main eschatology camps, Preterism and Futurism, part company. In the debate between the two camps, the crux issue is *which* generation "will not pass till all these things be done". Is it a generation already past or one in the future?

According to Preterism, the generation of Israel that saw Jesus' Palm-Sunday entry into Jerusalem, and the A.D.70 Destruction by the Romans, was the generation of the Olivet Discourse. As for the Second Coming, classic Preterits argue the destruction of Jerusalem and the Temple as the 'judgment-coming' of Christ upon an apostate Jewish nation. With the Temple destroyed, representing the abolishment of the Sinai Covenant and "the end of the [Jewish] age", the New Covenant comes into matured manifestation for all future time. The Second Coming (Rev. 19), the New

Heaven and New Earth (Rev. 21:1) serve only as allegories to that finished manifestation.[63] In connection, the perception that the 'End of days' was just over the contemporary horizon is represented in more than a few passages of the New Testament.[64] Moreover, expectation of a soon-coming 'End' was not exclusive to first generation Christianity. As evidenced in the Dead Sea Scrolls, the Judaic Qumran community, clear contemporaries to the Apostolic Church, held similar expectations that the 'End of days' was nigh.[65]

In response, and with references from the Gospels and Acts,[66] Futurists state that the Second Coming shall be a literal event in future history. According to the Discourse, immediately after the Tribulation, the sun, moon, and stars go dark to herald Jesus' glorious and literal return (Matt. 24:29–30; Mark 13:24–26). Since no such an astronomical event was ever seen and recorded following the A.D. 70 Destruction, Futurists maintain that the generation in question still lies in the future. In addition, from Jesus' parting address to the Nation (Matt. 23:39; Ps.118:26), Futurists assert that the Jewish nation accepting Jesus as the Messiah and the Son of God shall precede the Second Coming.[67]

On historical grounds, that there was a standing Temple to be desecrated and destroyed via Daniel's prophecy makes the Preterist claim valid: The generation of the Olivet Discourse was the generation of Israel that witnessed the coming of Christ and the A.D. 70 Destruction. Nevertheless, the Futurists maintain a very defendable position that the Second Coming of Jesus Christ shall occur in the future, and preceded by the Jewish nation recognizing him as Lord and Messiah. With both eschatology camps having sound arguments, which one is representing prophetic truth in accordance with Scripture: Preterism or Futurism?

Interestingly, perhaps both camps own a share of that truth.

As believed by both camps, the Olivet Discourse serves as a base to the Revelation. However, with that base, the Discourse also provides historical reference for the paradox in the Revelation. In a sentence, the paradox is the following: Immediately *after* the Temple *was* destroyed in A.D. 70, Jesus *will* return—incarnate and in glory—and to be seen by a welcoming Jewish nation and the redeemed from among the Gentiles. This being the paradox, all in Christ must ask the question Nicodemus asked: How can these things be? How can the A.D. 70 Destruction be immediately followed by a literal and future Second Coming of Jesus Christ?

According to Mark 13:3, the Olivet Discourse places Peter, Andrew, James, and John exclusively at the scene with Jesus. The peculiarity of this is that while the three synoptic Gospels contain the Olivet Discourse, it is absent in the Fourth Gospel, traditionally credited to John, who was present at the Discourse. Using parallel passages, John's account *should* contain the Olivet Discourse between the Palm-Sunday entry (John 12:12–19) and preparation for the Last Supper (13:1–2). It is not there, making the absence odd. Even so, there are other Gospel episodes illustrated in the synoptic accounts that go unmentioned in the Fourth Gospel (the Nativity, the Wilderness Temptation, the Sermon on the Mount, the Transfiguration, and the institution of Communion).

But again, what makes the oddness a bit more conspicuous is John 12:31, and is located at the same general narrative point where the Olivet Discourse is found in the synoptic Gospels. In that passage, Jesus speaks of immediate judgment befalling the World and Satan, demonstrating that a contemporary eschatological concept was on the author's mind at that point of the text. Yet, the author refrains from including the Olivet Discourse in the Fourth Gospel. If, on the other hand, the book of Revelation, also credited to one named John, is an explanation of the Olivet Discourse, then its' absence in the Gospel of John begins to make sense.[68] If the Revelation is to explain the Olivet Discourse, then Revelation's author had the same expository inclination as the author of the Fourth Gospel in clarifying particular sayings of Jesus.[69] Not only can this account for the absence of the Olivet Discourse in the Gospel of John, but suggests the original parchments of the Revelation and Fourth Gospel had the same owner, named John.[70]

But how does the Revelation, with all of its' elusive symbolisms, explain the A.D. 70 Destruction to be *immediately* followed by a future and literal Second Coming of Jesus Christ? The next step in learning and resolving this paradox, a particular item in the Revelation must be found and put to sure use.

Specifically, an item called a *key*.

CHAPTER 2

A Key in the pages

The basic mechanics of a key are impressive; perhaps even prophetic. In standard locks, when the correct key is inserted into the matching keyhole, its' distinct edge-pattern causes a series of pins holding the lock's bolt to re-align. Once the key aligns the pins to free the bolt, turning the key causes the bolt to rotate and the lock to open. The explicit reference to keys is found only eight times in the Bible, but with half in the book of Revelation.[71] In the Revelation, keys are seen near the beginning, about middle, and toward the end of the text. Further, the book portrays a variety of parties possessing keys: the demonic claws of a fallen angel, the radiant hands of a heavenly angel, and the pierced hands of the Risen Christ (Rev. 1:18; 3:7; 9:1; 20:1).

During his own time (250AD), and after speaking of all the attack on the book of Revelation by fellow Christians, Dionysius of Alexandria said he would never reject the book as Holy Writ. Rather, he viewed it largely a mystery. Further, he believed that the book's true message was present within its pages but hidden: "some deeper sense is enveloped in the words".[72] Closer to present times, James Stewart Russell (1816–1895) advocated that some kind of *key* was hidden away in the book: "When the right key to the Apocalypse is found it will open every lock".[73]

At the beginning of the Revelation, John offers a blessing to those who read, hear, and keep the things that are written in the book "for the time is at hand" (Rev. 1:3). Near the close of the book, and in contrast to the book of Daniel that was sealed until "the time of the end" (Dan. 12:4, 9), John was instructed to *not* seal up the Revelation, "for the time is at hand" (Rev. 22:10). Does this mean the book is unsealed, or perhaps the book *is* sealed, but the means to unseal it is readily available within its very pages, provided one knows where to look? Such a provision would technically leave the book *unsealed*, as instructed to John.

If a key is truly hidden somewhere in the Revelation to decrypt the book, to "open every lock", it is for the reader to find that key. Still, where in all the sights and sounds of the Revelation can there be a key found to unlock the book? To determine if something is missing or hidden the proper approach is to take an inventory. Question: Is there anything clearly illustrated in the Revelation, yet its underlying meaning *explicitly* concealed? The answer is *yes*, such a situation is found in the book of Revelation: specifically, in Revelation 10.

Standing on the beach of Patmos, John saw a being that he called an "angel" descend from Heaven. Touching down, the Being placed one foot in the sea, the other on the land, and with a loud voice gave off a sound like a lion's roar. Making this sound, *seven thunders* uttered their voices. Hearing the seven thunders, John began to write down what they said. As he did, a Voice from Heaven commanded John to conceal what the seven thunders uttered and not disclose their meaning. Next, the Being lifted his hand towards Heaven, and swore by the Eternal who created all things in Heaven and Earth, "that there should be time no longer" (Rev 10:1–6). Then the Being added, "But in the days of the voice of the seventh angel, when he shall begin to sound, the mystery of God should be finished, as he hath declared to his servants the prophets" (Rev. 10:7).

Just what are these seven thunders? How are they connected with the announcement "that there should be time no longer"? What of the time period called "the days of the voice of the seventh angel" when "the mystery of God should be finished"? Perhaps the more immediate question is why the aesthetic existence of the seven thunders is allowed to be heard, but not their prophetic identity?

Although Scripture makes clear that God keeps particular things to himself,[74] the seven thunders of Revelation 10 need not apply to such a classification. Remembering that God's word does not return to him void, but will accomplish to where God sends it (Is. 55:10–11; note the seasonal features), the truth of the seven thunders is meant be found. Once the undisclosed seven thunders are presented, it is for the reader to seek out what they represent (Prov. 25:2; Matt. 7:7–8). By allowing the seven thunders to be heard, but their prophetic truth kept hidden, God is challenging, not forbidding, the reader to find what the seven thunders said and be blessed (Rev. 1:3). To be clear, the seven thunders are not some deep concept that only the learned and wise can understand, or some Sphinx-like riddle where the answer eludes any and all.

Truly, their discovery is in much simpler terms:

> "When it is evening, ye say, it will be fair weather: for the sky is red. And in the morning, it will be foul weather today: for the sky is red and lowering. O ye hypocrites, ye can discern the face of the sky but can ye not discern the sign of the times.[75]

Generally put, the closer one approaches the summer season the more prone thunder and lightning is encountered. Therefore, the seven thunders of Revelation 10 are *seven summers,* seven consecutive summer seasons, one week of summers. Repeatedly, Scripture illustrates and alludes to the summer as a time of divine judgment.[76] The most notable is the Babylonian Destruction of Jerusalem and the kingdom of Judah in the summer of 586 B.C. and the commencement of the Seventy-year Exile in Babylon (II Chron. 36:15–21; Jer. 52:4–14). In the Gospels, the Isaiah-based parable of the vineyard (Is. 5:1–7; Matt. 21:33–48, Mark 12:1–11, Luke 20:9–18), associates the summer vine harvest with the time of judgment. In the land of Israel, the grape crop ripens and is gathered during the Hebrew months of Av (July/August) and Elul (August/September).[77] In addition, since Elul was the last month of the Jewish agricultural/civil calendar, that closing summer month was naturally perceived as the annual time of 'the End'.[78]

Like a key going into the right keyhole to realign the bolt pins, the seven summers realigns the chapters, seals, trumpets, and bowls of the Revelation into the correct chronological sequence. Once done, the book of Revelation is unlocked, decrypted, and ready to be read. However, if the seven thunders do represent seven summers and is the key to the book of Revelation, the next task is to find the keyhole. Where in the near two-thousand year history of the Church do the seven summers belong? Which year matches with the first summer for the remaining six to follow?

With the generation of the Olivet Discourse cautiously identified as the generation of Israel that saw the coming of Christ and the A.D. 70 Destruction, the first summer must lie between A.D. 33 and 70.[79] This nicely reduces the search parameter from some two-thousand years to thirty-seven years, or about the middle third of the first century A.D. In addition, such a time period aligns with the short-term temporal theme of the Revelation in that the book's prophetic events are to "shortly come to pass", and "the time is at hand". To narrow the search further, the author of Revelation provides clues to identify the first summer.

These clues are the passages of Revelation 13:18 and 17:9–10 that have the attached prefix or the like, "Here is wisdom…" The first passage, Revelation 13:18, names a particular ruler known unflatteringly as "the beast". According to the passage, this ruler owned a name equal to a specific numerical sum:

> "Here is wisdom. Let him who hath understanding count
> the number of the beast; for it is the number of a man;
> and his number is Six hundred threescore and six [666].
> Revelation 13:18.

Since Greek is the text language of Revelation, the premise went that finding the number-name of "the beast" depended on counting the letters of the Greek alphabet in their numerical value.[80] However, and despite labored attempts, no recognizable name has ever been deciphered from this premise. Yet, while Greek is the textual language of the Revelation, another language is also found in the book. Repeatedly, the author of Revelation employed Hebrew or Aramaic with respect to persons (*Abaddon*, Rev. 9:11), places (*Armageddon*, Rev. 16:16), and proclamations (*Hallelujah*, Rev. 19:1–6).[81] When applying the letter-number values of the Hebrew/Aramaic alphabet to the sum of 666, a specific name does add up. A name owned by a Man well known to Roman, Jew, and Christian alike.

The Name: *Nero Caesar,* or in the Semite phonetic, *Nrwn Qsr* (רסק נורנ). [82]

$$\text{נ (N)} = 50 \qquad \text{ק (Q)} = 100$$

$$\text{ר (R)} = 200 \qquad \text{ס (S)} = 60$$

$$\text{ו (W)} = 6 \qquad \text{ר (R)} = 200$$

$$\underline{\text{נ (N)} = 50} \qquad \underline{}$$

$$306 \quad + \quad 360 \quad = 666$$

The above spelling for 'Nero Caesar' not only matches passages found in the Talmud, but also from an Aramaic document among the Dead Sea Scrolls of Wadi Murabba'at. Further, said document (Mur. 18) has been dated to the second year of Nero's reign (A.D. 55–56) and thus contemporary to the Apostolic Period.[83] However, since one can do almost anything in number-letter arithmetic, other names can creatively add to 666: the Papacy, Napoleon, Hitler, Henry Kissinger, and Ronald Reagan. To eliminate a who's who lottery with the number 666, a second 'here is wisdom' passage is provided.

> "And here is the mind which hath wisdom. The seven heads are seven mountains…And there are seven kings: five are fallen, and one is, and other is not yet come, and when he cometh, he must continue a short space. Revelation 17:9-10

Regarding this beast of seven heads and ten horns (Rev. 13:1–8), the above passage provides further details, with a chronology. Not only does the author identify them as seven "mountains", a clear reference to the Seven Hills of Rome,[84] but also as seven "kings". Of the seven, five kings have already "fallen", one presently "is", and the seventh and final king is yet to come, but when he comes, "he must continue a short space".

With the name *Nero Caesar* equal to the 666 sum, and the seven "mountains" as Rome, it is imperative to find where Nero was chronologically standing in the early history of imperial Rome. Starting with Julius, the first Roman ruler to bear the name "Caesar", which quickly became synonymous with 'emperor', the five who are "fallen" are Julius (reigned 49–44BC), Augustus (43BC–A.D.14), Tiberius (A.D.14–37), Caligula (A.D.37–41), and Claudius (A.D.41–54). The "one is", the ruler who reigned during John's vision-experience on Patmos was *Nero* (A.D.54–68). Following Nero, the next ruler of Rome who owned the name "Caesar" was Servius Sulpicius Galba. While declared emperor by the Senate in June of A.D. 68, Galba was assassinated in January of A.D. 69, his reign lasting about seven months, or "a short space". With Galba as the seventh king "not yet come", Nero was the sixth king who "is" ruling at the time John witnessed the Revelation.

The passage of Revelation 17:9–10 provides the chronological setting for Revelation 13:18, thus confirming Nero Caesar the owner of the 666 number-name, and the sixth king that "is" ruling. With Nero identified as the "beast", the first of the seven summers is to be found inside the years of his reign. Nero was declared 'Caesar' by the Praetorian Guard and Senate immediately after the death of Claudius Caesar on October 13, A.D. 54. With Nero's suicide on June 9, A.D. 68, this tightens the search area for the first summer from thirty-seven to thirteen years.

As a final lead, Revelation 13 describes the beast being given the power to wage "war with the saints, and overcoming them" (Rev. 13:7). As Caesar, Nero was the first Roman emperor to persecute the Church with deadly force, and never stopped of his own volition. Moreover, Nero began this lethal attack on the Christians so to ostensibly blame them for a great fire that destroyed more than half of Rome. When did this burning of Rome happen?

Answer: July 19, A.D. 64.

Thus, the seven thunders of Revelation 10:3-4 are the seven summers of A.D. 64–70: the key and keyhole to unlock the book of Revelation. It is now time to put the key into the keyhole, turn the key, and begin a new journey into the book of Revelation. Starting in A.D. 64, that new journey begins with the infamous reign of Nero Caesar, the burning of Rome, and that Caesar's monstrous "war with the saints".

CHAPTER 3

Anno Domini 64: The First Summer

The young Caesar stood high at his choice location, plying the strings of his harp so to produce the right musical note. For this particular occasion, the appropriate musical piece was the *Sack of Ilium* and the burning of Troy. As he prepared, the emperor's select audience of 'yes men' sat and waited for this singing performance to commence, and while glancing at the city with the greatest worry. A warm summer wind caused the smell of smoke to breeze past Maecenas Tower where the artist-emperor chose as the setting for his nocturnal piece.[85] With another tug at the harp strings, he was ready. Dressed in tragic costume, Nero Caesar began his harp and singing recital this evening. All the while, the city of Rome burned before him in a blazing spectacle of fiery destruction.

The first five years of Nero's reign were credited as the most stable and successful in the history of imperial Rome.[86] Tax collectors were busy in the provinces, commerce ran smoothly, Rome's famed roads reached across the empire, and well-trained and combat ready legions guarded the frontiers with negligible opposition. From recently conquered Britain, Western Europe, the Balkans, Greece, the whole Mediterranean and islands, the Anatolia (Turkey), Syria to the Euphrates, Egypt and North Africa, the Arabian frontier, and the land of Israel, the dream of Julius and legacy of Augustus prevailed: Rome ruled the civilized world.

Nero was not yet seventeen when he became Caesar and sole master of the Roman world. However, his accession to imperial power was not by his own merits, but the relentless ambition of his mother: Agrippina the Younger.

19

The great-granddaughter of Augustus Caesar, daughter of the war-hero Germanicus,[87] and sister of Caligula Caesar, Agrippina married emperor Claudius Caesar, her uncle and twenty-five years her senior.[88] The following year (A.D. 50), the emperor officially adopted her son, young Lucius Domitius Ahenobarbus; an adoption that included a new name: Nero. In A.D. 53, Claudius married Nero to his own daughter Octavia, thereby establishing for Nero a direct link to the immediate imperial family. Further, Claudius permitted Nero to address the Senate, made him Consul-Elect, City-Prefect, and granted him the title *princeps iuventutis* (prince of youth). When hosting a series of games in the Great Circus, Nero entered the imperial stands clad in triumphal robes whereas Britannicus, Claudius' own son, accompanied wearing the attire of a minor. Clearly, all of consequence saw Nero as Rome's a new and rising star.[89]

As the story goes, on the evening of October 12, A.D. 54, after Nero's position as heir was certain, a dinner party was held. During the meal and festivities, Agrippina gave Claudius a plate of mushrooms. As she hoped, Claudius ate the poisoned delicacies, which brought about his end later that night. After death was confirmed, come noon the next day, a detachment from the Praetorian Guard[90] escorted sixteen year-old Nero to their barracks just beyond the city walls, and declared him Caesar. The Senate followed up with an official statement of recognition.[91]

With the death of Claudius Caesar, Nero's attainment to the imperial power was definite and announced to the Roman world (This also marked *the* moment from II Thessalonians when the 'restrainer' [Claudius] was "taken out of the way", and "the mystery of iniquity" through the new reign of Nero, began unfolding to its diabolic climax.[92]).

Under the responsible guidance of the philosopher Seneca, Praetorian Prefect Sextus Burrus, and a cordial Senate, Nero ruled Rome and the empire soundly. To their credit, Seneca and Burrus were initially successful in isolating the young Caesar's vices (like leading fellow youths about the city and attacking passersby) from disrupting the business of government.

However, though adored by Nero at first, Agrippina's constant pursuit of power, even to the point of making a display during official proceedings, created a friction with Nero and his staff.[93] Viewing his arranged marriage to Octavia as a political formality, Nero began a relationship with an ex-slave girl named Claudia Acte. In time, the affair turned into love. Once

Agrippina learned of Acte, she vehemently confronted Nero about the affair as a mockery of his marriage to Octavia, which gave legitimacy to Nero's claim to the Purple. Despite repeated objections from Agrippina, not only did Nero refuse to send Acte away, but his devotion to her grew stronger.[94] Feeling her hold on Nero slipping away, Agrippina considered Britannicus, Claudius surviving son, as potential leverage. Three years younger than Nero, it was at Britannicus' humiliating expense that Nero came to power. During another heated exchange, Agrippina threatened to take Britannicus to the Praetorian Camp and call on the Guard to recognize him as the true heir of the now deified Claudius Caesar.[95]

However, before Agrippina moved on such a threat, Nero moved first. In February of A.D. 55, only four months into Nero's reign, Britannicus collapsed and died at a banquet. As he went into convulsions at the emperor's dinner couch, those present and wise enough to keep their composure carefully sent their eyes over to Nero. The young Caesar continued with his meal unabated, though lightly commenting that his step-brother was simply having one of his natural fits of epilepsy. The attending servants took the poisoned body away, followed by a burial that night.[96] With Britannicus dead, and Agrippina deprived of a counter-move, the young Caesar sent a stinging message to his mother that, like herself, he too was willing to kill for power.

Trapped as Nero's wife, and seeing the death of her brother before her eyes, Octavia endured these acts with silent horror. Although, knowing that her marriage to Nero was vital to him being Caesar, Octavia may have taken some solace that her own life was safe. The best she could do was to hide her fear, and ignore Nero's further crimes.

Later in the year, Nero finally banished Agrippina from the imperial palace.[97] Soon after, Agrippina faced an accusation of harboring sedition with a distant member of the imperial family. Remembering her threat with Britannicus, Nero viewed the charge as plausible, and opportune. Quickly, Caesar appointed as commission to investigate the allegation, with Burrus in charge of the case. Since the accusation was based on hearsay testimony and from a hostile party, Agrippina persuaded the commission from making any formal indictment. Such deprived Nero of a singular chance to lawfully dispose his mother.[98]

Come A.D. 58 however, a new situation developed, and when brought to fruition would change Nero forever. During a social function, a friend named Marcus Otho introduced Nero to his wife, Poppaea Sabina. Not only did the beautifully seductive woman make an impression on Nero, Poppaea ambitiously saw the young Caesar an opportune trade up. In short order, and along with dismissing Acte, Nero dispatched Otho to govern the province of Lusitania (Portugal). There, Otho was to guard and administer that far-off province on the Atlantic, and was soon joined by Servius Sulpicius Galba to govern Spain. Meanwhile in Rome, Nero and Poppaea began sharing a bed.[99]

Enthralled by his latest and most gorgeous mistress, Nero and Poppaea began to talk about marriage. As with Acte however, Agrippina sharply opposed any idea of marriage, saying it necessitated a divorce of Octavia. Poppaea fired back, taunting Nero that he was afraid of his mother, thereby mocking his manhood. Finally, she threatened to leave Rome for Lusitania to rejoin Otho as his wife.[100] Nero refused to allow that.

The deep fissure that began between Nero and Agrippina soon after his accession became a vast chasm. The emperor now saw his mother as more a burden than ever a benefit to his rule. Nevertheless, as a descendant of Augustus and the daughter of the famed Germanicus, Nero knew Agrippina was still not without friends, influence, and more than a few favors yet called in. Further still, being in her mid-forties and with food testers ever at her service, Nero foresaw that his mother would be around for quite some time.

Unless, of course, there was some sort of... *accident.*

At the popular resort town of Baiae on the bay of Naples, Nero and Agrippina came together to celebrate the festival of Minerva (March 19–23, A.D. 59). There, over dinner, Nero offered tender words of reconciliation to his lately estranged mother. As mother and son talked into the evening Nero's demeanor appeared pleasant; perhaps even quiescent. If Poppaea and Octavia were brought up, they likely did not discuss them for very long. As the hour grew late, the two parted company, but only after Nero offered Agrippina another ship for the journey home. The vessel that brought her to Baiae was oddly damaged after making port. When he saw his mother off on the new ship, Nero kissed her a fond farewell. That night, the young Caesar did not get a minuet of sleep.[101]

After the ship departed for home across the bay of Naples, Agrippina reclined on her high-armed couch under a most ornate canopy. She felt confident of her new sway on Nero. All conflict and sharp resentment between mother and son had been seemingly dispelled by this joyous holiday celebration. Soon, Agrippina mused, her re-established position in the imperial court would be known again.

Then, as planned, it began.

Above Agrippina, a heavy weight slab in the disguised canopy collapsed, instantly killing one of her maidservants. Nevertheless, with the high arms of her couch absorbing most of the impact, Agrippina escaped the collapse with only an injured shoulder. Next, she quickly discovered that her new ship was sinking. In the wild confusion of crew and staff, Agrippina jumped into the frigid March water. Despite the sabotaged vessel sinking beneath her and the water so cold, Agrippina knew how to swim and kept afloat until picked up by a passing fishing boat. After being brought ashore, Agrippina reached her villa with probable hypothermia plus the hurt shoulder.

While the house physician tended her, Agrippina replayed the whole festival in her mind, and concluded the worst. Nero, her son to whom she gave life and the Empire, was now trying to kill her. However, Agrippina thought, if she announced such an impression too soon and to the wrong parties, such would only be at her peril. Instead, feigning ignorance, she sent a messenger to inform Nero she escaped a terrible sea accident and that she was safe. Yet, Agrippina added, his immediate presence was not required during her convalescence.[102]

When the courier reached Nero with this news, the emperor was struck dumb. If Agrippina thought the sinking was an attempt on her life, what would she do with that thought? Would the fond memory of her father sway the Senate? Even worse, might the Guard take her side? Fear, if not outright panic, began to take hold of the young Caesar. During these moments, Nero summoned Seneca and Burrus to brief them on the situation. While the two lead advisors may not have been privy to the plot, they knew it now and decided that the young Caesar had reached the point of no return: Nero had to finish what he started. Seneca turned to Burrus and asked if the Guard could carry out a summary execution. Since the Praetorians were sworn to the protection of the imperial family and not just a single member, Burrus was unable to guarantee the Guard's loyalty to such an order.

With the Guard uncertain, Nero called upon fleet admiral Anicetus, who produced the mocked up ship to serve as Agrippina's deepwater tomb. That plot having failed, Nero now had to improvise, quickly. On Caesar's order, Anicetus led a detachment of marines to Agrippina's home.

Later, as Agrippina lay exhausted in bed at her villa, she looked up, and saw Anicetus and his men enter. Not saying a word, the men surrounded her bed. Suspecting on why they came, Agrippina tried a desperate bluff, saying her son would never order her execution. At Anicetus' nod, one of the soldiers produced a baton and struck Agrippina in the head. Despite the blow, Agrippina remained conscious. Though dazed from the hit, she knew what was next. Resigned, but to send a vindictive farewell to her son, she pointed to her anatomy that gave birth to Nero. Doing so, to her executioners she simply said "Here".[103]

Anicetus looked at Agrippina, and nodded to his men again. They all drew their swords. As the blades came down on her, the last thought that likely flashed across Agrippina's mind was a horoscope given to her years ago. When the astrologers told her that Nero would one day become emperor, they also warned he would kill her. Agrippina's reply: "Let him kill me, so long as he rules."[104]

When Nero was briefed that his mother was dead, Burrus added that the loyalty of the Guard remained intact, to the young Caesar's great relief. In a subsequent report to the Senate, Nero accused Agrippina of plotting to overthrow him, which included an assassination attempt. In addition, Nero gave the Senate a list of abuses and outrages his mother committed in life, which merited her end as ordained by the gods. Though the Senate officially accepted the report, few actually believed it. One senator, Publius Clodius Thrasea, stood up and walked out of the meeting chamber in protest, and to Nero's unfavorable notice.[105]

Though he retained the loyalty of the Guard and the well wishes of the Senate, the guilt of matricide ate at the young Caesar. In his nightmares, the ghost of his mother and the Furies, she-demons of Greek myth, were tormenting him with whips and torches. So horrifying were these nightmares, Nero hired a team of Persian magi to exorcise Agrippina's spirit and implore forgiveness.[106] Nevertheless, with the disposal of his own mother, Nero was also coming to a dangerous realization that, so long as a semblance of formality was maintained, he could do anything he wanted.[107] Moreover, the execution of Agrippina also sent a chilling message to all of high station; senators, governors, legion commanders, and vassal royalty: No one was safe.

Early the following year (A.D. 60), and after a memorable sea voyage from Judea, the apostle Paul disembarked from the Alexandrian ship *Castor and Pollux* at the port city of Puteoli. In custody, Paul and his missionary aide Luke proceeded down the *Appian Way* for Rome. Upon reaching the Appii Forum and the Three Inns, members of the Roman church arrived to provide Paul a welcoming escort into the city (Acts 28:13–15).

The origin of the church in Rome remains largely a mystery. Most likely, it began with Jewish Christian missionaries from Judea during the Claudius years (A.D. 41–54).[108] These missionaries were evidently successful in making evangelical inroads into the city's Jewish community, which had been well established since at least the mid/late first century BC.[109] From Paul's letter to the Romans, and information gleaned from the book of Acts, a Christian community consisting of both Jews and Gentiles flourished in Rome.[110] However, when writing to them, Paul never addressed the faithful of Rome as a *church* as he does with the congregations of Corinth, Galatia, Thessalonica.[111] Rather, he writes "To that be in Rome beloved of God, called to be saints" (Rom. 1:7). This suggests that, while there was a high number of Christians in Rome, they were scattered groups, consisting of house-groups and semi-congregations throughout the city and its environs. Further, these groups may have ran along ethnic lines of Jewish Christians, Gentile Christians converted to Judaism, non-Judaic Gentile Christians, Greek-speaking Hellenists, and Latin-speaking Romans. If so, these fellowships likely lacked a central authority such as a bishop or presbytery (eldership) to unify the groups into a single ecclesiastical body.[112]

On the other hand, they all shared the common faith that Jesus of Nazareth was the Son of God and the Risen Lord. Through the Son, the Faithful are redeemed and may partake in the fruitful communion of the Holy Spirit in keeping the commandments, and call the One True and Invisible God their Father.[113] From the perspective of the Mother-Church in Jerusalem, and unlike the closer-to-home churches of Judea, Galilee, and Antioch, the Roman community was a cabin in the woods. The Roman Faithful made for a remote outpost of first generation Christianity in the wilderness of Roman heathenism, yet situated in the capitol of the empire. Under these circumstances, the faith of the Roman Christians was of world renowned (Rom. 1:8).

Upon arrival in the city and initial processing, Paul was permitted to remain under house arrest pending his appeal trial, which was one among other cases awaiting the legal proceedings. It was only a matter of time before Paul's case would reach the imperial docket and be heard. During the first few days of house arrest, Paul requested a meeting with representatives of Rome's Jewish community. The purpose of the meeting was for Paul to address the reason for his coming to Rome: his appeal to imperial authority as a Roman citizen on the charge of violating Temple laws in Jerusalem.[114] Before the Jewish delegation, Paul insisted that the charges laid against him by the Jerusalem leadership were groundless. Such, Paul explained, was borne out by the fact that the Roman provincial government of Judea was poised to release him from custody. But because Jerusalem objected, pressed for charges and the death penalty, Paul appealed to Roman justice (Acts 25:1–12; 26:30–32; 28:17-20).

Hearing this, the delegation told Paul they were unaware of his appeal case by way of letter or person out of Judea, nor heard of any adjoining malice against him. However, the delegation did wish to hear more from Paul about this new sect of the Christians. The delegation then added "We know that every where it is spoken against." (Acts 28:21–22)

The final statement was not totally without foundation. Already there have been riots in Ephesus and Jerusalem, and Paul at the center of both uproars (Acts 19:23–41, 21:27–22:29). In Rome itself, the Church's relationship with the city's pagan institutions, and its' general Jewish population, were tense at best. Because of the successful evangelism of their Christian counterparts, resentment from the pagan establishment ran high. The more the Roman church grew, the more the Greco-Roman temples lost patrons. In addition, many aspects of Roman life that the general public accepted and encouraged the Church shunned: pagan festivals, sexual license, the homage to the genius-spirits of families, and the pantheon of gods. Further still, many Romans, including the Senate-aristocracy, made good-will offerings to Nero's "divine" voice, to which the Christians would have no part. As a result, the Christians were viewed and despised as anti-social and anti-Roman malcontents. Nevertheless, the Christian community in Rome continued to grow among the rich, poor, slaves, and even members of "Caesar's household" (Phil. 4:22).[115]

The Jewish community-proper in Rome was also known for their stand-offish attitude to the city's social and religious norms, and thus viewed similarly. However, the Jews were mainly an ethnic group who worshipped their One all powerful God, had a far longer history in the city, which included sympathies from both Julius and Augustus Caesar. Moreover, in Jerusalem, the Jewish priests offered sacrifices on behalf of the emperor twice-daily in the Temple of their God.[116] Because of these factors, Judaism earned a legal status of toleration in Rome. Among the Jews in Rome, debate over Jesus as the Messiah grew intense. So great was the rancor over the Nazarene, the results were disturbances of the peace that reached a breaking point for many Romans. In response, Claudius Caesar ordered all Jews expelled from Rome (ca. A.D. 49).[117] Though the order was eventually rescinded, and the Jews allowed in the city again, tensions between the Church and Synagogue remained.

For the Romans', this belief among the Jews of a coming king sent by their lone and unseen God and called 'the Messiah' was a mild but persistent irritant. In Roman eyes, it is best for the Jews to remember that such beliefs not interrupt Roman interests, such as in Judea where their Temple stood. If there was a name that had the favor of Heaven to bring peace, law, order, and civilization to the world, that name was Rome. That some descendant of a Hebraic dynasty, stripped long ago of all sovereignty, yet given divine sanction to become the ruler of the World was just annoying to the Romans. May such Jewish fantasies, whether from Jerusalem, Nazareth, or anywhere never antagonize the order of the day, and for the present that order was Rome.

After a date was set, a second meeting was held at Paul's residence. The discussion covered the belief that Jesus of Nazareth was the Messiah as foretold by Moses and the Prophets, and through him the truth of the One True God will be revealed to the Gentiles. As Paul maintained this position, the Jewish delegation discussed these points among themselves, going back and forth, some supporting Paul while others did not (Acts 28:17–24).

Watching the debate, and the meeting about to break up, Paul interjected by citing Isaiah, saying that Israel had failed to listen and understand those things that God had shown them (Is. 6:9–10).[118] Attached to this prophetic indictment was a warning of judgment-destruction upon the Land and a removal of the people (Is. 6:11–12). Nonetheless, the people will endure and thrive in the Holy Land (Is. 6:13). Finally, Paul cited his life-mission: that salvation was now open for the Gentiles to hear. On that note, the meeting ended, all sides agreeing that they disagreed (Acts 28:25–29).

For the next two full years (A.D. 60–62), Paul waited for his appeal-case to be heard and a ruling made.[119] Meanwhile and remaining under house arrest, Paul continued his missionary work in preaching the Gospel message, "no man forbidding him" (Acts 28:30–31).[120]

By A.D. 62, the warm radiance of monarchy that welcomed Nero at the start of his reign had darkened to a cold overcast of tyranny and murder. During that year, Guard Prefect Burrus died of a seeming throat infection.[121] Because of his untimely (or very timely) death, Burrus was replaced by two men to serve as dual commanders of the Guard. One was the popular Faenius Rufus, previously in charge of grain shipments to Rome. The other was the ambitious and despicable Gaius Sofonsis Tigellinus, who would become Nero's chief adjutant in all crimes. The rise of Tigellinus also saw the resumption of the treason courts that flourished under Tiberius, and the on-going assassination of select persons that Nero saw as potential threats.[122]

Seeing the obvious handwriting of despotism on the wall, Seneca decided on retirement, leaving Nero and his new inner circle to their devices and fate.[123] After Seneca's departure, Faenius Rufus found himself the subject of blackmail by Tigellinus, who discovered that Rufus was a lover to Agrippina, Nero's executed and denounced mother. Such coerced Rufus into recognizing Tigellinus as lone *defacto* ruler of the Guard.[124]

Now being emperor for over seven years, and confident that his political position no longer required a marital bond to Octavia, Nero decided on divorce. However, like Agrippina's loud objections, Octavia's high popularity among the Roman public frustrated Nero from divorcing her outright. So much the case, even then Praetorian Prefect Burrus once warned Nero that in order to divorce Octavia, he would have to give back her dowry; for "dowry", read "Empire".[125] But now with Burrus gone, and a more compliant man at the Praetorian helm, Nero tried to force 'confessions' from several of Octavia's servants. With their statements as evidence, Nero could accuse Octavia of adultery as grounds for divorce. While some broke under the tortures of Tigellinus, the leading ladies-in-waiting refused to betray their mistress. Aggravated by such loyal insolence, Nero opted to a lesser charge in Octavia's failure to produce children during their nine-year marriage. Shortly after, and under close surveillance, Nero banished Octavia to the southern region of Campania.[126]

Only twelve days later, Nero and Poppaea were married. However, when news of the marriage became public, citizens came out in large droves to protest and proclaim their love for Octavia. During the demonstration, a rumor circulated that Nero rescinded the marriage, recalled Octavia, and restored her as his wife. Hearing this, crowds joyfully filled the temples and thanking the pagan gods on the emperor's decision. All the while, they smashed the statues of Poppaea in the Forum and replaced them with Octavia's. So out of control were the crowds, they nearly forced their way into the palace on the Palatine. Though the Praetorians were successful in pushing the demonstrators from the imperial grounds, the entire scene rattled Nero.[127] Seeing his reaction, Poppaea quickly pleaded with Caesar in not restoring Octavia as his wife, which would remand Poppaea back to being the 'other woman'. Moreover, Poppaea reminded Nero of her ability to provide an heir, whereas Octavia was barren.[128]

With this latest unrest, Nero knew that Rome's collective love for Octavia was without question. It was not enough for Nero to remove Octavia from Rome; he had to remove her favored impression from the people of Rome.[129] At this point for Nero, calculated guile was needed to achieve a more decisive end.

As in the death of Agrippina, fleet admiral Anicetus came forward with a solution. He 'confessed' to having a sexual relationship with Octavia, which allegedly involved conversations of treason. Because of this so-called affair/conspiracy, Anicetus was 'exiled' to Sardinia, where he lived comfortably until he and his iron-seared conscience departed this world.[130]

This new charge gave Nero the opportunity to make the definitive move against Octavia. To start, Nero exiled her to the dreaded island of Pandateria, where other women of the house of Caesar where imprisoned over the years. Only days after her arrival, an imperial dispatch arrived on the island ordering her execution on the charges of adultery and treason. Hearing the order, Octavia protested for her innocence to the guards. Despite her pleadings, and what may have been a valiant effort on Octavia's part, the guards tied her up, and sliced open her wrists. Either from her tight bindings or her body going into shock, Octavia's bleed out went very slow. To quicken things, the executioners lowered her into a steaming hot bath, resulting in a faster bleed-out. Finally, as specified in the execution order, Octavia's head was cut off and sent to Rome. There, and like a newly won trophy, Poppaea held the severed head in her hands to sadistically gloat over.[131]

Britannicus, Agrippina, Octavia, other members from the imperial house, all put to the sword at Nero's command. However, the liquidation of his own family was not only to preclude any chance of a rival to the Purple, but assure that the Julio-Claudian line of the Caesars could only survive through him alone.[132]

By A.D. 64, with Tigellinus and Poppaea now at his side, plus a network of informants throughout the city, Nero ruled Rome in a climate of fear, suspicion, and murder. Soon, however, *someone* more ruthless than Tigellinus, more seductive than Poppaea, and far more ancient than the legendary Romulus himself will make the young Caesar his pawn and knight.

On the night of July 19, A.D. 64, a fire broke out in the neighborhood of the Great Circus. As it raged more and more out of control, the blaze soon became "more terrible than any other which has befallen the city by the ravages of fire."[133]

With the help of a hot, dry summer wind, the fire spread quickly. To escape the fast growing inferno, citizens ran helter-skelter inside Rome's close quarters and narrow streets. Doing so, and while waiting for the young and old to catch up, many carried their cherished possessions in the hopes of saving them from the flames. But because of the fire's speed and the city's enclosed urban throughways, those who tried to flee the fire were trapped and burned alive. One of the more vital losses during the blaze was several of the city's grain supply. Despite being built with stone, the fire claimed a number of the granaries, which raised the fear of a food shortage in Rome as well as fire.[134] Also in the chaos, there came those opportunists who saw the city's conflagration as a chance for gain. Not only was there looting, but some even fed the flames so to keep it growing. When confronted with this insane behavior, those that threw the torches said they were doing so under orders.

With the fire eating everything in its path, some scrambled on to the larger stone monuments while others even broke into rock-cut tombs to escape incineration. Many got clear of the more tightly urban areas of the city where the fire was at its' best. Others retreated to the open fields beyond the city walls, but the safest option was to cross the Tiber River by one of several bridges. As the inferno swept across the city, throwing off stifling heat, plumes of smoke with waves of fire, and thousands poured across the Tiber bridges and into the *Transtiberim* district. From that opposite side of the river, the inferno's heat and lambent glow licking their faces, the escaping multitudes watched the burning of Rome with horrified awe.[135]

Nero himself was at the summer palace of Antium when informed of the fire, but it was only the news of the imperial palace on the Palatine going ablaze that prompted his return. On his arrival, Nero took charge of fire control and relief efforts. He ordered Mars' Field and his own private gardens on Vatican Hill to serve as refugee camps for the now thousands of homeless. Because of the heavy damage to the granaries, Nero ordered food brought in from Ostia and the neighboring towns, plus lowering the price of grain by a quarter.[136]

For nearly a week, the inferno raged and destroyed until fire brigades managed to get it under control. Even so, the damage to Rome was extensive. The fire gutted the most populated sections of the city, many of which were low-income residence. Of Rome's fourteen municipal districts, three were totally destroyed; seven were severely damaged, while the remaining four received minimal to no damage. Age-old buildings, works of art, and long-venerated documents of Rome's glorious past were lost. The number of dead, injured, and homeless went into the thousands. Cost estimates would be staggering.[137]

However, along with the collateral damage and heavy loss of life, Nero quickly discovered that he had another type of disaster on his hands. During the week-long fire, witnesses claimed to have seen the emperor plying his artistic talents by dressing in costume, playing a harp, and singing of the burning of Troy to match the burning of Rome. This caused suspicion that Nero ordered the fire set.[138] Such was further compounded by previous gossip that he wanted to rebuild Rome to his liking, even to the point of renaming it *Neropolis*.[139]

After six days, the inferno appeared extinguished, but even before any damage survey could be attempted, the fire sprung back to life. Catching all off guard, the new blaze spread and burned additional areas for several more days until exhausted fire brigades put it out at last. The first fire could be deemed a tragic accident assisted by Rome's hot and dry summer climate; a second fire so soon after had the look, feel, and smell of arson. Moreover, what made this second fire appear even more suspicious was that it originated on the property of Tigellinus, Nero's Praetorian confidant. The fire now directly linked to the emperor's inner circle, many who only suspected were now convinced: Nero ordered the burning of Rome.[140]

Whether Nero had actually ordered the fire is unknown; what mattered was that the public began seeing him as the author the blaze. Less than three months was the *Ludi Decennales,* when the tenth anniversary of Nero's reign would be celebrated with games. Near year's end, December 15th, was the emperor's 27th birthday. The *Neronia*, a Roman-styled Olympics that Nero established in A.D. 60 and to take place every fifth year, was to commence next summer. During those games, the artistic Caesar intended his public singing debut in Rome. Also a coronation ceremony was planned in the Forum, where a Parthian royal named Tiridates would be crowned king of Armenia by Nero before the vast crowds. Finally, a tour of Greece, where Nero would demonstrate his artistic, athletic, and equestrian talents before the Greek people, was high on the schedule. The last thing Nero wanted was the stigma of arsonist to eclipse these coming events.

Rome, the capitol of law, civilization, and order, the city that Augustus found in brick and left in marble, Nero is now seen as turning to soot and ash. Even before the Fire, there were already groups within Rome's upper echelons that loathed Nero for executing Agrippina, Octavia, and possibly Burrus. To the suspicious and conspiracy-minded, the fire served as an ideal pretext for Nero to recreate Rome in his own image, and woe betide any that dare stand in his way. Inevitably, the circles of Nero-haters increased and extended to every corner of the city.

Recalling the demonstrations in response to his marriage to Poppaea only two years earlier, Nero knew the situation with these arsonist rumors was precarious to say the least. The longer he delayed to address the arson allegation, the guiltier he will appear. Worse, such will spread and even permeate among the nobility and general public. If so, Nero was in danger of losing something an artist dare not lose: his audience. Whether an artist's work is viewed as wonderful or awful, let it never be ignored or treated with indifference, and all because of a suspicion of arson. Whatever damage control that could salvage his public image, Nero dare not waste any time.[141] The quickest way for the emperor to draw attention away from himself was to find a seemingly guilty party to blame for the conflagration. By doing so, Nero would demonstrate that he was at work capturing and punishing the 'real' perpetrators of the fire, thus projecting a semblance of control over the disaster. For the charge to look plausible however, Nero needed a group people already marginalized in the eyes of the general public. Even better, Nero entertained, a resented group and relatively new to the city.

Sirius rose brilliantly in the dawn sky to herald another dog day of August and the people of Rome emerged from the shock of the great fire. Work crews cleared the Forum and main streets of debris. The Urban Cohorts (city police) and the Praetorian Guard took positions at key points to prevent further looting. Among the ruined sections of the city, fire brigades made certain the last smoldering of the blaze was put out forever.

On the Tiber, grain barges came up from Ostia to deposit their precious cargo at the relief camps on Mars' Field and Vatican Hill. Once their storage holds were empty, they were filled with rubbish and debris from the fire for deposit at the Ostian marshes. At the camps, the dead were disposed, the injured and maimed were treated; those who suffered loss of family, home, and possessions painfully dwelt on their new position. All the while, everyone viewed Nero as the summer of their discontent.[142]

In temples and altars that survived the blaze, sacrifices were offered to Juno (goddess of heaven). Passages from the Sibyl were read, and prayers lifted to Vulcan (god of fire), Ceres (goddess of agriculture), and Proserpine (goddess of springtime, and queen of Hell).[143]

Meanwhile, city leaders, landowners, representatives of the Senate and the imperial government gathered and agreed on reconstruction efforts.

New fire codes would be enacted to prevent future disaster. New structures are to be spaced at a fixed distance; walk-ways made far wider; building materials flame resistant; water more easily accessible; and a discouraged use of wood. Even at this early stage, Nero may have already designated a destroyed tract of the city, where many of the working-class lived, as the site to rebuild the imperial palace on a grandiose scale.[144]

With these initiatives also came an official statement on the cause of the fire. As widely suspected, the cause was indeed arson. The statement also included the general identity of the guilty party, and would be punished to the furthest extent of Caesar's justice. The first wave of arrests began with openly known members of the sect called the *Christians*. From their information, more arrest followed in either the relief camps or the house-churches were they met to worship their God and Christ. In short order, the Christians were ceased in large numbers and charged in the burning of Rome.[145]

Of those arrested, Christians who were Roman citizens were probably taken to the *Castra Praetoria*, the barracks of the Praetorian Guard. There, they were likely given a much summarized measure of due process, followed by a conviction of arson. Next, they were taken to local jails, such as the dreaded dungeons of the *Tullian Keep* near the Forum. Incarcerated with the looters and common criminals, the Christians sat in chains while prayerfully awaiting the outcome of this sudden and horrid turn of events. Non-Roman Christians, foreigners and slaves, were immediately imprisoned. In short order, Roman and non-Roman Christians alike would be sentenced for the burning of Rome. In the case with the Roman Christians, death was to be quick and painless: beheading. For the non-Roman followers of the Christ, Nero might have stayed their executions, for the moment. The artistic Caesar had something singular, and most creative, for their disposal.

As August gave way to the start of September and the final weeks of summer, Nero prepared his private race track at the Vatican Gardens.[146] When the arena was ready for sporting events, chariot racing in particular, Nero opened it to spectators; fire victims from the near-by Vatican relief camp being the preferred attendees. While the crowds filled the stands and took their seats, a line of condemned prisoners carrying cuts of timber were led into the arena. Before the audience, they were crucified at set points about the track and stands. The sound of hammers striking iron spikes, accompanied by loud shouts of pain, were heard as guards nailed the condemned their crosses.

Crucified, naked, scourged, male and female, the Christians were lifted up in full view of the audience, causing the more pious and cultured Romans indignant to the grizzly sight. Odd, others thought as the crosses rose around them. Usually those sentenced to crucifixion were placed along the main roads and cross ways for all passersby to see. Why crucify them in the emperor's private arena, where it was comparatively secluded?

With the sun setting and twilight filling the stadium, each of the condemned hung in agony on their cross. From some of them, perhaps many, the soft sound of singing could be heard escaping their lips. Meanwhile, work crews approached and soaked each of the crucified in oil, then wrapped waxed sheets around them. Next, a torch was lit and carried into the arena. The torch bearer approached each cross and lit it on fire. The crosses flashed brilliant aflame to provide evening light for the emperor's nocturnal sport performance. Once lit, the night air was ripped apart by screams of blinding agony as the crucified Christians were burned alive. Seconds later, the screams faded to a horrible silence, replaced only by the hiss and crackle of burning wood and sinew. Seeing this, the entire audience, both cultured and common, sat hushed at the sight, the fiery crosses lighting up the arena in a rippling ambiance of diabolical surrealism.[147]

Next was a rushing sound of trumpets, quickly followed by a single chariot driving out on to the race track. Posed in the four horse vehicle, and clad in the leather riding habit of a charioteer, Nero Caesar stood reins in hand and proudly looking back at his dear audience.[148] Now the emperor would provide the crowds with an evening of equestrian skill and competition under the radiance of burning Christian carcasses. At his signal, other charioteers came out into proper formation in the first of several races this night. Throughout the evening, Nero maintained his duel roll of chief executioner and ring master to this unholy exhibition of *bread and circuses*.[149] Between heats as the torches burned, the reek of burning flesh creeping into the stands, Nero dismounted his chariot and entered the stands to cordially mingle with the spectators.

So began Nero's war with the Christians; a war the young Caesar was determined to win. To the fire victims in the stands, it was clear: the Christians were guilty of the burning of Rome, and to be executed in a manner on par to their accused crime. If Nero could sway the fire victims that the Christians were guilty of the great fire, and he the righteous judge to dispense the proper retribution, the rumor that he started the fire would be deflected and thus neutralized. As long as Nero was emperor, the hunt, capture, and death of Christians will be made a spectacle of terror. Tonight and onward, the Christians would be crucified, set upon by wild dogs, beheaded, and, as seen this evening, made into human torches. Though many saw the Christians as deserving such punishments for their anti-Roman sentiments, they were at the same time pitied. Many knew that such a gruesome array of punishments upon the Christian only served Nero's sadistic grandstanding, and not the betters of Roman law and justice.[150]

As the summer of A.D. 64 drew to a close, a dark winter fell on the Christians of Rome. News of Rome's great fire and the Christians the accused arsonists swept across the eastern Mediterranean, and was followed with anti-Christian hostilities wherever the new Faith made a home. The degree of these hostilities would vary from public distain, slander, arrests, and even death.[151]

Upon this new Anti-Christ reign, the Faithful in Christ lifted up prayers to God. Should not the Lord return at this time and end Nero's Rome? Did he not foretell that such things would happen, to be followed by his glorious return? Where is he then? If this all powerful and invisible God is their Father in heaven, then why does he permit his children to die at the sword of Nero? Such would be the questions and prayers of the Faithful at this dark hour, but a question means little if there is never an answer. Yet an answer was coming, from God the Father and his Son, Jesus the Christ.

Truly, Jesus would return, but not for all to see; not yet. At present, only one man would witness the Risen Messiah stand on the Earth again, and that would be on a small island out in the Aegean Sea called Patmos.

CHAPTER 4
Judea to the Aegean

The waves surged on the beach with a mild roar, its' sands baking unchallenged under the Mediterranean sun and the Apostle, John b. Zebedee, walked pensively along the island's shoreline. His eyes panning over the sea, then back to the rugged landscape, he may have considered these surroundings as harsh yet charming, grim but peaceful. John had seen worse; a far better place than that holding cell he shared with his apostle-brethren so many years ago (Acts 5:18). Nevertheless, he may have appreciated the hard beauty of this place, had it not been for the dire circumstances that brought him here.

Unlike Paul's arrival on Malta, John's presence on Patmos had nothing to do with irate weather on the high seas. Rather, John went from a hard-earning ministry in the land of Israel to this island solitude in the Aegean because of a death: a horrible murder. Moreover, a murder committed where the One True and Invisible God dwelt among his people.

Two years earlier, in A.D. 62.

While Peter, John, and the surviving Twelve announced the Gospel in the towns and villages of Israel, some better, some worse (Matt. 10:6–23), Paul awaited trial and proclaimed the Gospel in Rome. During this same time, a home front mission for the Good News was conducted in Jerusalem, and in the very courts of the Temple of God.

James, senior elder of the Jerusalem church, the 'brother' of the Lord Christ (Gal. 1:19), and recipient of the latter-on appellation 'the Just',[152] ascended the steps of the Temple each morning. By himself, yet with many other Jews flowing in with him, James entered the inner precinct of the

Temple called the Court of the Israelites. Inside, and on well calloused knees with the linen *tallit* prayer-shawl draping his head, James spent mornings lifting up prayers for friends, family, the Church, and the Jewish nation (James 5:16). With the very Sanctuary before him where the Covenant-Presence dwelt and fellow Jews about him, James gave glory and praise to the One True and Invisible God of Israel.[153]

Finished with prayers, the brother of Jesus left the inner courts via 'the Beautiful Gate', where Peter and John healed the lame beggar years earlier (Acts 3:1–2). From there, he proceeded to the outer courts to have discussions, debates, plus question and answer exchanges with other Jews. The nature of such active dialogue was to invite all to believe that Jesus of Nazareth is Lord and Messiah as promised by Moses and the Prophets.

In both the spoken and written word,[154] James reminded the people of Jesus' words of the great commandments to love God (Deut. 6:4–6), and your neighbor (Lev. 19:18). Such were the fulfilling essence of Torah, or as James called "the perfect law of liberty" and "the royal law" (James 1:25; 2:8, 12).[155] James proclaimed that the true keeping of Torah was the living and fruitful result of faith (James 2:17–26). Faith in *Yeshua HaMashiach*, Jesus the Messiah, whose coming introduced a new covenant to Israel (Jer. 31:31–34; Heb. 8:1–9:28). In his suffering and death on the Roman cross bought the remission of sins to Israel and the nations (Is. 52:13–53:12; Acts 8:32–35). This ended the animal sacrifice for sin-atonement as evidenced by the ripping of the veil in the Holiest Place upon the moment of Jesus' death on the cross. The ripped veil represented the Holiest Place and the Presence of God now open to the repentant sinner by way of the Messiah's death.[156] All of which was certified by God the Father raising Jesus from the dead in fulfillment of Psalm 16:8–11.

During these talks, representatives of the Pharisees, Sadducees, and other Judaic sects would approach James and ask him the same question again and again: "What is 'the Way of Jesus'"?[157]

First called *Christians* in Antioch (Acts 11:26), and *Nazarenes/ Nazoraeans* in Jerusalem (Acts 24:5), the self-given name to the Jerusalem church was simply called 'the Way', or 'the Way of Jesus' (Acts 9:2; 19:9, 23; 24:14, 22). It is this *way* that survived the persecution of Saul, and was now being embraced by congregations from Jerusalem to Antioch, Athens, and Rome. It is in these locations that the Holy Spirit has been poured out, leading the Faithful in all truth that Jesus of Nazareth is Lord, Messiah, and Savior (John 16:13–14; Acts 21:17–20). Truly, the prophecy of Simeon, spoken to their mother Mary was now coming to pass: "A light to lighten the Gentiles, and the glory of thy people Israel" (Luke 2:25–32). The 'Way of Jesus' is true. Let no man interfere.

Hearing their question, James gave the same answer Peter and John gave to the Sanhedrin years earlier: Jesus is the Savior of Israel. Let all the people and tribes of Israel repent and seek God's forgiveness in his name (Acts 5:30–31). Not only did James declare that the God of their fathers validated Jesus as the Savior by raising him from the dead, but testified that he actually eye-witnessed that miraculous event (I Cor. 15:3–7[158]). Along with declaring Jesus risen from the dead, James also asserted that Jesus would return, and soon, to be seen again by the Jewish nation as Ruler and Judge (James 5:7–9). In his discussions and debates with sect members, and the Roman fortress of Antonia standing ominously at the Temple's northwest corner, James caused many to wonder and consider. Could the Nazarene Carpenter have been the one who will restore the kingdom of David to Israel, and bring the light of God's truth to the Gentiles (Amos 9:11–12; Acts 15:16–17)?[159]

Each day, and most certainly on Sabbaths and the pilgrim-feasts, James would enter the Temple and lift up prayers for the Jewish nation and 'the Way', followed by proclaiming Jesus the King-Messiah to the people. The most likely location of James' ministry was Solomon's Porch: a beautifully high double colonnade portico along the eastern edge of the Temple's outer court. This porch ran north towards the pools of Israel and Bethesda (John 5:2), and to the southeast corner of the Temple Mount where a great drop off into the Kidron Valley lied beyond.[160] It was also in Solomon's Porch that Jesus was seen during the Feast of Dedication prior to the Passion (John 10:22–23), and where the Twelve frequented for prayer and ministry (Acts 3:1–11; 5:12).

As a result of his discussions, debates, and Scripture-based message, James brought many to the faith that Jesus is the Risen Messiah. For James, doing this manner of missionary work in the courts of the Temple, and in the blessed communion of the Holy Spirit, such was a glimpse of Paradise (Ps. 84:10).

To the resurrection-denying Sadducees of the Sanhedrin however, this obstinate belief in the Crucified was the sharpest stick in their eye. It was some thirty years since the Nazarene's death, yet the movement created by his followers, declaring that God raised him from the dead, keeps growing, to the frustration of the Sadducean leadership. While there were reports of Gentile-sustained converts among the *Diaspora* beyond the land of Israel, in Judea the vast majority of adherents of 'the Way' were Torah-observant Jews. In the general neighborhood of Jerusalem the number of those belonging to 'the Way' went into the thousands (Acts 21:20). Finally, their leader, James the Just, was ever proclaiming Jesus as King-Messiah in the Temple. To the public, including the more affluent families in Jerusalem (John 12:42), James' message had an appeal and assurance that was hard to dismiss.[161]

For the Sadducees and the other anti-Jesus factions of the Sanhedrin, the demise of the Nazarene sect was imperative. The Sadducees' puzzle: How to go about it? Aggressive action was already attempted against 'the Way' but failed. The frenzied killing of the deacon Stephen and the execution of the 'envoy' James b. Zebedee by (the late) Herod Agrippa I, only caused the movement to spread rather than be hindered (Acts 9:31; 12:20–24). And woe to anyone who even speaks of that traitor of traitors, Saul, now named Paul (Acts 9:23–24; 23:12, 21). Also, since as a standard rule the Sanhedrin could only carry out a death sentence with the approval of the Roman governor of Judea, Porcius Festus, such was far from promising. After the commotion attached to Paul and his appeal to Caesar, Festus would likely throw any further cases against 'the Way of Jesus' movement out of court, just as Gallio did in Corinth (Acts 18:12–17). In the end, with the Romans ever close by plus a sympathetic public even closer (Acts 2:47; 5:26), a hostile approach was not only impractical but proven unsuccessful.

Neither did the arena of debate offer a sure option; as repeatedly seen, James was too knowledgeable of Scripture, and articulately agile to prophetically apply them to Jesus. To have yet another open disputation with him would run the risk of more Jews coming to the messianic belief in his Nazarene kin. Most significant, James' definite assertion that he saw Jesus alive after his crucifixion gave credence to similar claims made by those twelve envoys of Jesus years earlier (Acts 2:22–36; 3:12–26; 4:8–12; 5:29–32).

For many Jews, this explained why 'the Way of Jesus' sect endured while other messianic groups lapse into insignificance after their 'deliverer' is killed, or when said leader abandoned his followers.[162] Such an observation was made by Rabban Gamaliel, the lead Pharisee on the Sanhedrin. During a session of that high council, he offered some sage advice and warning involving 'the Way of Jesus' movement. If 'the Way' was initiated by men, it will become nothing. If it is sanctioned by God, it can't be defeated, and those who try to defeat it will find themselves at war with God (Acts 5:34–39).[163] In essence, the question Gamaliel was asking the anti-Jesus parties on the Sanhedrin was if they were sure they God's instrument, or God's enemy, in their driven opposition to 'the Way of Jesus'?

The Sadducee response offered a more subjective yet frightening appraisal of the situation. If left alone, and a critical mass of the Nation recognizes the Nazarene as King-Messiah, a hostile Roman reply would be tantamount to spiritual genocide for Israel (John 11:48). Definitely, the Sadducees insisted, along with an invasion of legionary troops from Syria, the Romans would impose martial law throughout all Judea. With a complete lock down of the Temple, causing all sacrifices and priestly duties to cease, the pilgrim-feasts to Jerusalem as commanded in Torah would be banned. The Sanhedrin and the priestly families would be arrested and confined. There would be an army presence to the point of Roman military occupation in both Judea and Galilee. Under this dire forecast by the Sadducees, Israel would cease being God's covenant-nation, *if* the Nation accepts the Crucified as King-Messiah.

To prevent such a scenario, then High Priest during the Passion, Joseph b. Caiaphas called for decisive action. In a flash of prophetic insight, Caiaphas ruled that the Nazarene had to die in order to save the Jewish nation (John 11:49–51). Further, if Jesus had to come to an end, the Sadducees insisted, so must 'the Way of Jesus" movement, who were the provocateur-agents that will antagonize the Romans to respond in the above manner. In the Sadducees' mind, to save Israel from Roman invasion and destruction, the 'Way of Jesus' movement had to be eliminated. To defeat 'the Way of Jesus' movement however, a different kind of approach besides brute force or clever debate had to present itself. What the Sadducees were seeking now was a unique third alternative.

Early in the year, Roman governor Festus, who sent Paul to Rome for his appeal-trial (Acts 24:27; 26:32), died suddenly, thereby leaving a Roman authority vacuum in Judea. When informed of Festus' death in Rome, Nero appointed Lucceius Albinus as his replacement, who was in Alexandria when given the order.[164] Therefore, while the business of Roman government was addressing this change of the provincial post, a window was opening for the Sadducees to definitively deal with 'the Way of Jesus' sect.

The newly appointed High Priest, Annas b. Annas, was not only an anti–Jesus Sadducee, but the son of the High Priest Annas b. Seth, and who had Jesus arrested thirty years prior. Further, since Caiaphas was married into the Annas family, such made Annas b. Annas and Caiaphas brother-in-laws (John 18:12-14).[165] This also made him the brother-in-law of Joseph b. Caiaphas, High Priest during the Passion events and who married into the Annas family (Matt. 26:57; John 18:24, 28). When news arrived that Festus was dead, and his Roman replacement weeks away from arriving in Judea, Annas assembled the Sanhedrin with an idea.

With no Roman judicial presence to stop them, and knowing that he came to the Temple every morning, Annas and the Sanhedrin ordered the arrest of James the Just. Upon the order, the Temple guards began a search for the brother of Jesus throughout the Sanctuary complex. Once found, James and several others who bravely stood with him were arrested. While his companions were likely put in prison for future punishment, James was taken before the Sanhedrin for immediate trial.[166]

Before the council, consisting of no less than twenty-three members present and Annas the presiding chair, James was charged as an apostate of Torah, but also with sedition to the Roman peace. The probable nature of the sedition charge: proclaiming a king in Judea other than Caesar (John 19:12, 15). After deliberations for acquittal and conviction were made, and hearing the testimony of witnesses, a verdict was rendered and announced the following day. James was probably acquitted of the apostasy charge, but convicted of sedition by a two-plus majority vote and thus sentenced to death by stoning.[167]

However, before led away for execution, James was ordered to remain before the council. Standing alone, probably in chains before Annas and the other members of Sanhedrin, the Lord's brother was offered a reprieve, but with a singular condition. In exchange for the death penalty to be dismissed, James must go into the Temple, likely Solomon Porch, and address the people who were now arriving in the city for Passover. Standing high where all could see him, James had to denounce that Jesus was not the Messiah. To receive the clemency of the Sanhedrin, James had to publically declare that he never saw Jesus alive again after his death on the cross and he is not returning to be seen again by Israel as King-Messiah.[168]

As a member of Jesus' family, a leader in 'the Way' sect and with many Jews belonging to 'the Way' arriving in Jerusalem for the Passover, for the Sadducees this was the perfect storm. By denouncing Jesus from being the Messiah before all, it would demoralize 'the Way' movement to the point of implosion throughout the land of Israel. Soon after, the missionary congregations that reached out to Gentiles in the *Diaspora* will follow suit and evaporate into heathen nothingness. Like a falling star plunging to Earth, 'the Way of Jesus', burning bright for a moment, will sputter into dark insignificance and never to be seen again. Once done, the Sadducees hoped, the Jewish nation will be safe from any Roman military reprisal as provoked by 'the Way of Jesus'. It all depended on James taking the bait. For his death sentence to be annulled and released, he had to publically deny Jesus as the suffering, raised, and coming King-Messiah.

Hearing the offer and what might have been a long staring contest with Annas, James finally asked to be brought to Solomon's Porch. With lifted eyebrows, and thinking this might actually work, Annas granted James' request. Under heavy guard and with fellow Sanhedrinists in tow, a confident Annas led James to Solomon's Porch. A public denouncement of his Nazarene brethren for a dismissed death sentence, Annas wasn't too surprised at James' decision. Now, with his own life at stake, James will offer a different oratory that what he and his listeners were accustomed. Besides, Annas recalled, betrayals and denials of the Crucified have happen before, and by those who were his closest disciples. Why should this James be any different?

Under escort of the Temple guards, the Sanhedrin led James to the great eastern portico where he was habitually found proclaiming Jesus as the Messiah. There, after stacking a few wooden crates from the nearby shopping bazaar in the outer court, the guards placed him on the makeshift platform for everyone to see. Once done, and generally known by the public, a crowd of citizens, Passover pilgrims, and many of whom were fellow believers in Jesus, gathered to James. On the platform standing high, James saw those many faces he had debated and enjoyed company over the years. Perhaps even the Twelve, who were just arriving in the city for Passover and only learning of James' arrest, saw him standing on the platform under guard. With more and more people flowing into Solomon's Porch, the multitude growing larger and larger, the Sanhedrin took their positions at the front of the great gathering and closest to James.

Finally, a representative of the Sanhedrin came forward. As planned, he asked the same question that was put to James time and again: "Tell us what is 'the Way of Jesus?'" With the whole crowd quiet, and likely a Sanhedrin scribe ready to write down his denial of Jesus for mass copy and distribution, all waited on James' reply.[169]

Standing high on the wooden platform and bracketed by Temple guard, James heard the question as he did so often before. Only this time his answer was going to be different. All eyes on him, Solomon's Porch silent for the answer, the Lord's brother took a breath and spoke. "Why do you ask me about the Son of Man?" he said "He is sitting at the right hand of the Great Power, coming in the clouds of heaven."[170]

Like Jesus at his trial, James cited Daniel 7:13 as fulfilled in Jesus: The Divine King who is given "dominion, and glory, and a kingdom, that all people, nations, and languages, should serve him".[171] As James lived and breathed, his Lord and brother will not be betrayed and denied a second time. Hearing James bravely confess Jesus as King-Messiah, the multitude in Solomon's Porch rejoiced and shouted "Hosanna to the Son of David!"[172] Hearing their praise to Jesus, James was thankful to be worthy to keep the faith and speak the truth, and assuring all that Jesus, whom God raised from the dead, was Lord and Messiah. Maranatha! But because of his answer, James tragically knew, they would never ask him about 'the Way of Jesus' again.

Blinded by rage, Annas and his fellow Sanhedrinists realized that James turned the tables and used their reprieve offer as his opportunity to openly proclaim his brother King-Messiah. For the Sadducees, such a foolish and obstinate act, and under the threat of death, aroused their fury to the breaking point. With the crowds giving Davidic-messianic praise to Jesus, an enraged Sanhedrin ordered the Temple guards to cease James and take him out of the Temple courts for immediate execution. In the heat of his seizure, and with the people wanting to save James, his forced removal quickly turned into a massive brawl in Solomon's Porch (Acts 5:26). Fearing a sustained uproar will draw a response from the Romans at the nearby Antonia (Acts 21:27–34), the Sadducees ordered the guards to execute James right then and there in the eastern portico. Quickly, and for a hurried execution, several guards gathered armfuls of discarded stones from an in-court worksite for the Temple's renovation (Ps. 118:22; 127:1). Once the guards pulled James off the makeshift platform and threw him down on to the court flagstones, they surrounded him and began pelting him with the wayward rocks. Knowing his hour had come James went on his calloused knees and prayed in the Temple for the last time.[173]

As the stoning continued, persons from the surrounding crowd, one of them from the priestly Rachab family, broke through the guard line and grabbed several rock-bearing executioners to stop the stoning.[174] Seeing this and thinking a full scale riot in the Temple was certain, to be followed by bloody Roman intervention, one of the Temple guards decided to improvise. He turned and rushed over to the shopping bazaar and a fabrics kiosk with a washing station. Dodging quickly through the fast growing chaos, the guard reached the shop and grabbed a stone-carved fuller's pin to wring out wet wash. Again quickly, he maneuvered in behind a kneeling and praying James. As they stoned him, and the Temple guards trying to keep the frantic crowd back, the one guard took aim at the back of James' head with his new club. He drew back, and with all his strength, found his mark.[175]

Instantly, James dropped dead on the Temple's stonework floor to the sudden freeze of all in Solomon's Porch. For several silent seconds, the crowds, Sadducees, guards, everyone, stood motionless and looked at the lifeless body of James the Just. Seconds later, the silence was broken by a member of the Sanhedrin screaming at the Temple guards to get the body away. He loudly insisted to the guards that the body would defile the sanctity of the Temple (Lev. 21:11), to say nothing if the Romans show up and see all this.[176]

Promptly, the guards lifted the body, and clearing a path through the shocked crowd, they began for the nearest gate to exit the Temple courts. As they did so, they were chided again by the Sadducees. Looking this way and that, and fearing the Romans would become wiser any moment,

Annas and the Sanhedrin knew they had to get the body out and away from the Temple in the quickest time. They turned to the guards carrying the body and motioned them to follow. Panicky, ever looking toward the Antonia for Roman activity, the Sadducees proceed to the southeast corner of the Temple complex at a brisk pace. As the guards followed behind with their murdered burden, the sound of crying and the ripping of clothing could be heard among the surrounding multitude in Solomon's Porch.

At the southern end, and after climbing a flight of stairs, the perpetrators reached the roof of the grand galleria that spanned the entire southern end of the Temple complex.[177] At the southeast corner, and the Kidron Valley far below, the now winded guards carrying the body approached the roof's mid-high containment wall, or *parapet*. At the order of the Sadducees, the guards lifted the body, and rolled it over the wall, to which it plunged some 450 feet into the Kidron.[178]

With the body disposed, the fear of the Romans fading from their minds, Annas dismissed his fellow Sadducees and departed the Temple both frustrated and resigned. What he wanted was a public denouncement of the Crucified, not a heroic martyr to glorify him and that same public looking on with praise. Now with the people hearing James' messianic affirmation for Jesus and witnessing his courage in the face of death, 'the Way of Jesus' movement will no doubt strengthen and spread. What started as the crucifixion of a messianic imposter from Nazareth has blossomed into a death-defying faith that began in Jerusalem then out to Judea, Galilee, Samaria, and even to the Gentiles. Unless they can eradicate 'the Way of Jesus' and soon, Annas dreaded, this martyrdom of James will become like those of the Prophets: remembered for ages to come. Was Gamaliel's advice-warning correct? No matter for the moment. Annas was out of ideas. What were they to do now? How can he and Sanhedrin defeat 'the Way of Jesus', and save Israel from the Romans?

After witnessing such a travesty in the Temple, and hearing that the new governor was in route to Judea, a delegation of Jews went out to meet with Albinus. On the road, they informed him of everything that happened in Jerusalem with Annas' execution of James. Likewise, another group contacted King Herod Agrippa II, who probably just arrived in the city for Passover when told of the events. Since only the Roman provincial government can grant a capital sentence, Herod Agrippa II quickly removed Annas from the office of High Priest. Still traveling to assume the governor's post, Albinus sent a letter to Annas, threatening that he would receive punishment for his actions.[179]

Before any of these reprisals and retributions reached him, Annas likely ordered James' companions released from custody with no questions asked or answered. Why make a bad situation even worse? The less the Romans and Herod Agrippa saw from this fiasco the better. Truly, when all is said and done, there would be damnation to pay.

Meanwhile, members of the Holy Family and the Jerusalem church retrieved the body of James from the bottom of the Kidron. They performed the proper Jewish burial and his body was interred in a sepulture close to the Temple Mount.[180] After a time of mourning, and in an undisclosed location in or near Jerusalem, the Twelve, the Holy Family, and remaining elders of the Jerusalem church secretly gathered. With such a monstrous act in the Temple, they knew that the murder of James changed everything. Though Annas was removed as High Priest, and the new governor not necessarily hostile to the Jerusalem church, the Twelve knew they were in a dangerous position. Because their ministries were oriented toward their fellow Jewish countrymen in the Holy Land, the Twelve were known by the Sanhedrin and the still powerful Annas family (Acts 4:1–6; 5:17–18). In addition, the execution of Church leaders was welcomed by the more vicious anti-Jesus circles in Judea (Acts 12:1–3). Further, and according to reputation, Albinus was prone to enforce Roman justice for the right price.[181] Because of these factors, the Twelve made a fateful decision.

The Twelve decided to leave Jerusalem and the land of Israel, and visit the numerous churches among the Gentiles, or even journey to Gentile lands where the Gospel was yet to be heard. By leaving Judea and going out to the Gentiles, not only will the Twelve be out of reach of the Sadducees and their anti-Jesus comrades, but also a pliable Roman governor. Further, by going to the Gentiles, they can fulfill the commission from the Risen Lord to the letter: "Go ye therefore, and teach all nations, baptizing them in the name of the Father, and of the Son, and of the Holy Ghost" (Matt. 28:19).[182]

Before the meeting ended, the Twelve selected a tentative leader for the now seemingly underground Jerusalem church. The agreed appointment was Symeon b. Cleopas, a cousin to the Holy Family. Considering all things, it was only right that a relative of the Lord's family be the chief elder of the Jerusalem church. Add to that, Symeon, like the Twelve and James, may have had an eyewitness testimony of the Resurrection (Luke 24:13–34). In the cautious glow of lamp light escaping darkness, all gathered around Symeon and laid hands (Acts 6:6). After the lifting of prayers for the guidance of the Holy Spirit, Symeon was made acting leader of the Jerusalem church. Once the situation becomes more favorable in Jerusalem, the Twelve will reconvene and confirm Symeon's position as permanent before the whole congregation.[183]

That is, *if* the situation becomes favorable.

Soon after, the surviving Twelve bid each other a loving and likely tearful farewell, and set off to their foreign destinations. Will they ever see each other again? God only knew. Likely via the churches of Antioch and Corinth, Peter headed to Rome. Andrew journeyed to the Scythian frontier. Bartholomew went to far-off India. Thomas traveled to Parthia.[184]

For John, the son of thunder, "the disciple whom Jesus loved", his goal was the province of Asia.[185] A Roman possession since the late second century BC, Asia was one of the most prosperous and beautiful regions in the empire. Further, with a subsequent infusion of Roman culture and colonies, Asia also became one of the most Romanized. Though made a senatorial province by Augustus and therefore having no legions present, Asia was an active center for Roman emperor-worship.

Upon his arrival in A.D. 62–63, John took up residence among the Christians in Ephesus; the seeming lead-church in the province.[186] With John in Ephesus, and as one of the original Twelve, such was likely a great consolation for those Christians, since many of them may have still suffered from the loss of Paul years back (Acts 20:18–38). Once settled in his Gentile home away from Israelite home, John resumed his apostolic ministry. He would visit churches, organize new ones, encourage elders, and exhort the people to believe in the name of Jesus Christ in the good times, and the bad.

When news of Rome's great fire reached Asia (September/October, 64), followed up by Nero's arson charge against the Christians, public animosity towards the churches likely surged in province; Ephesus in particular. A few years back, and in the wake of evangelical success in the province, the Christians of Ephesus created a great celebratory bonfire. They gathered a collection of pagan and mystic literature valued at 50,000 silver pieces (ca. $1.4 million) and put the whole pile to the torch (Acts 19:18–20). Remembering this fiery spectacle, many believed the arson charge against the Christians in Rome. Further, since Ephesus and other Asian cities actively worshipped both Caesar and Rome as gods, a hostile response against the Christians of Asia was inevitable. Such entailed general harassment, anti-Christian denunciations, and even Christians taken into custody.

Shortly after this unfavorable turn of events, the Apostle John vanished from Ephesus. Whether he went into hiding or was arrested, the Apostle was suddenly absent from Asia. Having disappeared, as with Paul, the Ephesian Faithful suffered another heart-breaking loss of a great leader in Christ. Though gone from Asia, John's next address would be a small island out of the Aegean Sea. Located approximately 35 miles off the coast of Asia, the volcanic island of Patmos is part of the Dodecanese island group, and with only about 13 square miles of land. By Roman-era standards, the island would be deemed distant, perhaps remote, from the Asian mainland. This being the case, Patmos was an ideal location for those who merited the punitive status of banishment by the Roman State, or a preferred hiding place where one does not wish to be found. [187]

Whichever the case, after John arrived on Patmos, he seemingly had a high degree of outdoor movement and not confined to a dungeon, a cave, or some cruel mining quarry (Rev. 10:2, 12:1, 13:1, 17:3a).[188] With this free movement, John kept a wide berth from the island's law enforcement authority and Patmos' long established patron cult to Diana. Considering the recent history between the old cult and the new Faith (Acts 19:1–20:1), for John, avoidance would have been the better part of valor. Very likely, John took refuge at the secluded beach that would later be named *Psili Ammos* (Gk. 'fine sand'). Situated in a southwest corner of Patmos and closed in by hills, the beach was considerably isolated from the island's population center. This allowed for John to be comfortably removed from any passersby.[189] In such solitude, John remained in constant prayer, perhaps tried some fishing, but always waited on God to what lay ahead during the darkening hour of persecution.

As John walked along the Patmos beach, he must of pondered on the dire situation for himself and the Church. First was the death of Stephen, and followed by the persecution of Saul, which widely condemned captured members of the newborn Church. Next, John's own brother James was executed some twenty years ago by Herod Agrippa I. Recently, the horrible murder of James the Just in the very courts of the Jerusalem Temple, thus prompting the Twelve the depart the Holy Land. Now the emperor Nero had begun a deadly and wholesale attack upon the Faithful in Rome, and where Peter was now residing. What next?

One thing was certain: Before John leaves this small island on the Aegean, neither he nor young Christendom will ever be the same again.

Someone was approaching.

PART II
The Journey Begins

REVELATION·1

Patmos

Walking along the beach of Patmos, and though tentatively safe from his enemies, John may have feared that the absence of friends and family would eventually wear on him. Very soon, the Apostle would discover, such will not be the case.

Someone was approaching.

> "The Revelation of Jesus Christ, which God gave unto him, to shew unto his servants things which must shortly come to pass; and he sent and signified it by his angel unto his servant John: Who bare record of the word of God, and of the testimony of Jesus Christ, and of all things that he saw. Revelation 1:1–2

The book opens with a preamble and the word *apokalupsis* (αποκαλυψις), meaning "to reveal" or "unveil", hence "Apocalypse," or "Revelation". The book never identifies itself as the 'Revelation of John' as inaccurately titled in some Bible translations and commentaries. Rather, it is the "Revelation of Jesus Christ", which the Father gave to Jesus Christ, who in turn reveals it to John for him to give to the community of the Faithful. Unlike the Gospel, the Revelation is not (necessarily) a document for evangelism to the unsaved. Rather, the book is a prophetic disclosure to those who already accepted Jesus as Savior and Lord (I Cor. 14:22).

For many, the book of Revelation is on par with the so-called 'prophecies of Nostradamus' in that it is a collection of esoteric sayings and forecasts of the future leading to the end of the World. As a result, the word 'apocalypse' became synonymous with the fall of global civilization. However, the correct description of that last book of the Bible is more transcending in scope, richer in substance, and by far more beautiful in all things. In essence, the Revelation is the telling of a story; the story of Mankind's destiny in their relationship with God. Kept a mystery since the genesis of the World, and spoken of by the Hebrew Prophets, this story is now disclosed, *revealed*, to the community of the Faithful (Rom. 16:25–26; Eph. 3:3–10).[190]

In telling the story, the Risen Christ will send an angel to give John guidance on the two main features of the story. The first illustrates the destruction of the abominable "Whore" (Rev. 17–18), while the second proclaims the victory of the persecuted "Bride" (Rev. 21:9–22:5). These two female images of prophetic disclosure, the Whore and Bride, are the primaries of the book of the Revelation, which God gave to Christ to show to John as the premier recipient.

> "Blessed is he that readeth, and they that hear the words
> of this prophecy, and keep those things which are written
> therein: for the time is at hand. Revelation 1:3.

In verses 1 and 3, the foretold events of Revelation will "*shortly* come to pass" and that "the time is *at hand*". The Greek word in question is *en tachei* (εν ταχει), which has been the subject of much interpretation and debate.[191] Those who subscribe to a Futurist view for the Revelation insist that *en tachei* is a referent to *how*, not *when*, the foretold events of the book will occur. Once said events begin, they will happen *quickly* or *rapidly* to their conclusion. Therefore, according to Futurists, the events of the Revelation are yet to happen, but when they start to occur, they shall do so *quickly*.

Despite this assertion, there are more than a few English Bible versions that translate *en tachei* of Revelation 1:1 as a short-term *when* rather than a quick-paced *how*. To cite a few: *King James Version* ("shortly"); *Douay-Rheims Version* ("shortly"); *New International Version* ("soon"); *Revised Standard Version* ("soon"); *English Standard Version* ("soon").[192] In addition, verse 3 offers a second time indicator for fulfillment for the Revelation. Explicitly, verse 3 states that "the time is at hand", the pivotal word being *eggus* (εγγυς), which means 'near', 'within reach', or "at hand".

This same Greek word is also found at key points of the parable of the fig tree in all three synoptic accounts of the Olivet Discourse, and is also used in a short-term temporal sense.

> "Now learn a parable of the fig tree. When her branch
> is yet tender, and putteth forth leaves, ye know that
> summer is near [εγγυς]. So ye in like manner, when ye
> shall see these things come to pass, know that it is nigh
> [εγγυς], even at the doors. Verily, I say unto you, that this
> generation shall not pass, till all these things be done.[193]

Moreover, the Gospel of John also uses this same word as a near-to-be time indicator, and does so to specific calendar events: John 2:13 ("and the Jews Passover was *at hand*"); John 7:2 ("Now the Feast of Tabernacles was *at hand*"); John 11:55 ("and the Jews' Passover was *nigh at hand*"). Therefore, the most natural reading for the Revelation's opening verses attest that the fulfillment of the Revelation would happen *soon*, because the time was *near*.

> "John to the seven churches which are in Asia. Grace be
> unto you, and peace, from him which is, and which was,
> and which is to come; and from the seven Spirits which
> are before his throne; And from Jesus Christ, who is the
> faithful witness, and the first begotten of the dead, and
> the prince of the kings of the earth. Unto him that loved
> us, and washed us from our sins in his own blood, and
> hath made us kings and priests unto God and his Father;
> to him be glory and dominion forever and ever. Amen.
> Revelation 1:4–6

Not only does the author of Revelation identify himself as "John", he does so at least three times (Rev. 1:4, 9, and 22:8. Rev. 21:2 is textually questionable). Clearly, the author wanted no misunderstanding from his Asian readers on who was witnessing and writing the Revelation. If a second 'John' was prominent among the Christians of Asia, the "John" of Revelation would certainly have been more self-specific to prevent any chance of mistaken identity. [194]

As in most letters of the New Testament, John addresses the seven churches of Asia with an offered blessing, plus a doxology (a brief hymn of praise) to the three Persons of the Trinity. The description of He "which is, and which was, which is to come" speaks of the Father in the present tense of always having been, and shall be. The seven Spirits of God are the seven functions of the Holy Spirit to bring a dark and sinful World into God's brilliant and beautiful light (Is. 11:1–2). The reference to Jesus Christ being "the faithful witness" speaks of him as the only incarnate being to see and abide with the Father in glory, and thereby give testimony of that truth to the World.[195] The "first begotten of the dead" is a self-explanatory to Christ as the first participant of the Resurrection.[196] Like the more resounding "King of Kings and Lord of Lords" (Rev. 17:14; 19:16), "prince of kings" speaks of his sovereign rule above all rulers and kingdoms of the World.

John completes the doxology by citing the mission of Christ. In his love, suffering, and death, he brings redemption to all Mankind and the promise of sovereignty and holiness before the Father.

> "Behold, he cometh with clouds; and every eye shall see him, and they also which pierced him: and all kindreds of the earth shall wail because of him. Even so, Amen.
> Revelation 1:7

The author of the Revelation uses the visual imperative "Behold" to set the theme of the book; he is inviting all to look and see what the author is looking: the Messiah has come, and will come. In unison, Daniel 7:13–14, Zechariah 12:10, and Matthew 24:30, are echoed in that the Son of Man is coming in the clouds of Heaven to be seen by all. Yet, the families of the Jewish nation within the land of Israel shall mourn because of the pierced rejection of him. While the fathers of the Nation rejected Jesus of Nazareth to the point of calling for his crucifixion,[197] their children will sorrowfully regret that rejection, but shall see him return as the King-Messiah (Dan. 7:13–14). Truly, such will be hard but in the end an unimaginative blessing for the Jewish nation. John accepts what is to come as the sovereign will of God and for the good of the Nation (Rom. 8:28). He signified that acceptance with, "Even so, Amen."

> "I am Alpha and Omega, the beginning and the ending,
> saith the Lord, which is, and which was, and which is to
> come, the Almighty. Revelation 1:8

The book's preamble closes with this well known title of Hebrew monotheistic divinity. Based on Isaiah 41:4, 44:6, and 48:12, John illustrates the Lord God Almighty as the "Beginning and Ending", the Creator and Perfector of all his work. It is also He that transcends the temporal comprehensions of past, present, and future. This divine designation belongs to the Risen Christ in that he is of the Divine Nature with the Father and has ever been so, even before the Creation (John 1:1–3; 17:5; Heb. 1:2–13; 12:2). Not to say there are two gods and Christ is stealing the Divine Nature from the One True God. Rather, he is the Divine Expression, the *Logos*, the Word of God, emanating from the Father, who speaks to all Creation from Genesis thru Eternity.[198]

While the title "Beginning and End, First and Last" is from the above Isaiah passages, the Revelation was initially addressed to churches that were situated in the Greco-Roman cities of Asia. In those cities, their populations were naturally of Greek-speaking persuasion. For that reason, the Isaiah-Hebraic of "Beginning and End, First and Last" is given in a Hellenic expression, while using the first and last letters of the Greek alphabet: Alpha and Omega.

> "I John, who also am your brother, and companion in
> tribulation, and in the kingdom and patience of Jesus
> Christ, was in the isle that is called Patmos, for the word of
> God, and for the testimony of Jesus Christ. Revelation 1:9

If John was in hiding on Patmos from anti-Christian hostiles, he was now risking exposure to his location by writing to the Asian churches. If, on the other hand, the Apostle was exiled as church tradition asserts, then, not unlike Ovid during his life-banishment by Augustus (A.D. 8-18), John was at liberty to write to persons in Asia, regardless of his exiled status.

> "I was in the Spirit on the Lord's Day... Revelation 1:10a

Perhaps shortly after his arrival on the island, and probably on a Saturday or Sunday,[199] John walked along the Patmos beach. The Apostle pondered his situation and the latest horrid developments that befell the Church. It would not be the first time the Church suffered attack resulting in casualties; a fact John knew all too well (Acts 12:1–2). However, that a Roman emperor, a Caesar, was proactively involved in such an attack was unprecedented. Such an open display of aggression by Nero caused a baleful ripple effect upon the churches of the eastern Mediterranean.[200]

As he walked along the beach, John wondered: Is this the time the Lord Christ foretold on the Mount of Olives those many years ago? Will the Lord soon return and be seen by the Faithful? What about Nero and his reign of terror on the Faithful of Rome, where Peter was?

What about Israel?

Someone was approaching.

Still walking, it happened, as it happens to all who truly belong to Christ. John suddenly experienced that quickening, that stirring, of the Holy Spirit. That blessed touch of the living presence of God that elicits strength, purpose, guidance, joy, and in John's immediate case— communication.[201]

Someone arrived, and spoke.

> "…and heard behind me a great voice, as of a trumpet. Saying, I am Alpha and Omega, the first and the last:[202] and, What thou seest, write in a book, and send it unto the seven churches which are in Asia; unto Ephesus, and unto Smyrna, and unto Pergamos, and unto Thyatira, and unto Sardis, and unto Philadelphia, and unto Laodicea.
> Revelation 1:10b–11

Thinking he was alone, the powerful voice from behind no doubt caught John by surprise. Quickly, the Apostle spun about to face the owner of the Voice. While making the turn, a thought might have passed through John's mind: For all of its power and grandeur, was there something familiar about the Voice?

It was years ago, decades, along another shoreline, a young John walked with his friend and fellow fisherman Simon Peter. It was here, on the Sea of

Galilee, the two men worked their nets and made their living with John's father Zebedee as did many who lived on the great lake in northern Israel. Only now, they were made "fishers of men", and the gates of Hell never to prevail against them. As they walked, Peter and John were accompanied by their mutual best friend: Jesus of Nazareth, and recently risen from the dead (John 21:14–22).[203]

So much had happened, so much revealed. It was not many days since John saw Jesus hanging dead on a Roman cross outside Jerusalem. Now, the Nazarene was quite alive again, and walking along the Sea of Galilee with his closest disciples. Like Thomas, what the Twelve saw and heard overwhelmed all their doubts, sorrows, and fears, giving way to a new and glorious truth foretold by Moses, the Prophets, and David (Luke 24:44–48). In these past few days, for all time, the World had changed, and this small group of Galilean Jews were the first in the know.

But with their joyous bewilderment in seeing and being with their Lord again, wondrous questions remained. Will he now restore the kingdom of David to Israel (Acts 1:6)? Shall he destroy the Roman domination? Will the Gentiles see the glory of God?

After a meal, and walking along the shore, Jesus turned to Peter and asked him repeatedly if he loved him. Each time, Peter answered in the affirmative. Each time, Jesus told him to feed his lambs (or sheep). This exchange was not only a type of reconciliation for Peter's three-time denial on the night of the Lord's betrayal, but to tell Peter of his lead role in the newborn Church. Jesus then spoke of days further in the future. He told Peter that, in his old age, someone would bind Peter's hands and lead him to a place where he will not want to go. As though responding to that latter-day reluctance, Jesus said to Peter "Follow me". One day, the Risen Messiah said to the great fisherman, Peter would carry his recovered faith to the Roman cross, and while doing so glorify God (John 21:15–19; I Peter 4:12–19).

Peter then turned to John, who was trailing behind, and asked Jesus what would become of him. Jesus replied, "If I will that he tarry till I come, what is that to thee? Follow thou me" (John 21:20–22)

This saying became a kind of urban legend within the Church. To many, the Apostle John would live to see the Second Coming, and thus never die. In reply, the author of the Fourth Gospel disputes this interpretation, insisting that such were not the words of Christ, but only he was to "tarry" until he "come" (John 21:23). What was the saying's true meaning, the author never says, thereby preventing the saying from going anywhere in an expository sense. As a result, the saying remained cloaked in mystery.[204]

Then John heard the Voice, and made the turn.

> "And I turned to see the voice that spake with me. And being turned, I saw seven golden candlesticks; and in the midst of the seven candlesticks one like unto the Son of man, clothed with a garment down to the foot, and girt about the paps with a golden girdle. His head and his hairs were white like wool, as white as snow; and his eyes were as a flame of fire. And his feet like unto fine brass, as if they burned in a furnace. And his voice as the sound of many waters. And he had in his right hand seven stars: and out of his mouth went a sharp two-edged sword: and his countenance was as the sun shineth in his strength. Revelation 1:12–16

Following the Ascension, there is only one occasion when human eyes saw the Risen Christ stand in person on the Earth. Those eyes belonged to the Apostle John b. Zebedee during his stay on Patmos. Truly, John would "tarry" until the Risen Christ would "come", but not for the Second Coming.

Instead, there was a great task needing to be done.

After he heard the Voice from behind, John turned and came face-to-face with the owner. There was a visitor on Patmos. The Visitor appearance was reminiscent to the Transfiguration.[205] His face shined like the sun, his eyes blazed with fire, and his hair was brilliant-white as wool and snow. All illustrated the Shekhinah-Glory of God emanating from the Visitor's very being.

The description "one like unto the Son of Man" dovetails Daniel's vision of the Divine King whom God will give dominion over all (Dan. 7:13–14). The expression "Son of Man" is indicative to the *New Man*. Despite the musings of Marx, Nietzsche, and Hitler, the New Man, Mankind redeemed from the Old, begins with a New Adam. As the First Adam brought sin and death to all, the Second Adam brought redemption and a new relationship with the Creator-God (I Cor. 15:21-22, 45). It is through the striped flesh and shed blood of Jesus Christ, the New Adam, which the flesh-and-blood children of the Old Adam will be born-again and become new creatures. Through the Son, a new and redeemed Humanity shall stand righteous before the Father (II Cor. 5:17; Gal.6:15; Eph. 2:15).

Also reminiscent of Daniel (10:5–6), the Visitor's attire was a garment down to his feet and a golden sash draped across his mid-section, representing a priesthood (Heb. 7:1–8:1). Consistent to this sacerdotal image, the Visitor's feet glowed like hot brass from a furnace, which reveals the purity and holiness of his priestly status (Lev. 16:4). His standing among seven golden candlesticks recalls the seven-branched menorah in the Temple's Holy Place representing the illuminating Presence of God among Israel.[206]

The sword coming out of the Visitor's mouth depicts utterances of divine power and authority.[207] The voice with the sound of many waters, perhaps not too unlike the sea waves breaking on the Patmos beach, illustrates that the Visitor spoke with a voice that was both strong and majestic.

"And when I saw him, I fell at his feet as dead. Revelation 1:17a

At this initial stage, not knowing who or what stood before him, John was struck with sheer terror at the sight of the Visitor. Not unlike Moses when the Manifest-Presence of God passed before him (Ex. 33:21–34:8), the Apostle dropped "as dead" before the feet of the Visitor. From what he saw, John must have taken the Visitor as a being of supernatural origin, though the Risen Christ did not likely come to mind. Struck with a horror that strained his wits, heart racing, breath short, cold sweats, John trembled low before the Visitor. All that the son of Zebedee could do was to keep his face on the ground, remain absolutely still, and hope his terror would not carry him off.

What happened next was up to the good graces of the Visitor.

> "And he laid his right hand upon me, saying unto me, Fear not; I am the first and the last: I am he that liveth, and was dead; and, behold, I am alive for evermore, Amen; and have the keys of hell and of death Revelation 1:17b–18

As at the Transfiguration, the Visitor reached down and gently placed his hand on his horrified friend. He then comforted John by telling him to not fear, but to know that he is the First and the Last, thereby of the Divine Name and Nature. He then told John he is the same Jesus that healed the sick, raised the dead, and proclaimed the Kingdom of God to the people of Israel. The same Jesus that was crucified outside Jerusalem as Roman soldiers threw dice for his robe. The very Jesus that John saw alive again on the third day; the wounds on his hands, feet, and side giving chorus testimony to his eternal victory over death. Jesus also told John the benefit of his coming, death, and resurrection: His possession of "the keys of Hell and Death" attests to Christ capturing death and the grave at the Cross and Resurrection. Just as God raised Christ from the dead, so will all that belong him shall be raised up on the Last Day.[208]

With these words, and realizing that the Visitor was his Risen Lord and dear friend, John's terror was exchanged for astonished joy. Quickly, the Apostle got up, and happily welcomed his Lord. Next, the waves breaking on the beach before them, Jesus told John of what they must do as commanded by the Father.

> "Write the things which thou hast seen, and the things which are, and the things which shall be hereafter. Revelation 1:19

Through his Son Jesus Christ, the Father will disclose his relationship saga with Mankind to the Apostle John in a series of visions. Specifically, like God's time-transcending identification "which is, which was, and which is to come", John will receive visions that will disclose events belonging to the past, present, and the future. Further, the Apostle is to write down his God-given experiences, put his diaries together in a single volume, and then send it to the seven said churches of Asia. Before John received these visions, he must first compose seven cover letters to each church under Christ's dictation.

> "The mystery of the seven stars which thou sawest in my right hand, and the seven golden candlesticks. The seven stars are the angels of the seven churches: and the seven candlesticks which thou sawest are the seven churches. Revelation 1:20

Standing among the seven candlesticks demonstrated the illuminating light of the Holy Spirit dwelling in the hearts of the Faithful in Christ that comprised the seven churches (Matt. 5:14–16; Phil. 2:15). The seven stars are seven particular angels all sharing a common assignment in the service of the Risen Christ with respect to the seven churches.[209] From Patmos, John was to witness, write, and send to the Asian churches all that he was about to see and hear, starting with the Risen Christ's visit to John.

So began the great task for Jesus and John as willed by the Father: to witness, write, and send the final disclosure of God's relationship with Mankind to the Faithful in Christ, who now faced persecution. Nero continued his sadistic and deadly attack on the Christians of Rome, and on Patmos the Apostle John and the Lord Christ got to work.

REVELATION 2

To Ephesus, Smyrna, Pergamos, and Thyatira

Unlike the Gospel and Letters of John, the book of Revelation was written in a coarse quality Greek, yet also steeped with Semitic expressions and allusions of the Old Testament.[210] Such indicates that the author, most likely of Jewish background, was habitually exposed to Greek to allow a functional grasp of the language, though not highly proficient. This situation could apply to the surrounding region of Galilee in northern Israel with its many enclaves of Hellenism, and where John and the others of the Twelve once called home (Mark 1:16–20). Evidently, the author experienced the Revelation in his native Hebrew/Aramaic, and then crudely transposed that experience into Greek: the common language of the seven churches in Asia (Rev. 10:4; 14:13; 19:9; 21:5).[211]

Although he probably wrote the Gospel and Letters with the assistance of Greek-speaking Christians in Ephesus, John had no such luxury when writing the Revelation while on Patmos. Despite its place in the New Testament Canon, not only was it likely that the Revelation was John's first attempt to write a document that reached the Canon, but he wrote the book alone.

Almost.

Like Moses receiving divine instructions on Mount Sinai (Ex. 34:27–28), John took the Lord's dictation, writing down everything he said to the churches of Asia.[212] Together, with a roll of parchment and writing utensils at the ready, John and the Risen Christ began.

> "Unto the angel of the church of Ephesus write; These
> things saith he that holdeth the seven stars in his right

hand, who walketh in the midst of the seven golden candlesticks. Revelation 2:1.

For a long time, the seven stars in the right hand of the Risen Christ were interpreted as seven spiritual leaders of the seven churches. Essentially, the seven stars or "angels" were viewed as human beings, clergy or otherwise, through whom Christ spoke to each church.

However, when John saw the Risen Christ stand among the seven candlesticks, the seven stars were in his right hand. This indicates that the candlesticks and the stars, while having a common dominator in the Risen Christ, are distinct in their functions. The Risen Christ walking among the seven candlesticks represented his presence among the seven Spirit-lit churches of Asia that proclaimed his name (Matt. 5:14–16, 18:20; John 8:12). With respect to the seven *stars*, coming from the hand of the Risen and *Ascended* Christ, their purpose was of a more preemptive nature.

A city with a population of 250,000, Ephesus was the metropolis hub of Roman Asia. While Pergamos was the capitol, Ephesus was the chief seaport and the commercial/financial nerve center of the province.[213] Not only was the city home of the temple of Artemis (Diana), but also active in the Imperial cult with an altar and priesthood for the worship of the Roman emperor.

After several evangelical fits and starts, an organized congregation was established in Ephesus during Paul's third missionary journey (A.D. 53–57). Subsequently, with Ephesus as the flagship church for his work in Asia, Paul remained there for over two years until a civil altercation arose (Acts 18:19–21; 19:1–10, 26). Instigated by members of the local silversmith guild to the Diana cult, a riot broke out in Ephesus in response to Paul's evangelical activities (Acts 19:23–41). The result of the tumult was Paul's final departure from Ephesus, and the Ephesian Christians never to see him again. As a result of Paul's departure, many hearts among the Ephesian Faithful were sorely broken (Acts 20:18–38). Such likely repeated itself when John was gone from Ephesus for Patmos, causing many hearts, perhaps too many, to be broken a second time.

When news of the burning of Rome with Nero's arson charge on the Christians arrived in Ephesus, many anti-Christian parties remembered the bonfire in Ephesus years earlier (Acts 19:18–20). This caused an anti-Christian backlash that reverberated from Ephesus and out to all Asia, and where the other six churches resided. Hence, the Risen Christ dispatches seven *stars*, seven angels as heavenly escort to safeguard the delivery of the book and cover letters to their specific destinations.

> "I know thy works, and thy labor, and thy patience, and how thou canst not bear them which are evil: and thou hast tried them which say they are apostles, and are not, and hast found them liars. Revelation 2:2.

Not only was Ephesus the base for Paul's missionary work in Asia, but the church of the Ephesians was also traditional recipient to one of Paul's so-called 'prison epistles' (ca. A.D. 60–62). In his letter, Paul exhorts the church of Ephesus to be strong in the Lord and put on the armor of God so they may defeat the wiles of Enemy in the coming day of evil (Eph. 6:10–17). As John wrote, Christ commends the Ephesians for steadfast faith, abhorring of evil, and their rejection of false apostles, bringing to mind Paul's farewell-warning to the Ephesians (Acts 20:29–30).[214]

> "And hast borne, and hast patience, and for my name's sake hast labored, and hast not fainted. Nevertheless I have somewhat against thee, because thou hast left thy first love [agape]. Remember therefore from whence thou art fallen, and repent, and do the first works; or else I will come unto thee quickly, and will remove thy candlestick out of his place, except thou repent. Revelation 2:3-5

From the beginning, the Christians of Ephesus had a thriving *agape*-love for God and Christ, and reflected on to their neighbor. In those early days, with Paul as their inspirational guide, the Christians of Ephesus had a passion, drive, and fire to do the will of God as taught by his Son Jesus Christ. However, after the sorrowful departure of Paul years back, that passion began to retreat. Yet, with the welcoming arrival of the Apostle John, the Ephesian Christians began to recover from the loss of Paul and regain their focus in the Spirit. But again, shortly after the news of the great fire in Rome and the arsonist charge against the Christians, John disappeared from Ephesus. Whether he was hiding on Patmos or banished to Patmos by provincial authorities, the result was the same: the Christians of Ephesus was robbed of another beloved leader in Christ. This caused a second heart-breaking loss for the church at Ephesus. Soon enough, many in Ephesus became jaded, perhaps even hardened, in their faith. Such became like a bucket of water poured on that first fire of *agape*-love.

Doubtless, the Ephesian Christians maintained good orthodoxy with respect to doctrine and theology. Jesus was the Divine Son, sent from the Father, and to die for the sins of the World, and whom the Father rose from the dead and is alive forevermore; Amen. However, good orthodoxy, without the light and warmth of *agape*-love, makes only for a cold, dark, and empty cathedral (Matt. 7:21–23; I Cor. 13:1–3). What the Ephesians needed to remember and repent was that their personal fellowship with Paul or John, though a seasonal blessing, never defined their spiritual welfare. Only a relationship by faith with God's Son, Jesus Christ, their first love, and in a fruit-bearing communion of the Holy Spirit, makes for that welfare. Anything else is idolatry (Eph. 3:17–21; 4:1–7).[215]

> "But this thou hast, that thou hatest the deeds of the Nicolaitans, which I also hate. Revelation 2:6.

Irenaeus of Lyon (A.D. 185) identified the sect of the Nicolaitans as founded by Nicolas of Antioch, one of the seven original deacons of the Jerusalem Church. According to Irenaeus, Nicolas became an apostate from the Faith, and created a cult that practiced complete sexual license within its membership; hence the name *Nicolaitans*.[216] However, Clement of Alexandria (A.D. 190) was also aware of this origin story and made inquires. From his own investigation, Clement found no evidence of Nicolas having sexual relations besides his wife, nor did his children do anything scandalous. Finally, Clement found nothing to prove that Nicolas ever broke from the Apostles in Jerusalem. Based on these findings, Clement concluded that Nicolas of Antioch was never the sect's founder.[217]

Nevertheless, Irenaeus' base premise, that Nicolas of Antioch had *something* to do with the cult of the Nicolaitans, remains valid. When introducing Nicolas, Luke distinctly describes him as a "proselyte from Antioch" (Acts 6:5). Since the first deacons were appointed when the Apostolic Church still functioned inside Biblical Judaism (ca. A.D. 34),

Luke likely introduced Nicolas as a Gentile converted to Judaism. In connection, one of the great contentions in the book of Acts was the question of Gentile admission in the Church. For many of the Jewish Christians, the Gentile Christians were required to observe the practices of Torah, which included circumcision (Acts 15:1). Gentile converts must first become Jews before accepting Jesus as Lord and Savior, thereby maintaining the Church as a sect of Judaism. Both Acts and Paul speaks of these Torah legalists going as far as Antioch, Syria, Cilicia, and Galatia (Acts 15:23–24; Gal. 1:2–8). They insisted to the Gentile churches that Torah must be fully observed in order to be saved. Paul condemned such an assertion as an abrogation to the sacrifice Christ made on the Cross (Gal. 5:2–6; Eph. 2:8–9). Finally, the Apostles and elders of the Jerusalem church decreed that Gentile Christians need not practice circumcision and convert to Judaism as a requirement to accepting Jesus as Savior and Lord (Acts 15:19-31).[218]

Nevertheless, many Judaizing Christians may have continued to compel Gentile Christians to keep Torah. If there was such a group of Judaizing Christians, they may have adopted, exploited, Nicolas of Antioch as their proverbial poster-child. Using Nicolas as their example for Gentiles to keep Torah, then the "deeds of the Nicolaitans" was the use of Judaism as a prerequisite to salvation, and thereby making the Cross null and void.[219] The Risen Christ compliments the Ephesian church for disavowing fellowship with this group.

> "He that hath an ear let him hear what the Spirit saith
> unto the churches; To him that overcometh will I give to
> eat of the tree of life, which is in the midst of the paradise
> of God. Revelation 2:7

The invitation formula, "He that hath an ear, let him hear..." clearly echoes from Jesus' ministry, where he employed a similar saying when making a key point to his listeners.[220] That ministry fulfilled at the Cross and Resurrection, what the Faithful at Ephesus are to hear is the promise of restoration. Not a restoration of Paul or John, but the restoration to Paradise and the Tree of Life. Taken away from Mankind in the sin of the

First Adam, Paradise and the Tree of Life will be restored in Jesus Christ, the New Adam, to all who hear him and overcome.

> "And unto the angel of the church in Smyrna write; these things saith the first and the last, which was dead, and is alive. Revelation 2:8

Some 35 miles north of Ephesus, and because of its' size and beauty, the port city of Smyrna was dubbed "the crown of Asia." Founded as an Ionian colony as far back as 1000 B.C., the original city was destroyed at about 600 B.C. After that destruction, and for 400 years, the city remained in ruins.[221] It was only until ca. 200 B.C. Smyrna was rebuilt and became the jewel city of the province. So like the Christ, Smyrna was once alive, was dead, and is alive. Of the present day, Smyrna still stands as the Turkish port-city of Izmir.

In addition, Smyrna also had a history as a loyal provincial subject and beneficiary to Rome. In 195 B.C., the first Asian temple to Roma, the personified deity of Rome, was constructed. Later, temples to Augustus (27 B.C), and Tiberius (A.D. 37), were found in Smyrna.[222] With these temples, as in Ephesus, Smyrna was host to the Imperial cult with a priestly college to perform the regular offerings and related ceremonies to the Roman emperor: Nero Caesar.

In reply to such Roman-inspired idolatry, the Risen Christ identifies himself with the Isaiah-title of divinity "the first and the last" (Is. 41:4, 44:6, and 48:12). To the Faithful of Smyrna, the Risen Christ declares that he alone is the incarnate manifestation of the One True and Invisible God among men.[223]

> "I know thy works, and tribulation, and poverty, (but thou art rich)... Revelation 2:9a

One of the more striking features in the economy and religion in Asia were the trade guilds. Like the Ephesian silversmiths (Acts 19:24–28), the Asian trade guilds indulged in Greco-Roman pagan practices among their memberships. Such a circumstance would prove difficult for many Christians to find employment within those guilds. As result, many

Christians would resort to a more menial nature of employment in order to make a living and provide for their families. However, though they faced economic and social hardship, their relationship with God and his Christ was rich in the Holy Spirit, and for that they were wealthy and gave thanks (Matt. 6:20–21).

> "...and I know the blasphemy of them which say they are Jews, and are not, but are the synagogue of Satan.
> Revelation 2:9b

The other feature of Smyrna was the city's Jewish population. While some Jewish Christians may have resided in Smyrna, a majority of the city's Jewish community did not accept the belief that Jesus of Nazareth was the promised Messiah. As seen in other communities of the Hellenic Diaspora, some of the Jews in Smyrna may have been strongly, militantly, opposed to the belief (Acts 13:50; 14:2, 19–20; 17:13; 18:12–13).

Tragically, the above passage has been construed as an anti-Semitic battle cry by many Christians, and the cause of much suffering upon Jewish communities throughout Church history. However, the Risen Christ, the Risen Davidic Messiah, was never referring to the Jewish nation as a whole.

During a pilgrimage to Jerusalem for the Feast of Tabernacles, Jesus had a heated exchange with a group of Pharisees in the Temple (John 8:13–59). During the disputation, the issue of Abrahamic lineage came up, with the Jews making the claim that Abraham was their ancestral father. Jesus granted that they did belong to the flesh-and-blood lineage of Abraham. However, Jesus replied, in their desire to kill him, they were not doing the works worthy of Abraham: righteousness born from faith (Gen. 15:6; Rom. 4:1–23). As a result of this vindictive conduct, Jesus said they were doing the works of their *true* spiritual father: The Devil (John 8:39–44).

In light of this exchange in Jerusalem, the "synagogue of Satan" designation speaks *only* to those Jews who had a lethal grudge against the Christians, be they fellow Jews or Gentiles. Because of this behavior, such anti-Jesus Jews cease being the children of Abraham, and became the children of the Devil.

"Fear none of those things which thou shalt suffer: behold,
the devil shall cast some of you into prison, that ye may
be tried; and ye shall have tribulation ten days: be thou
faithful unto death, and I will give thee a crown of life.
Revelation 2:10

Once news of Nero's anti-Christian purge reached Smyrna, the temples
of Roma, Augustus, and Tiberius, became likely rallying centers against
the city's Christians. Add the enmity from the anti-Jesus factions within
the Jewish community and the civil atmosphere in Smyrna became toxic
for all who lived and breathed Jesus Christ as Savior and Lord. In the city,
such reproaches included public denouncements, arrests, incarceration,
even the execution of members the Faithful by local law enforcement.
Nevertheless, the Faithful will face such trials from these Satan-seduced
forces for a time, but not for very long.

In the face of such threats, the church was never to relent (Rom.
8:35–39); Jesus of Nazareth is Lord and Messiah, and Nero Caesar is not.
Whatever calumny and afflictions their enemies try to afflict on them, the
church of Smyrna should rejoice, for their reward is certain and eternal
(Matt. 5:11–12; Luke 6:22–23; I Pet. 4:14).

"He that hath an ear, let him hear what the Spirit saith
unto the churches; He that overcometh shall not be hurt
of the second death. Revelation 2:11

As the Faithful encountered great terrors in Rome, their fellow believers
in Smyrna will witness like dangers. If they stand in Faith, listening to
the voice of the Holy Spirit, the Faithful in Christ will look Death in the
face, and Death will blink (I Cor. 15:51–57; Rev. 20:13–14). Once done,
the Faithful of Rome and Smyrna will receive eternal life, and forever look
upon the beautiful and loving face of God the Father (Rev. 22:3–5).[224]

"And to the angel of the church in Pergamos write; These
things saith he which hath the sharp sword with two
edges. Revelation 2:12

With Ephesus as the economic nucleus, and Smyrna the aesthetic gem, Pergamos (or *Pergamum*) was the provincial capital of Asia. Located some 55 miles north of Smyrna, Pergamos was the proconsul's residence, and where Roman law was dispensed to the province. This setting in mind, the Risen Christ identifying himself to the church of Pergamos as "he that hath the sharp sword with two edges" illustrates his authority. It is the spoken word of the Risen Christ, and not Rome, that is the divine and final authority in Pergamos, Asia, and the entire World.

> "I know thy works, and where thou dwellest, even where
> Satan's seat is… Revelation 2:13a

Like the famed acropolis in Athens, Pergamos' religious center was situated on a high plateau, making the upper city an architectural marvel for miles around. One of those Greco-Roman structures was a great altar to Zeus, which, in the distance, appeared as a gigantic throne when one approached the city.[225] Clearly, the Greco-Roman deities of Zeus and Asclepius (the serpent-god of healing) had religious/liturgical homes in Pergamos, and were certainly blasphemies to the One True God. However, the reference to "Satan's seat" (aka "Satan's throne") in Pergamos had a far deeper meaning and history.

In the Garden, and while possessing the serpent, Satan tempted the parents of Humanity, Adam and Eve, saying:

> "Ye shall not surely die. For God doth knoweth that in the
> day ye eat thereof, then your eyes shall be opened, and ye
> shall be as gods, knowing good and evil.[226]

With such verbal seduction, to counterfeit God in defiance of his commanded word, Adam and Eve succumbed to the temptation of the Serpent. The inevitable result was the mortality of the sin-nature being passed on to Adam, Eve, and all subsequent generations of Mankind.

In another pivotal temptation moment, Satan led Jesus of Nazareth to a high mountain and showed him the kingdoms of the World in a moment's time, and said:

"All this power will I give thee, and the glory of them: for that is delivered unto me; and to whomsoever I will give it. If thou therefore will worship me all shall be thine."[227]

Unlike the First Adam and father of Humankind, the Second Adam and Son of God refused Satan's temptation in accordance to the written word of God, and thereby ruled the lives of all (Matt. 4:10; Luke 4:8). However, Man emulating God in the capacity of ruling the nations creates a demonic form of leader-idolatry that is reflected in Roman emperor-worship, beginning in Pergamos.

Along with being the capital of the province, Pergamos had a history of ruler-worship going back to the first anti-Seleucid potentate Eumenes I (263–241 B.C.). With this religious background, it would naturally follow that Pergamos be the first in the Empire to accommodate the Roman Imperial cult with a temple dedicated to the worship of Augustus Caesar (29 B.C.).[228] Soon after, all of Asia followed Pergamos' cue and was inundated with the religious devotionals of the Imperial cult, such as temples and altars.[229] This joining of the blasphemous worship of Man, constituting the worship of Satan, coupled with the Imperial cult's premiere status in Pergamos, identifies the city as "Satan's throne".[230]

"...and thou holdest fast my name, and hast not denied my faith, even in those days wherein Antipas was my faithful martyr, who was slain among you, where Satan dwelleth. Revelation 2:13b

In the face of the city's Roman emperor worship, the Risen Christ commends the church of Pergamos for their steadfast faith in him as Lord. So devout was their faith, a member of the Pergamos church named Antipas was martyred rather than acknowledge anyone else as Lord.[231] Further, the Risen Christ citing Antipas' martyrdom in proximity to "where Satan dwelleth" suggests that the Imperial cult may have had a degree participation in his death. Despite the killing of Antipas, the church at Pergamos remained unshaken.

> "But I have a few things against thee, because thou hast
> there them that hold the doctrine of Balaam, who taught
> Balac to cast a stumbling-block before the children of
> Israel, to eat things sacrificed unto idols, and to commit
> fornication. Revelation 2:14 [232]

Evidently, a corrupting element of paganism, via food rituals and sexual immorality, was being introduced to the church at Pergamos. The Risen Christ labeled it the "doctrine of Balaam", the prophet who persuaded the Israelites to those very deeds: fornication and eat foods offered to idols (Num. 25:1–2; II Peter 2:9–17; Jude 11). In essence, like the wandering Israelites who invited God's judgment (Num. 31:16), certain Christians in Pergamos were beginning to flirt with paganism.

> "So hast thou also them that hold the doctrine of the
> Nicolaitans, which thing I hate. Revelation 2:15

If the above definition for the Nicolaitans is correct, the full observance of Torah including circumcision as a requirement for salvation, then a notable presence of Judaizing Christians were among the congregation at Pergamos.

These two factions within the Pergamos church caused the congregation to become very polarized: Judaizing legalists ("doctrine of the Nicolaitans") and libertine pagans ("doctrine of Balaam"). Moreover, both factions of pagan Christians and the Judaizing Christians were in direct conflict with the decree of the Apostles and the Jerusalem church on Gentile admission into the church (Acts 15:1–29).

> "Repent; or else I will come unto thee quickly, and
> will fight against them with the sword of my mouth.
> Revelation 2:16

If the two opposing factions in the Pergamos church did not end their wayward practices, the Risen Christ would utter his divine word of judgment against them. The result of such a judgment would produce a disastrous outcome for both wayward factions. Like the oldest brother in charge of his younger siblings, if they misbehaved further, the Risen Christ had the authority from the Father to pass out retribution.

> "He that hath an ear, let him hear what the Spirit saith unto the churches; To him that overcometh will I give to eat of the hidden manna, and will give him a white stone, and in the stone a new name written, which no man knoweth saving he that receiveth it. Revelation 2:17

The "hidden manna" was the pot of food provided by God during Israel's forty years of wandering in the wilderness, and resided inside the Ark of the Covenant. The designated resting place for the Ark was behind the veil in the unseen Holiest Place of the Tabernacle.[233] Such Judaic imagery, and involving a sacred veneration of a food source, would have spoken to both deviant groups in Pergamos. Symbolically, through the cross of Christ, by faith and not works (Eph. 2:8–9), the saved sinner passes through the ripped veil and enters the invisible Holiest Place. Inside the Holiest Place, the pot of manna was found, and where the Covenant-Presence of God dwelt. There, the saved take part in the nourishing communion of the Holy Spirit and have eternal life (Heb. 10:19–20).[234]

Of the several proposed meanings of the "white stone", the best descriptive refers to a criminal trial where an accused party is found innocent of a crime. Once acquitted, the innocent are given a white stone, representing their acquittal (the convicted are given a black stone).[235] In accepting Christ, the sins of the repentant are placed on the Cross, and the repentant is justified before God. The "new name" on the white stone speaks of the new nature and life in Christ, which is attained by neither circumcision nor uncircumcision, but by faith.[236] That no else knows the new name, outside of the saved, tells of the intimate relationship between the saved and the Holy Spirit.

When the two factions, pagan Christians and Christian Judaizers, repent and shed their sinful weights, they will walk in the newness and freedom of the Spirit (Heb. 12:1). In that walk, they will discover that it is by faith that gives birth to good works that are deemed righteous and acceptable by a loving God.

"And unto the angel of the church in Thyatira write; These things saith the Son of God, who hath his eyes like unto a flame of fire, and his feet are like fine brass. Revelation 2:18

The above reference to the "the Son of God" is the only one in the book of Revelation applied to the Risen Christ, and attached to the first chapter descriptions of eyes of fire and feet of fine brass (Rev. 1:14–15). Further, the title was also a direct challenge to the paternalism of the Greco-Roman deities that were worshipped in Asia (Zeus/Jupiter, son of Cronus/Saturn; Apollo, son of Zeus/Jupiter).

While the letter to the church of Thyatira is the longest of the seven letters, the church and its' host-city are the least known.[237] Located some forty miles southeast of Pergamos into the Asian interior, Thyatira was commercial-based and the home of many merchants and artisans. This made the pagan trade guilds a high influence in the city's industry and economy.[238] As in the other churches of Asia, such a situation with the guilds would present a hard issue for all Christian households in Thyatira.

"I know thy works, and charity, and service, and faith, and thy patience, and thy works; and the last to be more than the first. Revelation 2:19

The Risen Christ compliments the Christians of Thyatira for their diligent service to the Faith. Unlike Ephesus, the Faithful in Thyatira did the works of *agape*-love in concert to being Christ-like examples to each other and all to see (John 13:34–35). Of the seven addressed churches in Asia, Thyatira was seemingly the one church that best grasped the vision of loving God, one's neighbor, in fulfillment of the Great Commandments.[239]

"Notwithstanding I have a few things against thee, because thou sufferest that woman Jezebel, which calleth herself a prophetess, to teach and seduce my servants to commit fornication, and to eat things sacrificed to idols. Revelation 2:20

For all their love and service to Christ and each other, something went wrong among the Faithful of Thyatira. Indeed, the twilight of dusk had fallen over that church.

From among the ranks of the church a particular person emerged, a woman, who seemed to have advocated some kind of compromise with pagan practices. Possibly, as a representative of the church, this woman may have begun some kind of dialogue for the admission of Christian artisans into the trade guilds. Such would have included some religious compromise. Perhaps a nominal donation for temple sacrifices, a purchased pinch of incense on an altar at the guild dinner-meetings, or the like. Once a compromise was reached and the Christians begin offering a religious token to the trade guilds, they could join the guilds and make a far better living for themselves and their families.

However, none of the above actions constituted the Old Testament nomenclature of "Jezebel" upon this woman. Jezebel, the wife of king Ahab, ruler of the northern kingdom of Israel, did aid false prophets and led Israel astray from God in the worship of Baal. Such deeds by Jezebel were called "whoredoms" and "witchcraft" (I Kings 18:19; II Kings 9:22). What earned this woman of Thyatira the name *Jezebel* was something darker and uglier.

> "And I gave her space to repent of her fornication; and she repented not. Behold, I will cast her into a bed, and them that commit adultery with her into great tribulation, except they repent of their deeds. And I will kill her children with death; and all the churches shall know that I am he which searches the reins and hearts; and I will give every one of you according to your works. Revelation 2:21–23

While standing on the Mount, Jesus taught his disciples to beware of false prophets who go about in sheep's clothing, but are hungry wolves underneath. He also instructed them to recognize these false prophets by their fruits, or their external behavior and what results from it. According to Jesus, identifying false prophets was less about what they said than what they did (Matt. 7:15–20).

Along with seducing Israel away from God, the other vile act that Jezebel committed was the most monstrous: Murder. With the killing of Naboth of Jezreel for the possession of his vineyard (I Kings 21:1–16), Jezebel also called on the execution of the prophets of God (I Kings 18:4, 13; II Kings 9:7). Further, after the victory at Mount Carmel over the prophets of Baal through God's lone prophet, Elijah (I Kings 18:20–40), Jezebel sent a message to Elijah threatening to kill him (I Kings 19:1–2).

If *Jezebel* of Thyatira was so named for such behavior, then it is likely that someone within the church at Thyatira, moved by the Holy Spirit, rose up to denounce her compromise with paganism. Whether it was a member of the clergy, laity, or a prophet from elsewhere sent by God, this person consistently spoke out against *Jezebel's* efforts to introduce heathen practices to the church. This messenger reminded the Faithful of Thyatira never to trade-off the purity of their faith for the polluted benefits of the world. Rather, it is the God and Father of the Lord Christ that is the true provider of their needs, not the seeming good intentions of the pagan trade guilds (Matt. 6:25–34, 7:7–11). Such warnings by this messenger was the "space to repent" for *Jezebel* to halt her efforts in bringing idolatrous practices into the church. Despite these warnings, *Jezebel* continued undeterred—and more.

Unable to silence or discredit this messenger, *Jezebel* resorted to a measure equal to the Jezebel of Scripture: Murder. To silence this messenger, *Jezebel* had the messenger killed. Moreover, it is likely that *Jezebel* and her accomplices made the messenger's death look like an accident. In doing so, it likely convinced most if not all in the church the messenger's death was a horrible tragedy and nothing more. However, such a crime did not escape the fiery eyes of the Risen Christ. The Risen Christ calls on the church with the visual imperative "behold", in that they will witness his judgment for such a diabolical act.

Surely, *Jezebel*, and all her accomplices before and accessories after the fact, will be recipient to his judgment. The image of them being cast into a bed to commit adultery with *Jezebel* is keyed on the principal "what they sow so shall they reap" (Gal. 6:7–8). All involved in the murder are committing adultery with *Jezebel*, and unless they repent they too will be struck with the same punishment she merited. The bed symbolism quickly shifts from a bed of adultery to a sickbed where the dead and dying are found. In whatever manner the divine judgment of Christ was dispensed, local plague, catastrophic weather, or earthquake, the end result will be equal to *Jezebel's* crime: Death.[240]

Once divine judgment came to pass, and death seen all about, the churches, and not only in Thyatira, will know that such was the justice of the Risen Christ. Immediately after, the church of Thyatira broke away from all paganisms, the trade guilds or anyone, and never fraternized with them again.

> "But unto you I say, and unto the rest in Thyatira, as many as have not this doctrine, and which have not known the depths of Satan, as they speak; I will put upon you none other burden. But that which ye already hold fast till I come. Revelation 2:24–25

For all the paganism, murder ("the depths of Satan") and deception that took place in Thyatira, the Risen Christ clearly indicates that not all in the church were participant to these acts. Rather, many in the church remained faithful and loving examples for Christ. For that, the exposure of the crime, followed by the horrid retribution for it, the Risen Christ refrains from giving the church any further admonitions. Moreover, he encourages those who were innocent of the deeds of *Jezebel* to hold fast to what they still have. Truly, in keeping their faith, they shall see Christ's provision come in the manner of blessed opportunities in their lives, livelihood, and families.

> "And he that overcometh, and keep my works unto the end, to him will I give power over the nations: And he shall rule them with a rod of iron; as the vessels of a potter shall they be broken to shivers; even as I received of my Father. Revelation 2:26–27

This echo of Psalms 2:8–9 links well with the Son of God identification of verse 18. The Risen Christ promises those who endure and overcome this dark time at Thyatira, and while abiding in the Faith, the same will inherit the Earth from the pagan and ungodly. Finally, just as the Risen Christ opened his message to the church of Thyatira as "the Son of God", he closes with his singular relationship with God ("my Father"), in that all the Faithful will rule with him.

"And I will give him the morning star. He that hath an
ear, let him hear what the Spirit saith unto the churches.
Revelation 2:28–29

In astronomy, the way to attain the "morning star" is to keep awake
(or wake up before its' too late) and watch for the brightest planet to rise
in the pre-dawn sky, which is soon followed by sunrise. The Christians of
Thyatira are keep awake in their faith, all the while hearing the voice of the
Spirit and looking to their Risen Lord, the Bright and Morning Star (Rev.
22:16; II Pet. 1:19). In doing so, they will see the long night of *Jezebel* come
to an end, and behold the daybreak of the Lord's blessings.[241]

REVELATION 3
To Sardis, Philadelphia, and Laodicea

Alongside the debated quote from Irenaeus,[242] many take the cover letters to the seven Asian churches as a tell-tale indicator to date the Revelation in the A.D. 90s. Since the churches were well established but encountering various issues, it would have taken considerable time for them to mature or decline to merit Christ's praise or admonishment. According to such a late-dating appraisal, such a situation with the Asian church places the Revelation in the A.D. 90s. However, when looking at the spread of Apostolic-era Christianity, which includes the evangelical missions of Paul in Asia, such may prove more a red herring than a rosette stone in late-dating the Revelation.

During his third missionary journey into Asia (A.D. 53–57), Paul remained in Ephesus for over two years. During which time "all they which dwelt in Asia heard the word of the Lord Jesus" (Acts 19:10). Further, with the remaining six cities on main roads, it is more than plausible that the Gospel message reached those locations during this early period of evangelism. In his letter to the Colossians (ca. A.D. 60), Paul cites a church already at Laodicea (Col. 4:13–16), which in geographic terms was the farthest church of the remaining six from Ephesus (some 110 miles). Add the fact that Paul neither founded the Colossian or Laodicean churches (Col. 1:4–6; 2:1), such indicates that the evangelization of Asia was beyond the efforts of Paul.

If the seven churches were founded during Paul's third mission-journey (53–57AD), it would provide adequate time (seven to eleven years) for the churches to be in the condition described in Revelation.

"And unto the angel of the church in Sardis write; These
things saith he that hath the seven Spirits of God and the
seven stars. Revelation 3:1a

Despite its' popularity, it is this author's view that the seven churches
of Asia do *not* symbolize seven succeeding periods of the Church-Age.[243]
While such makes for elegant dispensational drama, linking the Apostolic-
era to the End Times, the similarities are too vague to categorize whole
centuries of Church history into seven fixed periods. For example, to
apply the church of Sardis, which the Risen Christ faults as "dead", to the
Reformation is forced to say the least. When considering the historical
figures and events that contributed to the Reformation-Renaissance and
their impact, *dead* should be the last description applied Christendom of
that period.[244]

The Risen Christ greets the church of Sardis by citing images of his
initial appearance to John (Rev. 1:12–13, 16a). He is the one who possesses
the seven Spirits of God who gives light to a dark and sinful world (Is.
11:1–2). Again, the seven "stars" represent seven dispatched angels to
safeguard delivery of the Revelation and the adjoining cover letters to the
seven churches.

Located some thirty-five miles south of Thyatira, Sardis had a notable
history among the cities of Asia. Originally, the city was founded as an
acropolis-fortress built on the summit plateau of the Tmolus hill chain at
an elevation of 1500 ft. Sardis was also the capitol of the Lydian kingdom
under Croesus in the sixth century B.C. Although virtually destroyed
in the great A.D. 17 earthquake, the city was rebuilt with the assistance
of Rome. With the city-fortress surrounded by precipice with a single
but difficult ascent, Sardis was impregnable, seemingly. Notably, near
Sardis was a necropolis or burial ground of cave-tombs numbering in the
hundreds. Further, these tomb-caves would be used as places of refuge by
the locals in a time of emergency (Rev. 6:15–16).[245]

Probably a product of Paul's third missionary journey in Asia (Acts
19:10; A.D. 53–57), the church of Sardis began like most newborn
churches: with a desire and dedication to serve God and his Christ. In
time, however, the church of Sardis gave way to image and ceremony at

the expense of faith and substance. On the surface, the church at Sardis remained of good reputation, but the Risen Christ knew one better.

> "I know thy works, that thou hast a name that thou livest,
> and art dead. Revelation 3:1b

After greeting them, and unlike the other churches (save Laodicea; see below), the Risen Christ gives the Sardian church no compliment for their conduct. While the church was apparently active, in reality Christ tells them they are dead. This was not the first time Christ charged a religious group for being aesthetically favorable on the outside, but lifeless on the inside. Only days before the Crucifixion, and standing in the Temple, Jesus admonished the scribes and Pharisees with similar imagery:

> "Woe unto you, scribes and Pharisees, hypocrites! For ye
> like unto whited sepulchers, which indeed appear beautiful
> outward, but are within full of dead men's bones, and all
> uncleanness.[246]

The Greek word used throughout the Gospel accounts for "hypocrite" is *hupokrites* (υποκριτης) and is from *hupokrisis*, meaning *actor* or *performer*.[247] The church at Sardis had become mostly a community of 'Sunday Christians' in that they were active in their devotions of baptisms, communion, and hymns. Yet, on the other side, they lost that holy catalyst in accomplishing a true and fruitful Christian walk: *agape*-love, which comes from a prayerful communion in the Holy Spirit. Such dead faith amounts to nothing more than liturgical theater, to which the Christians of Sardis have become merely stage players, thus hypocrites.[248]

This is the distinguishing essence between Christianity as a religion of formula and ritual, and Christianity as a loving-living relationship with the one true God and his Son Jesus Christ. It is in that love of God and Christ that is to be reflected back on to one's neighbor in the dynamic guidance of the Holy Spirit, and thereby fulfilling the Scripture "the just shall live by faith" (Hab. 2:4; Rom. 1:17).

In short, and regardless of their surface devotionals, the faithful at

Sardis were spiritually dead and dying, which explains why Christ gave the church no acclamation of their works at the opening of the letter.

Nevertheless, the church was not yet lost from the Risen Christ.

> "Be watchful, and strengthen the things which remain, that are ready to die: for I have not found thy works perfect before God. Remember therefore how thou hast received and heard, and hold fast, and repent. If therefore thou shalt not watch, I will come on thee as a thief, and thou shalt not know what hour I will come upon thee. Revelation 3:2–3

As before, the Risen Christ gave the Sardian Christians a historical referent to give further impact in his message. Because of the high elevation and sharp escarpments of the fortress-city, Sardis was viewed as impervious to military attack. Nevertheless, Sardis fell to such conquest– twice. The first downfall came by Cyrus of Persia in 549 B.C., to be followed by Antiochus "the Great" in 218.B.C. On both occasions, Sardis was taken because its sentries failed to keep watch of enemy activity who found ways to climb up the natural escarpments protecting the fortress-city. Specifically, small crawl passages running up the rock face to the summit, and to the remissive of the guards.[249]

Such a historical background for the Faithful of Sardis gave added focus to Christ's warning of being "watchful, and strengthen the things which remain, that are ready to die." If the Sardian Christians failed to watch and repent of their lifeless faith, just as the city fell to Cyrus and Antiochus, the church will too meet with ruin by their enemies. Subsequently, they will also know all this was forewarned from the One who will bring that judgment: The Christ-Thief (Mark 13:35–37; II Pet. 3:10).

> "Thou hast a few names even in Sardis which have not defiled their garments and they shall walk with me in white: for they are worthy. He that overcometh, the same shall be clothed in white raiment; and I will not blot out his name out of the book of life, but I will confess his name before my Father, and before his angels. He that

hath an ear let him hear what the Spirit saith unto the
churches. Revelation 3:4–6

Not all of Sardis was akin to such sterile ritual in the name of Christ,
but there remained those few who maintained a Spirit-dynamic with
the Risen Christ and were called worthy. Yet, to those who do hear this
warning and exchange their dead faith for Spirit-living faith, they shall
then produce works of righteousness, which are the white and clean
apparel of the saints (Rev. 19:8; Jude 23).[250] Moreover, once this priority
is accomplished, and the Sardian Faithful walk in a newness of life in
the power of the Holy Spirit, then their well-kept liturgies will be taken
as perfect praise-offerings to the living God. Lastly, to those who do
overcome, the Risen Christ promises access to the Father, and their names
kept for all glory and eternity.

> "And to the angel of the church in Philadelphia write; These
> things saith he that is holy, he that is true, he that hath the
> key of David, he that openeth, and no man shutteth; and
> shutteth, and no man openeth. Revelation 3:7.

Nearly thirty miles east/south-east of Sardis, the city of Philadelphia
(Gk. *brotherly love*) had a comparatively small population. This was
due to seismic activity in the immediate area, resulting in Philadelphia
being destroyed by the earthquake of A.D. 17.[251] When the city was
rebuilt, it had so many pagan temples it was nicknamed "little Athens".
Nonetheless, because of the lingering fear of earthquakes, many lived
outside Philadelphia's urban area.

The Risen Christ identifies himself as "holy" and "true", which has no
illustrated parallel in Revelation 1, though the titles resurface elsewhere
(Rev. 6:10; 15:4; 19:11). The second self-identification, also absent in chapter
one, "he that hath the key of David, he that openeth, and no man shutteth;
and shutteth, and no man openeth." clearly echoes Isaiah 22:22. Further,
this identification belongs in the broader context of Isaiah 22:15–25.

Vainly confident that his position in the royal Davidic court was
secure, the ambitious and pliable steward to king Hezekiah, named
Shebna, planned to purchase a rock-carved sepulcher. At that time, God,

though the prophet Isaiah, approached Shebna and told him that he would be removed from high office, carried to a foreign land, and die in poverty (Is. 22:15–19). His post as royal steward would be given to one Eliakim b. Hilkiah, who shall prosper with great responsibilities to both Jerusalem and the kingdom of Judah (Is. 22:20–21). Of his duties, Eliakim will be the official who will grant or deny access to the king: "the key of David" (Is. 22:22). The royal steward will tend to many things of the Davidic household, right down to the table-ware (Is. 22:23–24). Nevertheless, the office and duties of the royal steward will one day be brought down and ultimately destroyed (Is. 22:25). This came to pass in the Babylonian Destruction under Nebuchadnezzar in 587 B.C.[252]

However, in the coming of Jesus Christ, the branch from the cut down stump of David, in whose resurrection the flesh of David did not see corruption, the "key of David" now belongs (Ps. 16:8–11; Acts 2:25–32). In the Risen Christ, not only shall the kingdom of David be restored, but *through* the Christ is the only entry into that kingdom, and not by any other name under Heaven (Acts 4:12).[253]

> "I know thy works: behold, I have set before thee an open door, and no man can shut it: for thou hast a little strength, and hast kept my word, and hast not denied my name. Revelation 3:8

Because of the relatively small population of the city, the church at Philadelphia appears to have been the 'baby of the family' to the seven churches. Even so, the church also had the greatest faith by keeping to Christ's teachings, and calling him the holy and true Lord. Like the church of Smyrna, the Risen Christ never faults the church at Philadelphia. Instead, the Risen Christ offered the Philadelphian faithful "an open door and no man can shut it". Such is an opportunity to escape the city before a catastrophe strikes them.

> "Behold, I will make them of the synagogue of Satan, which say they are Jews, and are not, but do lie; behold, I will make them to come and worship before thy feet, and to know that I have loved thee. Revelation 3:9

Despite the high level of paganism within the city, there was little to no anti-Christian sentiments in Philadelphia. Tensions, however, may have possibly been with the city's Jewish residency, which were probably vying with the Christians for converts among Philadelphia's citizens. When news of Nero's persecution reached Philadelphia, the public mood may have begun to shift against the Christians. This may have been further aggravated by anti-Christian factions inside the city's Jewish community. Before such a situation became dire, the Christians departed Philadelphia to its' outskirts. The "open door" that the Risen Christ promised the Faithful is an opportunity to spread the Gospel to the Asian hinterland beyond the boundaries of Philadelphia itself.[254]

The ultimate result of this opportunity is the same foretold by the prophet Isaiah. Those among the Jewish nation who harbored a hatred for the Faithful in Christ shall one day be made humble. Yet, wonderfully accept them as brethren in that Jesus of Nazareth is Lord and Messiah, and heir to the throne of David.[255]

> "Because thou hast kept the word of my patience, I also will keep thee from the hour of temptation, which shall come upon all the world, to try them that dwell upon the earth. Behold, I come quickly: hold that fast which thou hast, that no man take thy crown. Revelation 3:10-11

Nero's attack on the Roman Faithful reverberated into Asia and wherever Christianity took root (I Pet. 1:1–7; 5:8–9). During this encroaching time of persecution and danger, the Faithful will be tempted to abandon Christ. However, because of their great faith, the Risen Christ will spare the Philadelphian church from this dark time, while declaring his return imminent. Nevertheless, for the present, the Risen Christ exhorts them to hold on to what they have, and never to allow anyone to steal the blessed crown promised to them (James 1:12).

> "Him that overcometh will I make a pillar in the temple of my God, and he shall go no more out: and I will write upon him the name of my God, and the name of the city of my God, which is new Jerusalem, which cometh down

out of heaven from my God: and I will write upon him
my new name. He that hath an ear, let him hear what the
Spirit saith unto the churches. Revelation 3:12-13

While there will be no material temple in the New World to come
(Rev. 21:22), the Blessed Faithful, like tried tested stones, will make up a
new and living temple where God shall dwell forever.[256] Outside of John
20:17, the above is the only place where the Risen Christ calls the Father
"my God",[257] meaning, through the Son, the Almighty is Father and God
of the all the Faithful (II Cor. 6:18).

Under the Sinai Covenant, God's presence among his people was
isolated and access well regulated through the Levite priesthood. In the
New World to come, God's new and eternal home will be directly among
Redeemed Humanity (Rev. 21:3). In the New World to come, and as a
reward in overcoming, the Redeemed will have the Divine Name, the
name of his People, and the new name of his Christ, become part of their
very being.

"And unto the angel of the church of the Laodiceans write;
These things saith the Amen, the faithful and true witness,
the beginning of the creation of God. Revelation 3:14

The last of the seven churches, some forty miles south/southeast of
Philadelphia, Laodicea was situated in close proximity to the cities of
Hierapolis and Colossae. Because of their closeness, the Christians in
these three cities saw themselves as particular siblings in the Faith (Col.
4:13). Moreover and most curious, Laodicea was also the recipient of an
unaccounted letter from the Apostle Paul (Col. 4:16).

A wealthy city, Laodicea was known for its wool industry, a medical
school, and was home for an eye treatment facility. So prosperous was
Laodicea, when an earthquake devastated the city in A.D. 60, city leaders
passed on any financial assistance from Rome and funded reconstruction
efforts on their own.[258]

When addressing the Laodicean church, the Risen Christ identifies
himself as the "Amen" (Hebrew/Aramaic: *So be it*), indicating that through
him all things are affirmed and made so to the glory of God (II Cor. 1:20).

In echoing Revelation 1:5, Christ declares he is the "faithful and true witness". Meaning, he is the one incarnate being who saw and lived in the full glory of God the Father, and give testimony of that truth to a sinful and rebellious World (John 1:18).

In his next self-identification, the Risen Christ describes himself as "the beginning of the Creation of God".[259] Such a designation raises an interpretive specter that the Risen Christ had declared himself the first ever created being by God, and therefore non-divine. Such a view was not only espoused by Arianism of the Constantine-era Church, but by pseudo-Christian denominations of today. However, such identification should be considered in light of Paul's letter to the Colossians, which was read by the church of Laodicea, while Paul's (unaccounted) letter to the Laodiceans was read by the church of Colossae (Col. 4:16).

After offering prayer for the Colossian church (Col. 1:9–14), Paul cites a hymnal in praise of Christ:

> "Who is the image of the invisible God, the first born of every creature: For by him were all things created, that are in heaven, and that are in the earth, visible and invisible, whether they be thrones, or dominions, or principalities, or powers: all things were created by and for him. And he is before all things, and by him all things consist.[260]

In connection, when viewing the text of Genesis 1:1-4 alongside John 1:1-5, the similarities are striking:

> "In the beginning God created the heaven and the earth. And the earth was without form, and void: and darkness was upon the face of the deep. And the Spirit of God moved upon the face of the waters. And God said, Let there be light: and there was light. And God saw the light, that it was good: and God divided the light from the darkness.

> "In the beginning was the Word, and the Word with God, and the Word was God. The same was in the beginning

with God. All things were created by him; and without
him was not anything made that was made. In him was
life; and the life was the light of men. And the light shineth
in darkness; and the darkness comprehended it not. [261]

The Greek term "Logos" (Λογος) translated as "Word" in John 1:1 may
be conceptually based on the *Memra* as found in the Targums: Paraphrased
commentaries of the Old Testament in Aramaic. In the Targums, *Memra*
is repeatedly indicative to the self-expression of God to his Creation.[262] The
divine nature of the *Memra-Logos-Word* has preeminence before and above
all things, the prime mover of Creation, one with God the Father, and the
Divine Expression to all Creation (John 17:5).

> "I know thy works, that thou art neither cold nor hot: I
> would thou wert cold or hot. So then because thou art
> lukewarm, and neither cold nor hot, I will spue thee out
> of my mouth. Revelation 3:15-16

Like the church of Sardis, the Risen Christ gave no commendation
to Laodicea. Rather, he points out their fault up front. As he did with the
other churches of Asia, Christ cites a local feature that the Laodiceans
could immediately associate and understand.

Laodicea situated close to Hierapolis and Colossae, yet each city had
their own tell-tale water source. Hierapolis was a well known health resort
for its hot springs, whereas Colossae's water supply came from streams
that were cold and fresh. In Laodicea's case, there was no natural source.
Because of this situation, the city's water had to be brought in via aqueduct
from hot springs about five miles away. By the time the water traveled the
route and reached Laodicea, not only was the water tepid but because of
its low quality it had a tendency to being emetic (vomit rousing).[263]

The Risen Christ told the Christians of Laodicea they were neither
hot nor cold, to which he would prefer, but rather they were the undesired
lukewarm. While the waters of Hierapolis were therapeutically hot, and
Colossae thirst-quenching cold, both serving their natural and proper
purposes, Laodicea's water was brought in artificially. Once in the city,
the diverted water was tepid, *lukewarm*, with a sickening effect when

drank. This reflects the spiritual welfare to the church at Laodicea. Instead of trusting in God's provision and thus distant from the life-water of the Holy Spirit (John 7:37–39), the Laodiceans saw their own efforts and accomplishment as the definition of their prosperity. As a result, the spiritual life of the Laodicean church became lukewarm; devoid of any real faith and passion for the One God and his Christ. Like their town water, the Risen Christ warned the Laodiceans he would spit their unpalatable faith from his mouth.[264]

> "Because thou sayest, I am rich, and increased with goods, and have need of nothing; and knowest not that thou art wretched, and miserable, and poor, and blind, and naked. Revelation 3:17

The affluent station of the Laodicean Christians became their spiritual winter. Because they felt well enough in their material comfort zone, the church of Laodicea fell into a type of complacency, which robbed them of any genuine and precious faith in the Provider-God. From this passionless disposition, the Laodiceans became "wretched, and miserable, and poor, and blind, and naked". Such characteristics were antithetical to what the city was known for, yet reminiscent to the horrid scene of the earthquake that ruined Laodicea only a few years earlier.

> "I counsel thee to buy of me gold tried in the fire, that thou mayest be rich; and white raiment, that thou mayest be clothed, and that the shame of thy nakedness do not appear; and anoint thine eyes with eye-salve, that thou mayest see. Revelation 3:18

Talking to them in their own prosperous language, the Risen Christ invites the Laodiceans to "buy of him", tried-tested gold that will bring their faith back to true value. Like the church at Sardis, they too shall put on white attire, the righteousness of the saints (Rev. 19:8). Finally, if they seek him out, the Christ would anoint their eyes in the Spirit for them to see beyond their here-and-now materialism, and look upon those things that are true, priceless, and timeless.

> "As many as I love, I rebuke and chasten: be zealous
> therefore, and repent. Behold, I stand at the door, and
> knock: if any man hear my voice, and open the door, I
> will come in to him, and will sup with him, and he with
> me. Revelation 3:19-20

The letter to the Laodiceans begins transcending into an epilogue for all seven letters, declaring that Christ's rebukes and judgments are not simply to elevate shame, but to see his love. From such comes repentance from unworthy works with a rededication to faith and goodness. The image of Christ standing at the door knocking suggests a beautiful portrayal of the Gospel. He came and visited our 'house': the World (John 1:10–14; 18:37). His standing at the door and 'knocking' is his ministry, climaxed by the Cross, which will draw all to him (John 3:14–15; 8:28; 12:32–33). Those that open the door and let Christ in shall begin a friendship with him in the communion of the Holy Spirit (John 14:23–26;15:1–17).

> "To him that overcometh will I grant to sit with me in my
> throne, even as I also overcame, and am set down with
> my Father in his throne. He that hath an ear, let him
> hear what the Spirit saith unto the churches. Revelation
> 3:21-22

The constant theme from Revelation's seven cover letters can be summed up in one word: "Overcome". With that theme comes a singular *proviso*: "he that hath an ear, let him hear what the Spirit saith to the churches". To those Faithful who overcome by hearing and listening to the Spirit, the same shall be where Christ is: the Throne of Glory, and joyously beholding the face of God the Father.

Although they do not represent seven historical periods of the Church, the seven churches of Revelation 2–3 had daily issues that can be associated to any congregation of Christendom. Whether it is leadership, doctrine, external/internal threat, general morale, or just a focus of purpose, if they heed to what the Holy Spirit says, they will *overcome* those enemies and challenges. More so, God shall be with them and bless them for their faithful diligence. If not, and they take lightly what the Spirit says, Christ will turn away, leaving them exposed to their enemies and afflictions. In short, the seven letters to the Asian churches are as warnings, comforts, and promises to the historical churches to whom they are addressed. However, the letters also speak to the Church in general, which deals with the good, bad, ugly, and holy, on a daily basis.

The letters finished, John discovered the Risen Christ was gone. Looking about, John may have thought his Lord was ascending into Heaven once again (Acts 1:9–11). Quickly, John lifted his eyes upward. Looking into the sky, the Apostle was suddenly astonished. However, what John saw was not the Risen Christ in ascension—nor did he *yet* see an opened door in Heaven (Rev. 4:1). At this point, after writing the letters, John will now witness the things he had previously encountered and learned in relation to the coming of Jesus Christ and the newborn Church (John 1:14; 19:35; 21:24; Acts 4:19–20; I John 1:1–3). John will now experience "the things which thou hast seen" (Rev. 1:19a).

What the son of Zebedee saw in the sky was a woman giving birth (Rev. 12:1–2).

REVELATION · 12

Bruises

In the Beginning, God created Man, male and female, in his own image and likeness. He blessed them to reproduce, populate, and dominate the Earth (Gen. 1:26–28). Yet, God's intention for Man went beyond a prolific landowner on the third planet orbiting a yellow star careening through the Milky Way (Ps. 8:4–8).

Far beyond, indeed.

Before the Creation, before the reckoning of time, God decided to have a friend. In his infinite brilliance and wisdom, Eternal God destined a creature to become the closest to share his heart. A creature that God will engage in a unique and most loving relationship. From the moment God created them, Mankind's destiny was to be nearest to God, to abide in his glory, see his Face, and be joined in loving union. Such a destiny is the mystery of God, kept hidden since the Beginning and spoken of by the Prophets.[265] Though a mystery, an earthly reflection of Man's destiny with God is seen in the holy matrimony of husband and wife as ordained by God from the Beginning (Eph. 5:22–33). It is this matrimony-union of male and female, husband and wife, which are the foundation stones to create a family as the base unit of society and to perpetuate Mankind (Gen. 2:23–24).[266]

In his creation of Man, male and female, God made them free from bodily affliction, disease, or genetic defect. With this pristine physical state, Man was also created in spiritual innocence: not knowing sin. However, this physical and spiritual purity were just preliminaries for Man's relationship with the Creator-God; something had to be built on it. Though the ultimate goal of God's union with Man is perfection, the initial

97

goal was authenticity: Man's relationship with God must be genuine. Real. To accomplish this, not only did God create Man in innocence, he created them with free will: the choice to obey or disobey him. Man, for better or for worse, must choose, experience, and grow beyond their newly created innocence. Such a choice was presented in the home God provided Man.

In the region of Earth later to be called *Mesopotamia* (and much later Iraq[267]), eastward in the land of Eden, God planted a garden for Man to inhabit and tend (Gen. 2:8–15). The garden was adorned with a variety of fruit trees, plus a likely assortment of grape vines, berry bushes, and carpet-like green grass all in between. With a river flowing through Eden, and the Voice of God regularly visiting the Garden (Gen. 3:8a)—but never his Face—such a place would truly be a delightful paradise.

Standing in the center of the Garden were two particular trees (Gen. 2:9). One was the Tree of Life, which Man was free to eat along with all other trees of the garden, except one. The other was the Tree of the Knowledge of good and evil, which Man was prohibited by God not to eat under the penalty of death (Gen. 2:15–17). These two trees, the Tree of Life and the Tree of Knowledge, were the earthy manifestations of God giving free will to Man, and their adjoining benefits and consequences. In the strict sense, both trees offered the same thing: the knowledge of good and evil, but with one distinction. The Tree of Life represented trust and obedience to God. The result of eating the fruit of that tree would be the knowledge of good and evil by divine revelation, thereby giving Man the ability to live a holy life from sin, and never die. The Tree of Knowledge stood for disobedience to God. The detriment of eating the fruit of that tree was the knowledge of good and evil by first-hand experience: a sinful life, which results in God's stated punishment of death.

By placing the two trees in the center of the Garden, essentially next to each other, for Man to freely approach the Tree of Life, he must also draw near to the forbidden Tree of Knowledge. In short, God was creating the opportunity of choice for Man. The choice to trust and obey his word or not. Thus, God demonstrated that his relationship with Man was true and substantive, like the love and commitment between a husband and wife, and not the string tugs of a puppet-master on a marionette.

Nevertheless, God is not mocked. With free will, God also requires responsibility and accountability (Job 38:3; Luke 12:48b). Those who disobey God, those who reject him and his commandments, the same shall face his judgment and retribution. Yet again, God's destiny for Man never changes: Man is the Creature to whom God has ordained a loving and eternal relationship (Ps. 33:11; Job 23:13; Is. 46:10). Such is the grace of God.

In the creation of Man "God saw everything that he had made, and behold, it was very good." (Gen. 1:31). Within God's Heavenly realm, the angels sang in praise to the creation of all things (Job 38:6–7). However, in the creation of Man, not all of the Heavenly host was smiling. More than a few angels were surprised, even put upon, by God's creation and destiny of Man.

One angel in particular.

The great and beautiful angel Lucifer (Heb. *light-bearer*) had no other desire but to stand before the Throne of Glory and worship God. Joyously, he would approach the Throne and with his unique voice and offer glory to the Almighty without ceasing (Ezek. 28:13). With all that he was, Lucifer's one joyous thought for existence was to stand close to God and sing him praise without ceasing.

Then God said, "Let us make Man in our own image, after our likeness..." The creation of Man and his singular destiny with God had come. Like all the angels, Lucifer looked upon Man's destiny with desire (I Pet. 1:12). However, for Lucifer, mere desire was not enough. Since he and his fellow angels were the first beings created to serve and behold God, shouldn't they be the closest to God and his glorious favor? Yet, they are to stand aside for the being called Man, who was created *after* them but destined to have the greatest favor with God (Luke 14:8–11). Wonderful jars of clay (or according to secular dogma, privileged primates), Man, who has never seen God, but given the choice to glorify God? Such a Being was destined to be the closest and most loved by God? Even worse, if Man was to be the closest to God, the result being a union of the two. It follows that the angelic host of Heaven would be the servants of Man as they are the servants of God. In Lucifer's mind, that was the insult; the cheating, despicable, insult to his entitled due. The destined favor of Man by God jealously ate at Lucifer. Jealousy that gave way to spite then hatred, which in turn consumed the great angel.[268]

From that moment, Lucifer became Satan, the Devil, the Accuser and Enemy who comes to steal, kill, and destroy (John 10:10); the demonic monster of Scripture and fable. As such, Satan focused his power, his lusts, and vindictive will on one objective: the extermination of Mankind.[269] Once Man was destroyed, Satan mused, he and his fellow angels would take Man's place as the creature most favored and loved by God (Is. 14:12–14[270]). Truly, the ultimate love-hate triangle of the ages. To destroy Man, however, Satan must make the case before God that such destruction was justifiable. The annihilation of Man had to be divinely sanctioned.

In the Garden, a Satan-possessed serpent tempted the first parents of Man: Adam and Eve. As the Serpent, Satan enticed them to distrust God's spoken word and eat the fruit from the forbidden Tree of Knowledge, to which Eve, then Adam, relented. When that happened, just as God warned, the sin nature resulting in death immediately fell upon Man. Classically known as *the Original Sin*, once Man ate the forbidden fruit, Adam and Eve lost their newborn innocence (Gen. 3:1–7). With Man now subject to sin and death, they were required to leave God's provided Garden and their relationship with God was now only at a distance (Is. 59:12–13). While leaving the Garden, God sent fiery angels to keep Man clear from the Tree of Life, which was now closed off to them (Gen. 3:24).

Yet, before driven from the Garden, both Adam and Eve heard the Voice of God render judgment on the Serpent. After cursing the serpent to the ground, the Voice then spoke to the Demonic One who possessed and animated the serpent. The Voice told Satan of his ultimate defeat; a defeat that will come about by one of Eve's own children:

> "And I will put enmity between thee and the woman, and
> between thy seed and her seed; it shall bruise thy head,
> and thou shall bruise his heel. Genesis 3:15

Besides having children to multiply and populate the Earth, Eve's children, her "seed", will also inherit the sin-nature that she and Adam acquired with their disobedience at the Tree of Knowledge. The result of this generational sin-nature, as the Voice warned, is death, which is also the progeny of the Serpent-Satan (Gen. 2:17; Rom. 5:12; 6:23; Jam. 1:15; Heb. 2:14). Hence, all born into the Human race were also born with the sin-nature, which always brings death. This general *status-quo* of one birth-one death for Humanity is the "enmity" between Eve's "seed" and the Serpent-Satan's "seed".

The Voice continued, saying that from among Eve's children, there shall come One who will exchange 'bruises' or injuries between himself and the Serpent-Satan. The injury Satan inflicts on the coming Seed will be temporary, whereas the exchanging injury the Seed delivers upon the Serpent will be everlasting. Although driven from the Garden, Adam and Eve were driven with the knowledge of hope that from one of their children the way back to the Garden and the Tree of Life will be opened again (Rev. 2:7).

Further, having left the Garden, Man encountered that nature itself began illustrating harsh and painful features of a now sinful and rebellious world. Such entailed laborious reproduction on the female's part, and for the male the toiling for the provision food. In addition, Man's physical state would now be subject to aging, disease, infection, an inevitable host of cancers, the breakdown of bodily organs, and finally decomposition after death (Gen. 3:16–19).

With the advent of Sin, and in the duel roll of tempter on Earth and prosecutor in Heaven (Job 1:6–12; 2:1–7; Zech. 3:1–2), Satan now stood before the Throne of Glory. There, Satan ever accuses Man as corrupt, evil, and worthy of one thing: genocide. As Man multiplied and populated the Earth, Cain murdered Abel, and was followed by the increasing wickedness of human civilization. Such gave Satan abundant proof before God to merit the extermination of Mankind (Gen 4:1–24; 6:1–7).

Finally, save Noah's family, such proof became too abundant.[271]

The letters finished, John discovered the Risen Christ was gone. Looking about, John may have thought his Lord was ascending into Heaven once again. Quickly, he lifted his eyes upward. Looking into the sky, the Apostle was suddenly astonished. However, what John saw was not the Risen Christ in ascension—nor did he *yet* see an opened door in Heaven. At this point, after writing the letters, John will now witness the things he had previously encountered and learned in relation to the coming of Jesus Christ and the newborn Church. John will now experience "the things which thou hast seen".

What the son of Zebedee saw in the sky was a woman giving birth.

> "And there appeared a great wonder in heaven; a woman clothed with the sun and the moon under her feet, and upon her head a crown of twelve stars. And she being with child cried, travailing in birth, and pained to be delivered. Revelation 12:1-2

If illustrated alone, stars are a reference to angelic beings (Rev. 1:20). When presented in context with the sun and moon, they represent the tracking of time as decreed by God from the Beginning (Gen. 1:14–19). According to the Hebrew calendar, the setting of the sun, followed by the appearance of three stars in the waning dusk, marked the start of a new day. With the passing of each season, one set of three stars generally gave way to another. At the phase of the new moon was the beginning of a new month, and to keep the lunar and solar calendars in balance with the seasons, a leap month was added every two or three years.[272] In essence, the sky was the God-given clock for Man to measure time.[273] Such is seen in Joseph's dream of the sun, moon, and stars (representing Jacob and his family) bowing before him. This prophesied that the family of Jacob, through the prominence of Joseph, will go from a local Semite clan in Caanan to a nation that will endure and be known for all ages of time (Gen. 37:9–10; 46:1–7; Jer. 31:35–36; Rev. 21:12).

Only one generation removed from the divine cataclysm of the Flood, Man began lapsing back into apostasy as seen with the tower of Babel (Gen. 11:1–8). After fragmenting the Babel civilization through multiple languages and frustrating the tower's construction, God called on one man for a chosen task. God promised this man to be the father of a people that will be his example nation to the world (Gen. 12:1–3; Ex. 19:3–6). His children and descendants are to be a covenant people to show the nations of the Earth the truths of the One True and invisible God. The name of the man was Abram, whom God later renamed *Abraham* (Heb. *father of a multitude*). The example nation he would father, named after his grandson Jacob, and given a new name by God, is Israel (Gen. 28:1–15; 32:24–32).

The Woman, crowned with twelve stars, dressed in the sun and the moon at her feet, represents Mankind, the children of Eve, via the line of Israel though the ages of time.[274] The labor pains of the Woman attest to Israel repeatedly faltering in remembering God's covenant and keeping his commandments

(Gen. 3:16; Is. 26:12–21). These labor pains span from the days of Abraham's arrival in Canaan to the reign of Herod under Augustus Caesar (Matt. 2:1; Luke 1:5; 2:1). The Child the Woman delivers is Christ the Lord, King-Messiah, who will bring fulfillment of God's promise to Abraham, Isaac, and Israel: "in thee shall all the families of the earth be blessed".[275]

> "And there appeared another wonder in heaven; and behold a great red dragon, having seven heads and ten horns, and seven crowns upon his heads. Revelation 12:3

With the birth of the Christ Child, Satan's position as accuser before the Throne of Glory, so to justify Man's genocide, plunged into jeopardy. The seven heads with seven crowns of the Dragon were seven world-empires under Satan's influence.[276] Each head had a direct and long-term involvement with Israel: Egypt, Assyria, Babylon, Medo-Persia, Ptolemy, Seleucid[277], and Rome. The ten horns are ten rulers from among the seven world-empires who demonstrated lethal intent towards Israel from the days of Moses to the Apostles: Pharaoh of the Exodus,[278] Tiglath-pileser III,[279] Shalmaneser V, Sargon II,[280] Sennacherib,[281] Nebuchadnezzar,[282] Antiochus Epiphanes,[283] Herod 'the great',[284] Archelaus,[285] and Herod Agrippa I.[286]

> "And his tail drew the third part of the stars of heaven, and did cast them to the earth... Revelation 12:4a

In his effort to destroy Man, Satan seduced one third of the angelic host to abandon their service to God and join his deviant cause. After foreswearing God, Satan dispatched his dark angels to the Earth to further draw Mankind away from the One True God. Once done, Satan would then blame Mankind before God for such sinful conduct. Through persons receptive to their influence, these dark angels would employ tactics to entice people from the Creator-God and follow other beliefs and superstitions. These tactics included false gods, incantations, paranormal phenomenon, or just plain grifting.

> "...and the dragon stood before the woman which was ready to be delivered, for to devour her child as soon as it was born. And she brought forth a man child, who was to rule all nations with a rod of iron: and her child was caught up unto God, and to his throne. Revelation 12:4b–5

Knowing that the Newborn will be a threat to him, the Dragon-Satan moves in to eat the Child once he is born, which a clear representation of the slaughter of the Bethlehem innocence by Herod (Matt. 2:16–18). But to no avail: the Child lived and grew. Before God and *all* the angels of Heaven, Jesus of Nazareth, the incarnate Son of God through the virgin vessel of Mary, obeyed the will of his Father in a sinless life—and a sinless death (Mark 14:36; John 1:1-3,14; 17:5). The Child lifted to God's Throne illustrates the Risen Christ victoriously ascending into Heaven and taking his place at the right hand of the Father.[287] Further, in a bell-clear echo from Psalms 2, the ascended Child whom the Woman bore is to rule the nations with "a rod of iron", hostile world opposition notwithstanding, be it a Herod or a Caesar (Ps.2:1–2).[288]

> "And there was war in heaven: Michael and his angels fought against the dragon; and the dragon fought and his angels. And prevailed not; neither was their place found any more in heaven. Revelation 12:7–8

Begun during the ministry of the Baptist, who proclaimed "the kingdom of Heaven is at hand", the arch-angel Michael made the attempt to expel Satan and his dark angels from Heaven. Since Satan's condemnation against sinful Mankind remained principally valid, Michael's efforts proved unsuccessful (Matt. 11:12). Yet, as Jesus arrived at the waters of the Jordan and approaching the Baptist, all that was about the change.

At his baptism and Jesus coming out of the water, the Spirit of God descended upon Jesus and with that came the voice of the Father saying, "This is my beloved Son, in whom I am well pleased" (Matt. 3:16–17; Mark 1:9–11; Luke 3:21–22). This the moment when Jesus began his ministry by word and deed that the kingdom of God, the sovereign power of God, had arrived on Earth (Matt. 12:24–28; Mark 1:15; Luke 11:15–20). Once baptized, Jesus was led by the Spirit into the wilderness to face Satan. In his desire to thwart the Spirit-empowered ministry of Christ and exterminate Mankind, Satan tempts the Nazarene for forty days and nights in the Judean wilderness and the Jerusalem Temple. However, by tempting Jesus, the Devil committed himself to recognizing the incarnate Son of God as a member of Mankind. By doing so caused Satan to sow the seeds of his own undoing (Ezek. 28:18; Heb. 2:14–18; 4:14–16).

Following the forty days of Satan's profitless temptations, Jesus began his ministry in the power of the Spirit. During his ministry, Jesus healed the sick, cast out the demons, gave sight to the blind, raised the dead, and provided nourishment to both the starving body and depleted soul.[289] When this happened on Earth, Satan and his demonic minions began to weaken and fall to Michael's expulsion efforts (Matt. 10:1-8; Luke 10:18–20).

Finally, with God-given strength (Luke 22:43), Jesus provided the sin-sacrifice and salvation to all on the Cross. With Jesus' death on the Cross as instigated by Satan,[290] the death-penalty for sin was paid in full.[291] In the coming of Jesus Christ, God's love and destiny for Man, hidden in mystery, not only endured, but unfolded the more to the glory of God (Col. 1:26–27). With Christ paying the death-penalty for sin with his sinless life, Satan prosecution case against Mankind died on the Cross. Thus, Christ defanged the Devil of any further accusations to justify the genocide of Man before God, and God throwing Satan case against Man out of court, and more. Had the Devil knew what would result from the Cross, he would have never crucified the Lord Christ (I Cor. 2:7–9; Col. 2:14–15).

> "And the great dragon was cast out, that old serpent, called the Devil, and Satan, which deceiveth the whole world: he was cast out into the earth, and his angels were cast out with him. Revelation 12:9

Despite his memorable line from Milton, "It is better to reign in Hell than serve in Heaven",[292] being cast out from Heaven was the absolute last thing Satan wanted.

To validate Jesus' sin-sacrifice on the Cross for Israel and the World,

God the Father raised Jesus from the dead, soon followed by the Ascension. With his ascension into Heaven, the Risen Christ became the living intercessor for the repentant sinner who accepts him as Savior and Lord by faith.[293]

Only by the Risen Christ ascending incarnate to the Throne of Glory was Satan's ouster from Heaven fully achieved. Not only did the Heavenly arrival of the Risen Christ mean that Satan's prosecution against Man was at an end, but the Devil was now convicted of obstructing the will of God from the Beginning. For such a crime, Satan was banished from the Heavenly realm and Throne of Glory, forever. When standing before the Throne of Glory, one never wants to leave. If one does leave, it is only with God-given certainty one may return. To leave the Throne, glory, and Face of Almighty God and never return is epic torment without end. Considering Lucifer's first desire, to stand and praise God before the Throne, for Satan to be forcefully removed from Heaven by Michael and the loyal angels was a scene of absolute kicking and screaming. Once ejected out of Heaven for eternity, Satan and his fellow fallen angels were utterly enraged.

> "And I heard a loud voice saying in heaven, Now is come salvation, and strength, and the kingdom of our God, and the power of his Christ: for the accuser of our brethren is cast down, which accused them before our God day and night. Revelation 12:10

In the days leading to his suffering and death on the Cross during the Passion-Passover, Jesus addressed a group of feast pilgrims in the city, saying:

> "Now is the judgment of this world: now shall the prince of this world be cast out. And I, if I be lifted up from the Earth, will draw all men unto me.[294]

Soon after, at the table of the Last Supper/Passover Seder, Jesus told his Twelve Apostles (minus one; Judas having left the table) after his death and departure, the Holy Spirit will come and begin its' evangelical work in the world, because: 1) The world is in a state of sinful unbelief in him; 2) Jesus ascends incarnate to the Father and becomes the intercessor to all who accept him as Savior and Lord; 3) Satan, "the prince of this world" who accused all before the Throne for their sins, is judged and cast out of Heaven.[295]

Fifty days after the Passion and on the pilgrim feast of Pentecost, the Holy Spirit descended upon the Faithful in Christ. On that day, the Gospel message through the sacrifice of Christ on the Cross was first announced to a fallen and sinful world (Acts 2: 14–40). This *Good News* was made known via God's chosen delivery vehicle: the founding members of the Jerusalem church under the Twelve, which now represented New Covenant Israel. Such a situation constitutes "salvation, and strength, and the kingdom of our God and the power of his Christ" having entered the World.

In this historical setting, the above herald of Revelation 12:10–12 is the chronological marker to begin Revelation's prophetic narrative following the seven letters to the churches of Asia. Revelation 12 represents the happenings the Apostle John experienced and learned during his lifetime with the coming of Christ and the Spirit-baptized Church. Such comprises "the things which thou hast seen" (Rev. 1:19a).

> "And they overcame him by the blood of the Lamb and
> by the word of their testimony; and they loved not their
> lives unto the death. Revelation 12:11

In the outpouring of the Holy Spirit, the Apostolic Church in Jerusalem proclaimed the Gospel message. By word, deed, and power, they declared that through the suffering and death of Christ on the Cross, and validated by his resurrection, the power and kingdom of God had arrived on Earth (Acts 3:12–26). In the Great Commission, to announce the arrival of that Kingdom, the Apostles and Jerusalem Faithful began proclaiming the Gospel without compromise, and, if necessary, with their lives.

And such would prove necessary.

> "Therefore rejoice, ye heavens, and ye that dwell in them…
> Revelation 12:12a

Since the Fall in the Garden, the souls of all who died faithful to God were allowed to enter Heaven. However, because of the Fall, Satan stood before the Throne of Glory and accused all of being sinfully unworthy to approach. As a result, all Faithful pre-Cross souls in Heaven were confined from drawing near the Throne and behold the Face of God.

Once Jesus died on the Cross, his soul joined the souls of all the pre-Cross Faithful in Heaven. Among them, he declared his sinless nature and his sacrifice for the sins of all (I Peter 3:19). Next, the soul of Jesus approached the Throne. Satan, accusing all of being sinfully unworthy to approach, moved in and stood face to face with the sinless and divine Son. However, having no legitimate grounds to accuse, Satan grudgingly stepped aside and gave Jesus access to the Throne of Glory. The pre-incarnate Word from before the Creation, and the beloved Son of God, Jesus has returned to the Throne and finished the work the Father gave him: to destroy the works of the Devil.[296] That work now accomplished, the Father rewarded the Son for his labors: the first of the resurrection and the Conqueror of sin and death (Rev. 1:5; I Cor. 15:21–57).

After his resurrection, and the forty days with the Twelve, Jesus ascended into Heaven. There, the incarnate Risen Christ took his place on the Throne of Glory. When that happened, and Satan ejected from Heaven, all pre-Cross Faithful, from Abel to the penitent Thief (Gen. 4:4–8; Luke 23:40–43) were now at liberty to approach the Throne and look upon the Face of God the Father (I Pet. 3:19–22). In reply, all the souls of Heaven rejoiced at the arrival of the Risen Christ to the Throne of Glory. Upon his incarnate arrival, the Risen Christ freed them all from the Devil's imprisoning accusation from approaching the Throne. Now free to draw near and look into the beautiful and loving Face of God, all souls gave praise, "for Heaven's golden day has broken!"[297]

> Woe to the inhabiters of the earth and of the sea! for the devil is come down unto you, having great wrath, because he knoweth that he hath but a short time. Revelation 12:12b

With the ascension of Christ, the time of judgment for the *world* (*cosmos;* κοσμos) had commenced in Heaven *and* Earth (John 12:31). The first recipient of this judgment was Satan forever ejected from Heaven and cast down to the Earth. In fulfillment of Psalms 110:1, upon the arrival of the Risen Christ to the Throne of Glory, Satan became the first 'footstool' of Christ, who is now victoriously at the right hand of the Father. Soon after the ascension of Jesus Christ, the gifts of the Holy Spirit were given, while Satan and his demons, the accusing captors to all, went into captivity from the Throne forever (Ps. 68:18; Eph. 1:17–23; 4:8).

The time of judgment began in Heaven with Christ's ascension and Satan's ejection. On Earth, said judgment began with the Faithful in Christ. Banished from Heaven and never to return, an incredibly enraged Satan targeted those persons belonging to the Jewish nation of the "earth", or the *land* of Israel, and the *sea*, i.e. Gentiles (Rev. 17:15). Specifically, he plotted persecutions on those who believed and proclaimed that Jesus Christ is Lord to the glory of God the Father, and by no other name under Heaven by which all are saved (Acts 4:12; Phil. 2:6–11). The Woman, now the newborn Jerusalem church and New Israel, begins to face attack (I Pet. 4:12–19). Not too long after Pentecost, the Devil began to tempt and deceive worldly powers to attack the Jerusalem church. In his enraged mind, if Satan can stifle the fledgling Church from spreading the Gospel to Israel and the Gentiles, the result may still be the genocide of Mankind. Despite even the coming of the Christ, Satan desperately grasped, the extermination of Humanity may be salvaged.

However, Satan also knew that the clock to vent his rage was ticking. On the Mount of Olives, Jesus disclosed to the Twelve of a coming "tribulation" (Matt. 24:21), "affliction" (Mark 13:19), "the days of vengeance" and "wrath upon this people" (Luke 21:22–23). Contemporary to the generation of Israel that witnessed the coming of Christ (Matt. 24:34; Mark 13:30; Luke 21:32), but for the sake of the "elect", the Faithful in Christ, the time of the tribulation will be limited, otherwise none will survive it (Matt 24:22; Mark 13:20).

> "And when the dragon saw that he was cast unto the earth, he persecuted the woman which brought forth the man child... And the serpent cast out of his mouth water as a flood after the woman, that he might cause her to be carried away of the flood. And the earth helped the

woman, and the earth opened her mouth, and swallowed up the flood which the dragon cast out of his mouth. Revelation 12:13, 15, and 16[298]

Along with Satan falling from Heaven, the Holy Spirit descending from Heaven on Pentecost to guide, strengthen, and comfort the Jerusalem church. As a result, the Satan-spawned persecutions, lethal and horrible enough, proved counter-productive. Indeed, such attacks on the Faithful actually caused the Gospel message to spread across the land of Israel and go to the Gentiles countries.

Beginning with the stoning of Stephen, the deadly persecution of Saul began (Acts 7:54–60; 9:1; 26:10). In response, the Gospel went out from Jerusalem to Samaria, the Coastal Plain to Caesarea, Phoenicia, Cyprus, and Antioch (Acts 11:19-24). After Saul's interrupted journey to Damascus, the churches of Judea, Galilee, and Samaria were strengthened and given new resolve that God was with them: the Gospel spread and the churches grew (Acts 9:1–31). Not very long after, the house of Cornelius in Caesarea, converted and baptized by Peter, set the apostolic precedent for the Gentiles to receive the Gospel and be saved (Acts 10:1–11:18). When Herod Agrippa I executed James b. Zebedee (the brother of John) in A.D. 43, he planned to follow up by having Peter put to the sword. That execution was halted by divine intervention with Peter's escape and Agrippa's demise. Again, the Gospel message continued and the Church grew the more (Acts 12:1–24).

Soon after, Barnabas and Saul-Paul began their first missionary journey to the Gentiles of Cyprus (Acts 13:1–5). At the close of Paul's third missionary journey (ca. A.D. 57), and not without hostile resistance,[299] Christian congregations were founded in the Hellenic East, Macedonia, and Achaia (Greece). Finally, while Paul remained in Rome for his appeal-trial, the Sadducean authorities in Jerusalem executed James the Just in A.D. 62.[300] Responding to this execution, the surviving Twelve such as Peter and John went out to visit the Gentile churches to give them further edification in preserving and preaching the Word (I Peter 1:10–25; I John 2:1–17).

Despite Satan's attempt through the persecutions of Saul, Herod Agrippa I, the attacks on Paul, and the execution of James in Jerusalem, the Spirit-empowered Church endured and prevailed. By the power and guidance of the Holy Spirit, the Gospel went out from Jerusalem, across the land of Israel, and to the countries and peoples of the Greco-Roman world (Matt. 24:14; Mark 13:9–11).

> "And the woman fled into the wilderness, where she hath a place prepared of God that they should feed her there a thousand two hundred and threescore days... And to the woman were given two wings of a great eagle, that she might fly into the wilderness, into her place, where she is nourished for a time, and times, and half a time, from the face of the serpent...Revelation 12:6, 14

Soon after the failed persecutions on the Judean-Jerusalem church, the Jewish Christians were to quickly depart from the city. The Woman acquiring eagle's wings and flying into the wilderness, reminiscent to the Israelite exodus from Egypt (Ex. 19:4), represents the Jerusalem Faithful fleeing the city and its' environs (Matt. 24:16–18: Mark 13:14–16). Further, the woman departing the "face of the serpent" speaks of the Mother-Church of Jerusalem leaving the city because of a blasphemous yet seductive lie being enacted at Jerusalem. Such a lie, which, if it were possible "would deceive the very elect" (Matt. 24:24; Mark 13:22). Away from this profane slander, the Jewish Christians left the Jerusalem area and traveled to places where God will protect them from the coming tribulation, which will last no longer than 3½ years (next chapter).

> "And the dragon was wroth with the woman, and went to make war with the remnant of her seed, which keep the commandments of God, and have the testimony of Jesus Christ. Revelation 12:17

Frustrated by his inability to kill the Mother-Church, and time going more against him, Satan shifted attack strategies. He now makes ready to persecute those children-churches among the Gentiles who have accepted Jesus Christ as Savior and Lord. Churches founded by the Spirit-filled evangelisms of Peter, Barnabas, and Paul, and sanctioned by the Jerusalem Mother-Church.[301]

REVELATION 13:1-10

Pax Satanica

The Condemned were stitched into freshly killed animal skins, and then led out into the arena. As they stood out on the open playing field, they quickly became the object of jeers and 'boos' from the surrounding spectators in the stands. The Condemned, some fearful some brave, looked about and wondered what was next in this bizarre display of costumed theater.

A moment later, the far-end gates opened and dozens to hundreds of wild and starving dogs were released. The Condemned, followers of the Christ, saw the beasts emerge on to the field and knew what was to be. Smelling the animal pelts the Christians wore, the vicious canines focused on their quarry and charged. Seeing the dogs coming at full speed with teeth agape, the brave held the fearful with a promise of Paradise after a hard moment. The redeemed in Christ then closed their eyes with a final prayer. Lunging upon them, the dogs mauled the Christians to death with carnivore ferocity. This was done all to the cheers and look-away horror of those in the stands.

Nearby, on the slopes of Vatican hill, more followers of Christ were crucified in full view of the fire relief camp, illustrating the 'justice' of Nero. Finally, after the sun had set, those crosses were turned into Nero's torches to give light in his private gardens and arena during evening hours. [302]

Under that same evening darkness, in backrooms, cellars, and underground passageways in and around Rome, surviving Christians gathered for worship and prayer. As though an answer to those prayers, the latest news was that a founding member of the Jerusalem church had just arrived in the city, and would begin visiting the secret gatherings. At the meetings, Christians sat closely about while greeting each other with cautiously low voices. Shortly after, the special visitor entered. All eyes on him, the aged Apostle Peter came in and sat down among the Roman Faithful with his assistant Mark. As the Christians were hunted and killed for Nero's sadistic pleasure, Peter came to the city in perfect divine-appointed timing to give the persecuted Church guidance, comfort, and strength.

In the light of a single lamp or low fireside, the Christians gathered around Peter. With Mark taking valuable notes at his side, the aging Apostle began. He told these gatherings of his time with the Lord Jesus Christ: the Baptist at the Jordan, Jesus' ministry around the Sea of Galilee. He told them of the glorious sight on the mount of Transfiguration, his miraculous healings of the sick, lame, blind, and rising the dead. He told them of his parables, and teachings of the great commandments to love God and neighbor. As the Christians hung to his every word, Peter told them of Jesus' Palm Sunday arrival into Jerusalem, the night of his betrayal and Peter's three-time denial. Struggling because of those hard memories, Peter continued and told them of the Lord's crucifixion, and his resurrection appearances to Peter and the Twelve. But more than this, Peter also told them meaning of Christ's coming. Foretold by the Prophets, God the Father has expressed his mercy and grace to a sinful and rebellious world in the coming, death and resurrection of his Son Jesus Christ. Through Jesus' death on the Cross, the repentant sinner may have a relationship with the Father in the fruitful communion of the Holy Spirit and life eternal (I Pet. 1:2–4)

To the Christians of Rome, and the churches of the East, Peter told the Faithful on how the Prophets spoke and wondered of the coming salvation to Israel and the World. Yet, it wasn't for the Prophets' own day, but to those who now heard the message of the Gospel through Holy Spirit (I Pet. 1:9–12). This being so, then the Christian's faith was precious, and to be refined in the fiery trial of Nero's present attack on the Church, to which they should rejoice, proving their faith tested as fine gold (I Pet. 1:6–7, 4:12–13). He also spoke of the accusation that Christians were evil-doers (such as arsonist), and taught them to respond only with goodness, and obey all the ordinances of government (I Pet. 2:12–17). Peter told the Christians in Rome, and the churches of the East, that the terror and violence they were facing are the earmarks of the last days (I Pet. 1:5–6, 20; 3:12–15; 4:7).

Peter further described the latest attack on the Faithful as both Satan-spawned and the beginning of divine-appointed judgment. Yet, though this tribulation will be for a season, the Faithful shall receive a reward that will be for Eternity:

> "For the time is come that judgment must begin at the house of God: and if it first begin at us, what shall the end be of them that obey not the gospel of God? And if the righteous scarcely be saved, where shall the ungodly and sinner appear. I Peter 4:17

And elsewhere, Peter warns:

> "Be sober, be vigilant; because your adversary the devil, as a roaring lion, walketh about, seeking whom he may devour; whom resist steadfast in the faith, knowing that the same afflictions are accomplished in your brethren that are in the world. But the God of all grace, who hath called us unto his eternal glory by Christ Jesus, after that ye have suffered a while, make you perfect, stablish, strengthen, settle you. To him be glory and dominion forever and ever. Amen. I Peter 5:8–11[303]

At each gathering, probably including baptism, communion, and a hymn from the Psalms, Peter would lay hands on those present for God's anointing of the Holy Spirit. Finally, along with a peace-blessing to all in Christ (I Pet. 5:14), Peter would certainly led these clandestine groups in Christ in prayer before the gatherings concluded and dispersed. The most likely priority of prayer needs: To trust in God's provision in all things, and the end of Nero's reign of terror on the Faithful in Christ.

After that first meeting, Peter and Mark made sweet farewells to the gathering, and then carefully started back to the safe-house they were staying. Under cover of darkness, they edged and maneuvered through the alleys and back streets of Rome. As they did, Peter may have looked out towards Vatican hill and saw Nero's fiendish torches burning bright.

It was so long ago, during his younger years, when the center of Peter's world was the fishing nets and boats parked ashore at Capernaum on the Sea of Galilee. How much revenue the next haul would bring was the question of the day. Then the Man from Nazareth entered his life. Now in Rome, the capitol city of the world civilization, Peter proclaims that same Nazarene as Lord and Christ, in a time when being a Christian was tantamount to a death sentence. For Peter, these two worlds, the shores of the Sea of Galilee and magnificent Rome, were now brought together. Seeing where he was, the horrid things done to the saved in Christ, and advanced in his years, Peter wondered. Could this be the approaching time when the Lord will call him to the Cross and to glory, as the Risen Christ foretold on the seashore of Galilee (John 21:18–19; II Pet. 1:14–15[304])?

This also prompted Peter to think about other members of the Church during these dark times. His brother Andrew, who introduced him to the Lord (John 1:40–42), was in Scythia offering the Gospel to those equestrian-skilled barbarians and beyond the legal reach of Rome. Closer still, and aware of his appeal-case that brought him to Rome, Paul had left the city and was proclaiming the Gospel in the provinces (if his appeal ended in acquittal or was dismissed). Possibly, Paul went west to Spain (Rom. 15:24–28), but more likely back to the East (II Tim. 4:13, 20).

What about John, Peter wondered. It was that same seashore walk when the Risen Christ also foretold that John would "tarry" until he would come (John 21:21-23). Could the saying mean that John will live to see the Lord's return and thus never die? Perhaps, it meant something else. Maybe John knew, Peter wondered. Although the Great Fisherman may have known he was someplace in Asia, but where and what in Asia?

What was John doing at this very moment?

Hearing a cautious signal from Mark, Peter pulled his eyes from the Vatican and his thoughts to the immediate, and the two continued in their stealth maneuvering through the city. After cautiously making a corner, Peter and Mark vanished into the night darkness.

After witnessing Satan's failed attack on the Mother-Church, John stood in view of the beach on Patmos. As he looked out towards the waves, the Apostle saw something emerge from the water.

"And I stood upon the sand of the sea,[305]and saw a beast
rise up out of the sea, having seven heads and ten horns,
and upon his horns ten crowns, and upon his heads the
name of blasphemy. And the beast which I saw was like
unto a leopard, and his feet were as the feet of a bear, and
his mouth as the mouth of a lion: and the dragon gave him
his power, and his seat, and great authority. Revelation
13:1–2

This creature rising from the sea "was like unto a leopard, and his feet
were as the feet of a bear, and his mouth as the mouth of a lion". Such a
description makes for a prophetic echo of the four beasts from the book
of Daniel (Dan. 7:2–8), making that prophet's vision the prime lead to
identify this creature.[306]

In his night vision, Daniel saw four beasts emerge from the sea, each
animal representing an empire from among the Gentiles. The first beast, a
lion, symbolizes Babylon. The second beast, a bear, stood for Media-Persia.
The third creature, a four-headed leopard, represented the vast dominion
of Alexander the Great, and was divided into the four Hellenic states of
Hellas-Thrace, with the Seleucid, Ptolemaic, and Antigonid kingdoms.
Like the great four-staged statue in Nebuchadnezzar's dream (head of
gold, Babylon; upper body and arms of silver, Medo-Persia; mid-section
and things of brass, Greece; Dan. 2:31–43), the four beasts characterize
an age of foreign rule over Israel in four successive world-empires. This
foreign rule over Israel began with the Babylonian destruction and exile
by Nebuchadnezzar in 586 B.C.

While Cyrus of Persia ended the seventy-year exile for the Jews,
culminated by the rebuilding of the Jerusalem temple in ca.515 B.C. (II
Chron. 36:22–23; Ezra 1:1–3), such was only in geographic terms. The
exiled Jews did indeed return from Babylon and back to the land of Israel,
but since the Babylonian Destruction, the Jewish nation remained under
Gentile rule. In connection, the house of David never returned in any
sovereign capacity to Israel; the viceroy of Zerubbabel under the Persians
notwithstanding. In both Babylon and in the post-exile Holy Land, the
Jewish nation was passed from one Gentile dominion to another. Jesus

described this succession of Gentile domination in the Olivet Discourse as "the times of the Gentiles" (Luke 21:24).[307]

The fourth beast of Daniel's vision was a Gentile power unlike the previous three; it was "dreadful and terrible, and strong exceedingly" and had ten horns (Daniel 7:7). Further, John states this creature was "like unto a leopard, and his feet were the feet of a bear, and his mouth as the mouth of a lion" (Rev. 13:2). This attest to the fourth beast possessing territories once owned by the previous three. Such would include kingdoms and nations of the East, but most relevant was the land of Israel. Daniel also stated that the fourth beast "shall be diverse from all kingdoms, and shall devour the whole earth, and shall tread it down, and break it in pieces" (Daniel 7:23). In short, this fourth great empire of the Gentiles shall be one of conquering and destructive qualities, and to be remembered for all time.

Once a group of farms huts situated in and around seven hills, an unassuming village grew. In time, land was cleared and a town square, a *forum*, was laid. In addition, a bridge was built across the Tiber River to benefit travel, commerce, and troop deployment. On one of the seven hills, the Capitoline, a shrine to Jupiter was raised, which became a symbol to the proud patriotism of this growing metropolis: Rome.

After breaking away from their Etruscan masters and the founding of a Republic (ca.510 B.C.), the Romans dominated regions near, then far, and eventually all of Italy. Following the Punic Wars that saw the defeat of Hannibal and the obliteration of Carthage, a Roman empire took hold of territories in Spain, North Africa, and the greater islands of Sardinia and Sicily. Not long, the Hellenic lands of Macedonia, Greece, and western Asia fell to Rome's advancing legions. In 63 B.C., the Romans captured Jerusalem, thereby commencing Roman domination in the Holy Land for centuries.

By the dictatorship of Julius Caesar (reigned 49–44 B.C.), Rome's territorial possessions spanned the Mediterranean, Western Europe, territories in North Africa, the Balkans, and the Near East. Add the vassal kingdom of Egypt under Queen Cleopatra, and Rome was master of the civilized world.

"And I saw one of his heads as it were wounded to death...
Revelation 13:3a.

As previously indicated, the seven heads of the beast are seven mountains (the Seven Hills of Rome), and seven "kings" in a chronological context: five are fallen, one is, and another is yet to come (Rev. 17:9–10). These "kings" represent the first seven rulers of Rome that owned the name *Caesar*: Julius, Augustus, Tiberius, Gaius-Caligula, and Claudius (fallen), Nero (is), and Galba (yet to come). Of these seven heads, one of them is wounded to death, representing one of the Caesars brutally murdered. Although both Caligula and Galba met such a fate, the murder of a previous and "fallen" Caesar not only became the most infamous throughout history, but brought violent repercussions that lasted for years.[308]

On the morning of March 15, 44 B.C., the dictator-for-life, Julius Caesar, entered the Senate chamber in Pompey Theater. As all senators stood at his entrance, the eyes of a dozen of them coldly followed Caesar as he took his designated chair of state. Looking over session-documents before the call to order, the dozen edging around Caesar, Senator Tillius Cimber approached with a request. Though Caesar ordered Cimber away, the Senator drew close, grabbed Caesar's purple toga and pulled it off his shoulder: that was the signal. Quickly, the dozen produced their weapons and moved in. The first dagger came from Senator Casca, followed by Cassius. With them came another dagger, then another, and another, and the final blow from Brutus. Desperate in ridding Rome of this would-be king and his aim to destroy the Republic, the *Liberators*, senator-assassins, stabbed Caesar twenty-three times. After this moment of murderous frenzy and to the shock of the remaining senators looking on, a blood soaked Julius dropped at the foot of Pompey's statue and breathed his last. While Caesar lied dead on the theater floor, the Senate session broke up into chaos, which reverberated throughout the city. The theater deserted, no one present but the body, three slaves finally entered the empty senate chamber, placed the body on a stretcher and carried it home.[309]

If Brutus, Casca, and Cassius thought the assassination of Julius would preclude the rise of a Roman monarch named *Caesar*, they could not have been more magnificently wrong. After learning of Julius' murder, young grand-nephew, heir, and adopted son, Caius Octavian, returned to Rome from Epirus (northwestern Greece). Soon after, Octavian assumed the name *Caesar* as his own.[310] In Rome, Octavian, and with two of Julius' allies, Mark Antony and Marcus Lepidus parleyed. The three, eventually, decided to pool their forces and formed what would be known as the 'Second Triumvirate': a group dictatorship over the affairs of the Roman State and the military.[311] This included, as Octavian insisted, hunting down and killing Julius' assassins. It also entailed a bloody reign of terror upon the Roman aristocracy and affluent that listed hundreds to thousands for execution.[312] Such a horrific tactic was to single out and eliminate any sympathizers to Julius' assassination from the nobility, and was followed by the seizure of assets and estates of the condemned. Those blood assets and properties not only filled pockets but financed the legions of the Triumvirate who were now preparing a military expedition to pursue and crush the Assassins. With Lepidus as Consul to attend the affairs of Rome and Italy, Octavian Caesar and Mark Anthony lead their armies to the East, where Julius' assassins fled and amassed troops.

"And his deadly wound was healed: and all the world wondered after the beast. Revelation 13:3b

In the summer of 29 B.C., and after more than a decade of civil war, Octavian entered Rome in triumph. During those years, Julius' assassins, the treachery of Marcus Lepidus, and the rebellion of Sextus Pompey were defeated by Octavian (thanks mainly to Admiral Marcus Agrippa, Octavian's military go-to-man). More recently, the Eastern rebellion and personal betrayal of Mark Antony with Cleopatra were crushed at the famed battle Actium (September 2, 31 B.C.), and followed by the conquest of Egypt (30 B.C.). Subjugated, that ancient land of the Pharaohs became the very property of Octavian.[313] Now, sole military overlord of the Empire, Octavian Caesar rode into Rome to the cheers and praise as Rome's champion and savior. With Octavian's celebrated entry in Rome came the treasures of Egypt as war-spoils to serve as gifts to the public, friends, and the military. During the three-day Triumph, the new Caesar ordered the doors of the temple of Janus officially shut, declaring that peace, victorious peace, had come to Rome and the Empire.[314]

The following years consisted of calculated political maneuvers with a largely cowed Senate, a ceremonial respect to republican traditions, yet a relentless but patient pursuit for absolute power. For Octavian Caesar, now given the name *Augustus* (Lat. *sacred* or *revered*), such resulted in succeeding where Julius left off. Augustus' creation: a monarchy in Rome, where the notion of a king was loathed, yet one man was absolute ruler.[315] Further, the new monarchy of Augustus Caesar not only brought closure to years of unrest and civil war for Rome and Italy, but began the age latter known as *Pax Romana* (Lat. *Roman Peace*). This plateau of some two-hundred years spanned from Augustus to the death of Marcus Aurelius (A.D. 180). Such was a time when Rome, by and large, prospered at home, while conquering and annexing lands, kingdoms, and nations abroad.

In the rise of Augustus, despite the assassination of Julius and subsequent civil war, one named 'Caesar' would successfully rule Rome and the Empire to the awe and resentment of conquered peoples.

> "And they worshipped the dragon which gave power unto the beast: and they worshipped the beast, saying, Who is like unto the beast? who is able to make war with him? Revelation 13:4

The reverence of monarchs and rulers in the form of divine worship was well known in the ancient world, with a history going back to the Pharaohs of Egypt. By the time of Julius and Augustus such veneration became an accepted trait in Roman society.

In early 44 B.C. and shortly before the assassination, Julius was greeted by a group of loyalists during a pilgrimage to Mount Albanus. There, the devout locals praised Julius as a king. In reply, Julius said "I am not a king, I am Caesar." Soon after, during the festival of the Lupercalia, his lieutenant, Mark Antony, who was also consul that year, publically placed a crown on Julius' head, to which Caesar removed. He then insisted (in public, at least) that he would not revive the long abandoned idea of monarchy to Rome.[316] Nevertheless, given the status of 'dictator for life', his robes the traditional purple color of royalty, and his chair of state gilded gold at Senate meetings, Julius' was a king in every way but name only. But the name he would use in place of king would forever be *Caesar*.

The name 'Caesar' (probably derived from the Latin *caesaries*, meaning *fine head of hair*) was adopted by Julius' successors, making the name synonymous with 'emperor'. Further, Julius refusing the official title of 'king' or wearing a likewise crown, the author of Revelation may be engaging in a kind of word-play. Watching the beast rise from the sea, what John saw upon his seven heads were not crowns nor hair but the "name of blasphemy." Beginning with Julius, all subsequent Roman rulers bearing the name *Caesar* were, in one capacity degree or another, revered as gods.[317]

Although Julius never mandated worship of himself during his *defacto* reign in Rome, he did overtly entertain the idea. Along with insisting that his family line, the *Juli*, were descendants from the goddess Venus, he displayed his statue with the Greco-Roman gods, such as in the temple of Quirinus with the inscription "To the unconquered god".[318] Further, after the Triumvirate victory at Philippi which defeated Julius' assassins (October, 42 B.C.), Julius was posthumously declared a god by the Senate. In addition, one of the prime summer months, his birth month, was renamed after Caesar's family *Juli* (July).

Like Julius, Augustus also refrained from being worshiped as a god in Rome, but he did permit such devotional to be conducted elsewhere, and with a practical application. As a historical axiom, conquest is easy control is not, but if the conquered are invited to join in the culture of the conquerors, control may prove more feasible. Since leader/conqueror worship was well practiced in the East, the creation of an imperial cult, which the Roman emperor was worshipped as a god, could serve Roman interests. Such could encourage loyalty among the local nobility or inject a Roman element into the culture of subjugated regions. Along with numerous colonies, followed by impressive roads, trade, commerce, and tax collectors, an imperial cult for the Roman emperor could serve as a hearts and minds tactic in pacification. Such a religious cult would invite the populations of the provinces, vassal kingdoms, and occupied territories of the Empire to participate in the devotions and prosperous Roman world.

Of course, among the subject peoples, some ardent nationalists opposed such Romanization of their homelands. In response, troops and a Roman cross, many of both if necessary, would ...
native patriotisms.

In the founding of the imperial cult, divine devotions were joined with the worship of Roma, the personified ... In doing so, temples were built, statues and altars set up, organized, and the *Roma et Augustus* Cult spread ... and eventually in the West. In time, Augustus was ...

122

gods of Olympus.[320] One such place where Caesar was worshipped was Pergamos: the administrative capitol of Asia and home to one of the seven churches in Revelation. It was in Pergamos where 'Satan's throne' resided (Rev. 2:13), and in 29 B.C. the first ever temple for the Roman emperor was built.[321] In the Holy Land, Herod 'the Great' (37-ca.4 B.C.) transformed the unassuming seaside of town of 'Strato's Tower' into one of the most striking port cities of the East and renamed it *Caesarea*. Like Pergamos, one of the central fixtures of Caesarea was a temple to *Roma et Augustus*.[322]

As for the Jews of Judea and their uncompromising stance to worship their lone God to the exclusion of others, Augustus decided, an alternative approach to bring them inside the imperial cult was required (next chapter).

At the age of 75, having ruled for nearly sixty years since the Triumvirate, Augustus Caesar died on August 19, A.D. 14. Following the news of his death, not only did the Senate allow for a temple to be built for his worship as a recognized god in Rome, and the other prime summer month named after him (August). But the imperial cult he created would survive him under his successors, all bearing the name *Caesar*.

Across the Roman world, the man named 'Caesar' was revered a god in the bright light of day, but crotched deep in the shadow of Caesar, the dark prince of this world, Caesar's evil genius, received the real and blasphemous homage of godhood (Gen. 3:4–5; Luke 4:6).

The ten horns of the beast that both Daniel and John saw represent ten client kingdoms of the East that were given a degree of autonomy, but always remained compliant with Rome. Begun during the Republic and continuing under the Caesars, Rome's foreign policy included the use of vassal states to serve as buffer territories to enemy powers such as the Parthians. Also, the client kingdoms supplemented the Roman legions with respect to border infiltration and local disturbances. Usually, Rome would appoint a member of a local dynasty as a vassal-ruler. Such a ruler was given a measure of semi-independence, but always remained in obedient to Rome.[323] Such was the case with Herod "the great" in the land of Israel at the time of Christ's birth (ca.4–1 B.C.), and later by his grandson Herod Agrippa I during the Apostolic-period Church (A.D. 41–44).

By the reign of Nero Caesar, the sixth head/king that *is* ruling, the Eastern client states included Arabia,[324] Armenia Minor,[325] the Bosporan kingdom,[326] Comana,[327] Commagene,[328] the Herodian kingdom of Agrippa II,[329] Pontus,[330] Sophene,[331] Syria,[332] and the Teucrid principality[333]. From the statue of Nebuchadnezzar's dream, the legs or iron represented Rome. The feet and toes, mixed with iron and clay, spoke of the client kingdoms always submissive to Rome and Caesar (iron), but allowed that degree of autonomy (clay).

In addition, Daniel provides a detailed feature regarding the ten horns. Seeing the horns, Daniel also saw another horn: one that had eyes, a mouth that spoke great things, was stout, and overpowered three of the ten horns (Dan. 7:20). The stout horn Daniel saw was certainly one of the seven heads John saw, meaning that three of the Eastern vassal states will be taken over by one of the Caesars. In A.D. 62, and likely as a move against the Parthians, the Bosporan kingdom was placed under Roman military rule, effectively making that seaside principality one large Roman naval base.[334] In A.D. 64, again because of the Parthians, and for the kingdom's precious metal resources, the Pontus was annexed as Roman province.[335] In A.D. 67–68, and in response to Jewish revolt, the territories inside the kingdom of Herod Agrippa II, Galilee and Perea, were re-conquered by Rome.[336]

Finally, Daniel and John asserted this horn/head that subdued three of the ten horns would also make war with the saints and prevail against them (Dan. 7:21; Rev. 13:7). Along with subduing the three client kingdoms above, Nero's persecution of the Faithful in Christ will be on-going. As long as Nero lived and ruled the Christians died.

> "And there was given unto him a mouth speaking great things and blasphemies; and power was given unto him to continue forty and two months. And he opened his mouth in blasphemy against God, to blaspheme his name, and his tabernacle, and them that dwell in heaven. And it was given unto him to make war with the saints, and to overcome them, and power was given him over all kindreds, and tongues, and nations. Revelation 13:5–7

Like the stout horn Daniel saw speaking things against the Most High (Daniel 7:25), John saw the beast verbally blaspheme God "his name, tabernacle, and them that dwell in Heaven". He continued for "forty-two months" (3½ years), and made "war with the saints, and to overcome them". All these descriptions represent a triple-hat performance of Nero's own Anti-Christ megalomania.[337]

I: Like his predecessors, the imperial cult under Nero functioned unhindered throughout the empire (mainly in the East), in which Roma and Caesar were both worshipped as deities.[338] As an added feature, soon after the murder of his mother Agrippina (A.D. 59), and given his desire to demonstrate his artistic skills, Nero held a 'coming out' recital in his private arena on Vatican hill. After a musical performance of harp and singing, a select cheering squad called the *Augustiani* showered Nero with praise for his "divine voice" and comparing his musical talents to Apollo.[339] Eventually, a semi-liturgy for Nero's musical talent began. In Rome, and likely the Greek-orientated cities of Neapolis and Tarentum, sacrifice offerings were made to Nero's "divine voice." [340]

II: After the great fire destroyed over half of Rome in July of A.D. 64, Nero blamed the Christians for the inferno shortly after. He deemed them the enemies of all and began his war against them, to which he would never relent. Thus, the Christians, the new and incarnate temple-tabernacle of the living God by the indwelling the Holy Spirit,[341] were crucified, set on by wild dogs, made into torches at night, or beheaded. Once the martyred in Christ died under such methods, their released soul entered the Heavenly realm to approach the Throne of Glory and behold the Face. Next, the Father and the Son welcome them with a crown of life.

III: As the Mother-Church of Jerusalem departs from Jerusalem, God will keep them under his protection for 3½ years (Rev. 12:6, 14). This being the same 3½ year period that is the result of Israel being deceived into apostasy by false signs of the beast and thereby invite the tribulation. According to Daniel's 'Seventy Weeks' prophecy (Dan. 9:24–27), the Messiah would be revealed to Israel after a set time of sixty-nine "weeks" (483 years). During the seventieth and final week, the Messiah shall be "cut off", i.e. killed. But at the mid-point of that final "week", his death will validate a covenant with Israel that will end the required sin-atonement sacrifice in the Temple. For the remaining 3½ years of Daniel's final "week", and beast already becoming a profane catalyst in seducing Israel into Anti-Christ apostasy, God will dispense his judgment and wrath. But Israel and the Beast will be recipients of that judgment and wrath.

All the while, Nero's mind was progressively poisoned by the Ancient Serpent with desires of godhood, sadism, and lust for power. Also, he was allowed to rule a Roman Empire that dominated the nations, lands, peoples, and cultures; from Britain to the Euphrates.

> "And all that dwell upon the earth shall worship him, whose names are not written in the book of life of the Lamb slain from the foundation of the world. Revelation 13:8

Across the Empire, followers of the imperial cult made sacrifices and burned incense before statues of Roma and Nero. Even in the Holy Land, the Greco-Roman enclaves of Caesarea, Samaria, and the northern kingdom of Herod Agrippa II, temples, altars, and priests to gave religious homage to the cult of the Caesars.[342] In doing so, no patron to the Imperial Cult shall ever delight in the glory of the One True and Invisible God as was their destiny from the Beginning. Rather, to the unspeakable dread of their souls, when their time comes, they will go elsewhere.

> "If any man have an ear, let him hear: He that leadeth into captivity shall go into captivity: he that killeth with the sword must be killed with the sword. Here is the patience and the faith of the saints. Revelation 13:9-10

After disclosing the vision-scene of the beast rising from the sea, who blasphemed God, persecuted the Faithful in Christ, and ruled the peoples of the civilized world, John halts his narrative. With the familiar "he that hath and ear let him hear"[343], coupled with "all they that take the sword shall perish with the sword" (Matt. 26:52), the identity of the person who spoke this saying to John becomes clear. The saying is a promise: a promise from God given by the Risen Christ for all the suffering Church to hear. The beast that is hunting, killing, and terrorizing the Faithful in Christ shall meet God's judgment. Moreover, as Jesus taught "with what measure ye mete, it shall be measured to you again" (Matt. 7:2; Luke 6:38), the beast shall meet his downfall in a manner matching his attack on the Faithful. As the beast made Christians fugitives of the Roman State, so will the beast become a fugitive of said State; as the beast executed Christians, so will the beast become his own executioner. The saying concludes that those who belong to Christ and have the indwelling of the Holy Spirit are to stand firm and faithfully wait for that Christ-given promise to be fulfilled (Rom. 8:24-39).

God's promises are sure and never late.

Near Passover of A.D. 44, King Herod Agrippa I executed John's brother, the Apostle James b. Zebedee. As a sequel to please the anti-Jesus circles in Judaea who welcomed James' death, Agrippa planned on to execute Peter, whom he had in prison and under guard. However, through angelic assistance, the great fisherman escaped from his prison and went far-off into hiding (Acts 12:1–17). Not very long after, Agrippa traveled to the grand port-city of Caesarea. There, on the morning of a particular feast-day (possibly Claudius Caesar's 54th birthday: August 1, A.D. 44[344]), and decked in brilliant royal attire, Agrippa addressed the gathered multitude. Finished with his oratory, the applauding crowds cheered and exclaimed that Agrippa owned the voice a god and not a man. Agrippa neither rebuked nor welcomed such a blasphemous praise of deity. Yet, and with the blood of the Apostle James on his hands, Agrippa entertained a moment for such divine praise to be applied to him. Just then, before the elated crowds, official guests, and family at his side, divine agency struck and Agrippa immediately collapsed. Tormented with the sharpest pains in his stomach, the king was carried into the palace and to the care of doctors. He lived for five days in agony and finally died. Possibly from observations of his stool and urine, it was discovered that Agrippa's digestive track was infested with maggots.[345]

If Herod Agrippa merited God's judgment and wrath in the killing of the Apostle James and permitted only a moment of blasphemous praise be applied to him, how much more shall it be upon Nero, who well received divine acclaim from his *Augustini* cheering squad at his music recitals, and is now killing the Christians of Rome in great numbers? Just as the Risen Christ foretold above, Nero has a date with God's justice. Truly, the many sins of that Caesar will hunt him down and find him out (Numbers 32:23).

The ultimate outcome of the four beasts representing four world-empires of Daniel's vision, Nero's Rome in particular, though allowed to successively rule for a time, will be dethroned. The final and everlasting victor, "the Son of Man": the Divine King, seated at the right hand of God and seen coming in the clouds of Heaven, shall rule Israel and the World forever (Dan. 7:9–14). Again from Daniel, after seeing the great statue with the head of gold, arms of silver, mid-section and thighs of brass, legs of iron, and feet and toes of iron and clay, Nebuchadnezzar then saw an uncarved stone from a mountain striking the statue at the feet, causing the entire image to shatter and collapse into pieces. The remaining shards of the statue lay on the ground like chaff on a *summer* threshing floor to be blown away with the wind. The uncut stone however, grew into a great mountain: the kingdom of God to cover all the earth (Dan. 2:34–35).

In the days of Rome's eastern vassal kingdoms, the Divine Son, Jesus Christ, came to be the means of sin remission and create a new and eternal relationship between the saved sinner and God the Father. Such is the Good News that the Church is to announce to the World without failure or compromise. Be it the sunniest of days or the stormiest of nights, and to the death, the Faithful proclaiming the Good News is to endure, more forward, and prevail, and the gates of Hades powerless to halt the advance (Rom.8:35–39). Not only were the Faithful in Christ to survive Nero and Imperial Rome, but as the Risen Christ consistently encouraged in the cover-letters to the seven churches, they were to *overcome*.

Lastly, the promise of the beast's downfall and the saints faithfully patient for it, makes for the second chronological marker representing John experiencing, and writing the Revelation, on Patmos while Nero ruled Rome and killed Christians: "things things which are" (Rev. 1:19b).

Excursus

To the dating of the Revelation, traditional and conventional opinion maintains that the book's composition was done in the final years of Domitian Caesar (A.D. 81–96). This view is based virtually on one piece of external and non-contemporary datum: the much discussed passage from Irenaeus of Lyon and his work *Against Heresies* (ca. A.D. 180).

Interestingly, in the passages in question, Irenaeus' point of discussion did not involve to when the Revelation was written, but the 666 number-name of the beast in Revelation 13:18. Irenaeus stipulates the number-name as based on the letter-to-number conversion of the Greek alphabet. He then makes several attempts to construct credulous names in compliance to the 666 sum in the Greek. Finally, Irenaeus resigns that if the number-name was vital knowledge for the Faithful, the witness of the Revelation (John) would have disclosed it when he was with them. Then, in passing, Irenaeus adds, "For that was seen no very long time since, but almost in our day, towards the end of Domitian's reign".[346]

When a youth, Irenaeus was a listener of Polycarp's sermons, who was a companion of John, which places Irenaeus only one degree away from the one who saw the Revelation.[347] This makes the testimony of Irenaeus metal-clad proof that the book of Revelation is dated to ca. A.D. 95, "towards the end of Domitian's reign", thus ending all debate on when the book was written.

Seemingly.

When giving the passage a closer look, such metal-clad proof is not without rust. Considering the original Greek of the Irenaeus passages, the question has been raised on what, or *who*, was actually seen towards the end of Domitian's reign. Was it John who was seen, or the Revelation that was seen? [348]

As to the book of Revelation itself, when deciding on a date to the book, one aspect of internal evidence must be well weighed. Near the beginning of the book, John and the churches are facing persecution (Rev. 1:9). Moreover, a persecution which has reached deadly proportions at the time John experienced and wrote the Revelation (Rev. 2:10, 13; 6:9–11; 13:9–10; 14:13). Most notably, in Revelation 13, the beast is given the ability to "make war with the saints, and to overcome them", and shall do this while ruling "kindreds, and tongues, and nations" (13:7). Next verse, those who that worship the beast forfeit their names to be written in the book of life, as is Humanity's destiny from when God created them (13:8). Clearly, the beast that will "make war with the saints" is a world-ruler and is worshiped as a god. Remembering that the book's foretold events are to "shortly come to pass" for "the time is at hand" (Rev. 1:1–3; 22:6, 10), this beast can best be a Caesar. One who rules a vast empire reaching three continents, and is worshiped as a god via the imperial cult. Moreover, in his "war with the saints", the Revelation adds that he will "overcome them", meaning once he begins killing the Faithful, he will never stop of his own volition. Such detail is vital to the dating of the Revelation.

In the following verses, the persecuted Faithful are given a promise that the beast, who is making relentless war with the saints, ruling nations, and worshiped as a god, will meet God's judgment (13:9–10):

> "If any man have an ear let him hear. He that leadeth in captivity shall go into captivity: he that killeth with the sword must be killed by the sword. Here is the patience and the faith of the saints.

This promise, to which the Faithful in Christ are to trust and wait for its fulfillment, foretells the beast's downfall, which will match the manner of his persecution of the Faithful. As the beast made Christians fugitives, so will the beast be made a fugitive; as the beast executed Christians, so shall the beast become his own executioner. This promise, in conjunction with the above passages involving Faithful under deadly persecution, clearly speaks to the situation that the Church was under at the time the Revelation was being written.

When comparing theses passages of the Revelation with contemporary historical sources, the claim that Domitian was the beast that will "make war with the saints and to overcome them" becomes fragile.

According to sources contemporary to the reign of Domitian, Christian and pagan, there is a woeful plight of any corroboration that Domitian ever executed a single Christian during his reign. Suetonius Tranquillus (ca.A.D.70–ca.140), Roman biographer on both Nero and Domitian, clearly cites the Nero persecution but never one conducted by Domitian. Clement of Rome (ca. A.D. 40–101) is explicitly silent on the matter,[349] as is Ignatius of Antioch (ca. A.D. 35–ca.110).[350] Moreover, in A.D. 112, and as the governor of Pontus-Bithynia, Pliny the Younger and the emperor Trajan Caesar correspond via letters on how to deal with Christians, which included the death penalty. While doing so, neither cited any statutory precedent of lethal action against the Church by Domitian sixteen years prior.[351] Further, this is despite the fact that Pliny speaks of Domitian on other issues during his correspondence with Trajan.[352] Granted, citing the absence of a lethal persecution by Domitian by the above sources can be quickly dismissed as an argument from silence. However, that four sources (five, including Trajan's reply to Pliny), contemporary to Domitian, each speaking of Christian persecution elsewhere, creates a pattern that compels such silence to become loud and clear.

On the other hand, several testimonies from the late second/early third century speak of some manner of hostility against the Faithful during the Domitian years: Hegesippus (ca. A.D.175), Melito of Sardis (A.D.180) and Tertullian (ca. A.D.200). However, none of these sources make a clear reference to any deadly attack against the Faithful during Domitian's reign. Rather, according to Hegesippus, while he arrested and interrogated Christians—two of which included the grand-nephews of Jesus—Domitian became convinced they were not a threat to his rule. In short, he ended his pursuit of the Christians, and with no clear reference of a single Christian being put to death.[353] Such is corroborated by Tertullian, who stated that Domitian ended his pursuit of Christians soon after he started it.[354] Finally, while Melito compares Nero and Domitian in the same breath as does Tertullian, the only specific he describes that the two Caesars committed against the Christian were falsehoods and slanders.[355] If these testimonies are correct, then Domitian did initiate some form of aggressive, yet non-lethal, action towards the Church, and then ordered it stopped soon after it began. Such a situation could explain why a Domitian persecution is never cited by the contemporary sources. Moreover, according to Suetonius, for Domitian to end a persecution of Christians reflects with the early years of his reign when that Caesar was "most conscientious in dispensing justice".[356] In fact, it is not until the fifth century AD that a documented reference explicitly cites any attack on the Church resulting in fatality during the Domitian years.[357]

In light of the historical sources, the passages of Revelation indicating a deadly persecution at the time the book was written, and notably the prophecy downfall (Rev. 13:9–10), suits with the reign of Nero than ever Domitian. While Domitian briefly showed some form of hostile conduct towards the Church, he ordered it stopped shortly after, and was assassinated over a decade later.[358] Nero, however, murdered Christians with sadistic and unrelenting abandon. Less than four years later was declared a public enemy by the Senate, making him a fugitive on the run, to be soon followed by assisted suicide.[359]

Whether the Revelation or John was seen at "towards the end of

Domitian's reign", one sentence, written some eighty years after the death of John, should not be the dating absolute at the expense of the Revelation being allowed to speak on its own.[360] Clearly, the book and beast of Revelation matches well with the reign of Nero Caesar, who ruled the Empire while being worshiped as a god, who executed Christians for his amusement with no intention of stopping, and whose downfall was promised by prophecy. Lastly, the name, 'Nero Caesar', adds to the ominous number sum of 666 in Hebrew/Aramaic, and *not* Greek as was insisted by Irenaeus.

REVELATION 13:11-18

Sacrilege

Like his late cousin James, acting senior elder of the Jerusalem church, Symeon b. Cleopas, would regularly go to the Temple for worship. However, after James' murder two years ago, the Jerusalem church chose to be far more discreet in public activities, especially in the Temple courts.

When going up to the Sanctuary for morning or afternoon worship, Symeon would likely do so surrounded by a large delegation of Faithful. Crossing the broad expanse of the Court of the Gentiles for the inner precincts, the entourage would have looked rather conspicuous. Nevertheless, the Jerusalem Faithful were not going to allow another opportunity for the Sadducees or other factions opposed to 'the Way' endanger the chief elder. Entering the gates of the inner enclosures for the Court of the Israelites, the group did their best to avoid concentrations of the Temple guard and the Sadducees.

Inside the Court of the Israelites, their heads covered with *tallit* prayer shawls, and some probably wearing the traditional *tefilin* head and arm bindings, Symeon and the others took respectful places. Most likely commencing with the *Shema* (Deut. 6:4–6; Mark 12:29–30), followed by hymns and psalms in either Semitic tongue (Hebrew or Aramaic), 'the Way of Jesus' lifted prayers to God.

As they stood and knelt praying, Symeon and the others may have seen a particular sacrifice being prepared by the priests in the slaughter area, and then offered up on the great altar. This sacrifice was made twice-daily in the Temple, and carried out since the time of Augustus Caesar. The Rome-Caesar offering, a sacrifice of two lambs and a bull, was committed to smoke on behalf of the people of Rome and the emperor for the morning and evening burnt-offerings. Watching this offering-ceremony, the Lord's cousin suspiciously eyed the initial plumes of blue smoke rise from the great altar. Strange, Symeon thought as he watched the smoke go skyward. As he understood it, the Romans were not even paying for these offerings, but a special fund by the Jewish nation as a sign of national loyalty to the emperor, Nero Caesar, and Rome.[361]

Moreover, such a sight made for the sharpest contrast on what was happening of late in Judea and Jerusalem.

After James' death and the start of the new governorship of Lucceius Albinus, murmurs for armed conflict and the gathering of militant groups were heard and seen throughout the city. With Albinus' penchant for high taxes, bribery, and thus selective law enforcement, plus the ever disapproval to Gentile rule in the land of Israel, a new anti-Rome discontent took root in Judea. The Zealots, who were generally termed 'the fourth philosophy' of Judaism after the Pharisees, Sadducees, and Essenes,[362] became more pronounced and active. The terrorist-assassins called the *Sicarii* have been about for some ten years, but lately refined their terrorism with kidnapping and hostage taking. In southern Judea, a young maverick named Simon b. Giora began to gather followers, train and organize militia, and call upon what he and others saw as the inevitable: open war with Rome.

To the people, the rise of such war-factions became a constant fear, especially when said revolutionaries called upon the youth to join their militant cause. In reply, many fathers and family patriarchs refused their sons and grandsons to take part in such a dangerous calling, causing resentment and reprisals from the militants. A great dread and foreboding ran through the city and countryside. The sun had gone behind thunderhead clouds and a dark overcast shadowed the land, city, and Temple.

Something was coming, and it was not for the welfare of the Nation.

After worship, the senior elder and his escort exited the Temple's inner courts and returned to the city below. As they quietly departed the Sanctuary complex, work crews were making finishing touches to the Temple's long renovation. Elsewhere in the sacred enclosures, as Symeon and company passed, crowds gathered in the outer porches and listened to Zealot orators make venomous denouncements against Caesar and Rome.

Reaching the outer passages, Symeon and the others proceeded down the stairs and back into the city. As they descended the steps, the Lord's cousin heard something in the distance: a voice and it was shouting. It was that same loud and lamenting voice all Jerusalem heard every day for the last couple of years, and saying the same repetitive thing.

"Woe, woe, unto Jerusalem!"

Sensing something, John spun about and looked inland from the beach. His eyes quickly focused on one particular spot of ground: something was happening. Just then, the ground gave way and another horrid creature came rearing up before him.

> "And I beheld another beast coming up out of the earth;
> and he had two horns like a lamb and he spake as a
> dragon. Revelation 13:11

The first beast rising from the sea represented Daniel's fourth and great sovereign power from among the Gentiles: Rome. This second creature John saw emerging from the "the earth", or that is the land, the *Promised Land, the Holy Land*: the land of Israel. That it owns two horns like a lamb indicates a sacrificial offering, such as the Torah-stipulate twice-a-day offering in the Jerusalem Temple (Ex 29:38–39).

However, the creature speaking like a Dragon illustrates that the second beast brings a message that is nothing more than a great lie. Indeed, a lie deceitful enough, if possible, to deceive "the very elect" (Matt. 24:24; Mark 13:22). In essence, this second beast from the Land is a profane hybrid, an unholy alliance, the joining of the imperial cult of the Caesars and the priestly institution of the Jerusalem Temple. Their one inevitable commonality: slander towards the One True and Invisible God and his Risen Messiah.

Initiated by Augustus himself, a burnt offering on behalf of Rome and Caesar, consisting of two lambs and a bull, was made twice every day on the great altar of the Temple. Such an offering served as a surrogate in order for the Jews to participate in the Imperial Cult without violating the commandment to not have other gods besides the One True and Invisible God (Ex. 20:3). Instead of making sacrifices *to* Caesar as done elsewhere in the Empire, the Jewish nation was making a sacrifice *for* Caesar. By itself, this imperial offering in the Temple would not constitute a desecration of the Sanctuary, but rather the reverse. Since the Jewish nation was making burnt offerings on behalf of their Gentile rulers, it showed a prayerful hope that Rome and the emperor would come to know the One True God of Israel. Such sentiment, especially since the Romans initially paid for the offerings, would philosophically be in line with Jesus' teaching: "render to Caesar the things that are Caesar's, and to God the things that are God's" (Matt. 22:17–21; Mark 12:14–17; Luke 20:20–25).

However, once the Temple was rebuilt, plus the news of Nero's attack on the Christians reaching Jerusalem, the twice-a-day offering on behalf and Rome and Caesar became a malignant game-changer for all of Israel.

At about A.D. 64, around the time Nero began his persecution of the Christians, the long reconstruction of the Jerusalem Temple was completed.[363] Begun in the reign of Herod (ca.19 B.C.), the Temple and its large adjoining complex of courts, porches, gates, ritual chambers, and the great altar, were now a finished masterpiece of gleaming gold, fine-cut stone, and masterfully crafted wood. The sight was one of architectural splendor. Furthermore, since a rebuilt and functioning Temple was one of the Biblical signs for the coming of the Messiah (Dan. 9:26; Hag. 2:6–9; Mal. 3:1), such caused many to believe the Messiah was soon to appear.[364]

However, with the Temple rebuilt, the Sadducees and other anti-Jesus factions also came to a fanciful realization that the finished Temple was their answer. That was the third alternative they were seeking in putting an end to 'the Way of Jesus' sect forever. Why have one man denouncing Jesus as the Messiah in the Temple when the very Temple itself can accomplish the same feat?

During the first Passover pilgrimage of his ministry (A.D. 30), Jesus entered the courts of the Temple. There, he saw how the precincts were being used for commercial and financial gain with the sale of cattle, sheep, doves, and the coin exchangers. These areas within the sacred enclosures (most likely the court of the Gentiles) were actually leased-out and turned into a shopping bazaar. In addition, and according to rabbinical sources, this leasing may have been brokered by the priestly Annas family.[365] In an act of righteous indignation for such abuse of the Sanctuary, Jesus overturned the tables, poured out coinage, let loose the animals for sale, and chased out the merchants from the Temple courts (John 2:13–15).

Seeing this, many Jews took Jesus' behavior as a blatant act of disrespect to the status milieu of the Temple complex; confronting him, many demanded a *sign* from Jesus to validate his actions.

Jesus answered: "Destroy this Temple, and in three days I will rise it up."

Incredulous, his listeners replied, "Forty and six years was this Temple in building, and thou wilt thou rear it up in three days?" (John 2:18–20).[366]

While the Gospel of John refers this saying to Jesus' resurrected body (John 2:21), he adds that such explanation wasn't revealed to the Apostles until after Jesus rose from the dead, three Passovers later (John 2:22). This resulted in the saying, rebuilding a destroyed Temple in three days, to resonate throughout the Jewish nation for three feast-cycles. At the end of that time, the saying came back to Jesus during his trial (Matt 26:61; Mark 14:58), Crucifixion (Matt. 27:40; Mark 15:29), and to subsequent members of the early Apostolic church (Acts 6:13-14).

Once the Temple reconstruction was complete, a backlash of this saying about the Temple was inevitable.

The Temple rebuilt, and Jesus never returning to destroy and rebuild the Sanctuary in three days, this saying of Jesus was deemed by many as a false prophecy in accordance to Deuteronomy 18:20–22. Since the anti-Jesus factions tried to catch Jesus in his words so to find contradiction and fault (Matt. 22:15; Mark 12:13; Luke 20:20), this seeming failed prophecy by the Nazarene was their best opportunity. Acting upon this apparently false prophecy, the Sadducees and other anti-Jesus groups of Jerusalem and Judea likely took it as irrefutable proof that Jesus was never the Messiah and Son of God. He never returned from the dead, nor will he return to be seen by the Jewish nation as King-Messiah. When the Sadducees and their anti-Jesus associates made this charge, their evidence was, on the face of it, the best one could ever have: a beautifully rebuilt Temple for all to see, and an alleged risen Nazarene nowhere to be found.[367]

> "And he exerciseth all the power of the first beast before
> him, and causeth the earth and them that dwell therein to
> worship the first beast, whose deadly wound was healed.
> Revelation 13:12

In those areas of the Holy Land under Gentile persuasion (Caesarea, Samaria, The Herodian Kingdom of Agrippa II), the Imperial Cult functioned unaffected, where Caesar, ruler of the Roman Empire was revered as a god; an empire which, despite the assassination of Julius Caesar, Rome ruled the civilized world.

> "And he doeth great wonders, so that he maketh fire come down from heaven on the earth in the sight of men. And deceiveth them that dwell on the earth by the means of those miracles which he had power to do in the sight of the beast; saying to them that dwell on the earth, that they should make an image to the beast, which had the wound by a sword, and did live. Revelation 13:13–14

The word for "wonders", *semeion* (σημειον), is also used in John 2:18, when Jesus detractors demanded a "sign" to justify his cleansing of the Temple.[368] With the Temple rebuilt and Jesus never returning to destroy and rebuild it in three days, such was taken as a *sign* to disprove Jesus of Nazareth as the Messiah.

In connection, while there was a hostile demeanor against the followers of Jesus in Judea by the local powers, Jerusalem in particular (I Thess. 2:14–16), Roman judicial rulings repeatedly fell on the favor of the Apostolic-era Church (Acts 16:35–39; 18:12-16; 25:1–12). Most recent of these was the fallout from the recent death of James the Just.[369] Therefore, when the news of Nero's attack against the Christians in Rome reached Judea (late A.D. 64/early65), such appear to be a hostile change in Rome's approach towards the followers of Jesus. Moreover, this latest news from Rome also served as an independent *sign* to confirm Jesus' alleged failed prophecy to rebuild the Jerusalem Temple. For the Sadducees and others opposed to 'the Way', such was likely taken as providential in that Jesus was not, nor ever will be, the Messiah.

Given these two *signs*, and on the Scriptural authority of Deuteronomy 18:20–22, a majority of Jews in the land of Israel were persuaded away from the belief that Jesus of Nazareth was the Messiah. Rather, the Nazarene was just another false prophet that was trying to lead Israel astray. For the Sadducees and others, once 'the Way of Jesus' movement lapses into insignificance, it would demonstrate that it was only a product of Man in accordance to the advice-ruling of Gamaliel. Further, with 'the Way of Jesus' proven false and at an end, Israel will be safe from any Roman military reprisal provoked by the belief that Jesus is King-Messiah. Lastly, as an added bonus, these signs disproving Jesus as the Messiah would, at least in principal, vindicate the Sadducees in the execution of James the Just (John 16:2–3).

The image of fire coming from Heaven is to identify the location where these two slanderous signs were manifested to Israel. When brought together, the signs shared a common geographic center: the great altar of the newly rebuilt Jerusalem Temple. This was same general location where David purchased Ornan's threshing floor and made burnt offerings to God, to which David made an insisted point in paying for the offerings. Once David's paid offerings were ready, fire came down from Heaven and burnt it up (I Chron. 21:18–26). Years later, fire came from Heaven again at the same place when Solomon made the premier offering of the great altar of the first Temple (II Chron. 7:1).[370]

Further, the great altar was inside the Court of the Priest, which was directly adjacent to the Court of the Israelites, where only males Jews may enter to worship. This allowed the men of Israel direct viewing to the functions of the priests, including the daily burnt-offerings on the great altar. Thus, Rome-Caesar offering, representing the lies of the second beast, was burnt up on the great altar "in the sight of men".

Also, at the north-west corner of the Temple complex stood the Fortress of Antonia, where the Roman garrison was stationed with a commanding view over the city; essentially a military embassy for Rome in Jerusalem. On the Temple Mount, the Antonia had direct access to the Sanctuary complex, allowing for quick deployment of Roman troops during a time of crisis (Acts 21:31–40; 22:24).

The Antonia Fortress at the northwest corner of the Temple Mount, the smoke of the Rome-Caesar offering rising twice-a-day "in the sight of the beast", was a foreboding portrait of the Jerusalem Temple and her priestly institution joined, married, to Nero's Rome.

> "And he had power to give life unto the image of the beast,
> that the image of the beast should both speak, and cause

> that as many as would not worship the image of the beast
> should be killed. Revelation 13:15

In Rome, at the southern end of the Forum, towered a colossal bronze statue of Nero of about 103 feet, which, from foot to head, would stand close in height to a later-day Lady of Liberty.[371] Certainly, it was a sight that no one in downtown Rome could easily escape. While the "image of the beast" was seen by Romans in stone and metal, in Jerusalem that image was manifested in living flesh.

Within the courts of the Jerusalem Temple, the officiating priest who offers the sacrifice on the great altar served as the representative of the offering party. In the Rome-Caesar sacrifice, the offering party would be the emperor: Nero Caesar. Predisposed in rejecting Jesus of Nazareth as the Messiah, and learning of Nero's deadly attack on the Christians in Rome, the Jewish leadership in Jerusalem decided (if they even gave it a thought) that the twice-a-day burnt offering for Rome-Caesar will continue. As with the imperial cult proper throughout the empire, to halt the Rome-Caesar offering would be viewed by the Romans as an act of insurrection, and invite a Roman military reply.

To gain further mileage from such a dreadful scenario, a *third* sign, a self-provided sign to bring the two previous signs together, was manifested. When first established by Augustus Caesar, the sacrifice for the Rome-Caesar offering was originally paid by the Romans.[372] By Nero's reign and the final renovation of the Temple (A.D. 64), responsibility for payment was transferred from the Romans to the Jews themselves. This fiscal-liturgical decision was made as token (*sign*) of loyalty to the emperor Nero.[373]

With the manifestation of these three signs, their converging point being the great altar of the Temple, this makes for the defining moment of the "the abomination of desolation" foretold by the prophet Daniel and cited by Jesus. By proxy of the officiating priest, and the general consent of the Jewish nation, Nero Caesar entered the Temple and the Court of the Priests. He proceeds up the altar ramp, and stands upon the great altar. There, his hands running with the blood of murdered Christians, his voice hailed as divine, Nero Caesar makes an all-expense-paid offering to the One True and Invisible God and Father of the Lord Jesus Christ.

Sacrilege.

As Nero killed Christians in Rome, and the Rome-Caesar offering continued on the great altar the Jerusalem Temple became a false prophet institution of stone and flesh. Collectively, the Jewish nation had now denounced Jesus as the Messiah, and recognized Nero Caesar the ruler of the land of Israel (John 19:15; II Thess. 2:9–12). By doing so, the Nation committed both Anti-Christ and Anti-David apostasy before God (John 5:43).

In addition, it wasn't just the Jewish nation in general that was being persuaded away from Jesus by these Temple-signs. The Jerusalem church and the Jewish Christians across the land of Israel saw and heard of these signs as well. Add to this, they would become the recipients of 'gotcha' ridicule and derision on sides of Jewish society, thereby causing a massive strain on their faith in Jesus. Yet, this very situation was foretold by Jesus in order for the Jewish Faithful to take heart and stand firm to these deceitful signs being daily perpetrated in the temple against God and his Christ:

> "For there shall arise false Christs, and false prophets, and
> shall shew great signs and wonders; insomuch that, if it
> were possible, they shall deceive the very elect. Behold, I
> have told you before.[374]

By using the imperative "Behold" followed by his reminder that he spoke to the Twelve of these things prior, Jesus was assuring the Faithful that he was in front and above these heinous lies (John 16:1-4). Furthermore, as stated in the Fourth Gospel, the Faithful must also remember that the saying-sign of John 2:19 was not about Jesus replacing a destroyed Temple with a new man-made sanctuary in three days. Rather, his resurrection on the third day was God the Father validating him as a tried and tested chief corner stone to a new and living temple, not made with human hands, built up by the living stones of the Faithful in Christ. A new covenant and a new house of God, fashioned by God, indwelled by his Holy Spirit, and to endure for Eternity (I Peter 2:4–10). As to the newly man-made and now desecrated Temple: "not one stone upon another…" (Matt. 24:2; Mark 13:2; Luke 21:6).

> "And he causeth all, both small and great, rich and poor,
> free and bond, to receive a mark in their right hand, or in

their foreheads: And that no man might buy or sell, save
he that had the mark, or the name of the beast, or the
number of his name. Revelation 13:16-17

The word for "mark", *charagma* (χαραγμα), is the same to describe
the imperial stamp used on documents, and the image of the emperor on
coins.[375] First begun by Julius, and done with more explicit refinement
under Nero,[376] Roman and provincial coins illustrated an image of the
Caesars. On the obverse (front) side of the coins, the profile image shows
Nero wearing a radiate crown of sunbeams.[377] This headdress of sunbeams
was indicative to godhood by the wearer.

The imagery essentially made the coins religious icons to Nero's
seemingly divine status. By keeping the coins in circulation, the purchaser/
seller was essentially advertizing Nero's claim of godhood to the general
public. Even if the purchaser/seller did not believe the divine claim, if
one transacted with such coins and therefore keeping them in promoted
circulation, the "mark" was on their right hand, the common transacting
hand for the buyer/seller. However, if one actually believed in Nero's
divinity, whether they used the coins or not, the mark was on their
forehead. Therefore, the symbolic constant of the beast's mark in the hand
or forehead was Nero's claim to deity as illustrated on the coins in Rome,
the provinces, and vassal states.

As these coins circulated throughout the Empire, one shoreline of
commercial landfall was the market place, or at least the money exchange,
within the courts of the Jerusalem Temple. The same of market that Jesus
of Nazareth so proactively condemned near the start (John 2:14–17) and
conclusion of his messianic ministry (Matt. 21:12–13; Mark 11:15–17;
Luke 19:45–46). Thus, the "image" of the beast resided within the Temple
complex both at the great altar in the inner court where the priest made the
daily Rome-Caesar offering, and the Nero coins within the market place
of outer court of the Gentiles.

> "Here is wisdom. Let him that hath understanding count
> the number of the beast: for it is the number of a man; and
> his number is Six hundred threescore and six. Revelation
> 13:18[378]

As already shown, the name 'Nero Caesar' in first century Hebrew or Aramaic, when the letter-characters are converted to numbers, add up to the sum 666 (see figure 1).[379] Such being the case, and starting from the assassinated Julius, Nero "is" the sixth head/king bearing the name *Caesar* (Rev. 17:9–10). Further, while Nero was being hailed as a god in Rome and abroad, dogs ripped apart, the crosses rose, human torches burned, and the heads of the Faithful in Christ were chopped off unhindered. All at the order of Nero (Rev. 13:7). In the face of such terror, the Risen Christ promised downfall of the beast and in the manner as he attacked the Faithful (Rev. 13:9–10). Finally, as the desecrating smoke of Rome-Caesar offering rose from the altar of the Jerusalem Temple, Israel was deceived by false signs from the truth of Jesus of Nazareth was the Risen Lord and Messiah (Rev. 13:11–15).

Back on Patmos, after witnessing the frightful appearance of the two beasts, a likely overwhelmed John b. Zebedee needed a moment. With the sea breeze blowing over him, the waves roaring nearby, there was a slight return to normalcy. John looked up towards the Heavens to offer prayer. As he did so, another fantastic sight met the Apostle's eyes. It was happening again, John wearied with wonder. However, to his consolation, there was going to be a considerable change of venue.

> "After this I looked, and behold, a door was opened in heaven: and the first voice which I heard was as it were a trumpet talking with me; which said, Come up hither, and I will show you thee things which must be hereafter.
> Revelation 4:1

In his initial meeting with the Risen Christ, John was told to write down "the things thou hast seen, the things which are, and the things which shall be hereafter" (Rev. 1:19). This represents the chronological stages in John receiving the Revelation, in which the Apostle's own life experiences were vital to that reception.

The Woman giving birth to the Child, the Dragon being cast out of Heaven and trying to destroy her to no avail represented the coming of Christ, the persecution of the Jerusalem Mother-Church, and Satan failure to accomplish that end. These and related events are the things John had previously witnessed and learned in his lifetime, or "the things which thou hast seen".

The beasts of seven head and ten horns and rising from the sea, speaks of the Roman Empire under Nero Caesar as he blasphemed with self-proclaimed godhood. With this blasphemy, Nero persecuted the Christians with deadly and sadistic force on the heels of Rome's great fire in July of A.D.64. This general date being the first of the seven thunder/summers of Revelation 10:3–4, which will resolve the paradox of the book of Revelation. This was joined by the second beast rising from the land with two horns, representing Nero's burnt-offering profaning the Jerusalem Temple to the consent of a Messiah-rejecting Jewish nation. All happening while John was on Patmos experiencing and writing the Revelation: "the things which are".

Now, invited up into the Heavenly realm, the Apostle John will witness and write down "the things which shall be hereafter." From this point on, the son of Zebedee will behold events belonging to the future. A future of the remaining six summers and a future where the One True and Invisible God will unleash his vengeance upon an apostate Israel, a Christian-murdering Rome, and Nero the Beast.

And what of the Second Coming of Jesus Christ, when a welcoming Jewish nation and the redeemed from among the Gentiles see him in glory?

To be continued...

SELECTED BIBLIOGRAPHY
(* Recommended by the author)

Authors

Arnold, Eberhard. *The Early Christians: After the Death of the Apostles*. New York; Plough, 1972 (Second Edition). *

Berlin, Andrea M. and Andrew Overman. *The First Jewish Revolt*. London-New York; Routledge, 2002.

Blomberg Craig L. *Historical Reliability of John's Gospel: Issues and Commentary*. Illinois; InterVarsity Press, 2001.

Brown, Raymond. *An Introduction to the New Testament*. New York; Abrl-Doubleday, 1997.
    –*Death of the Messiah Vol. I*. New York; Abrl-Doubleday, 1994. *

Bruce, F.F. *New Testament History*. New York; Doubleday-Galilee, 1969, 1971. *
    –*Peter, Stephen, James, and John: Studies in Non-Pauline Christianity*. Michigan; Eerdmans 1980.

Bunson, Matthew. *Dictionary of the Roman Empire*. New York-Oxford; Oxford University Press 1991, 1995.

Carson, D.A. *The Gospel According to John; Pillar New Testament Commentary*. Grand Rapids/Cambridge; Eerdmans-Leicester England; Apollos, 1991.

Cary, Earnest (transls). *Dio Cassius: Roman History; books 61-70*. Loeb Classic Library. Cambridge, Massachusetts-London, England: Harvard University Press, reprint 1995.

Chilton, David. *The Days of Vengeance: An Exposition of the book of Revelation*. Texas; Dominion Press, 1987. *

Cruse, C.F (transl). *Eusebius: Ecclesiastical History* [History of the Church]. Massachusetts; Hendrickson, 2014.

De Selincourt, Aubrey, John Marincola (transl). *Herodotus: The Histories*. London; Penguin, reprint 2003.

Diringer, David. *The Story of the Alpha Beth*. New York: Thomas Yoseloff; World Jewish Congress, 1958.

Edersheim, Alfred. *The Life and Times of Jesus the Messiah*. Virginia; MacDonald Publishing 1983 reprint. *

—*The Temple: Its ministry and services as they were at the time of Jesus Christ*. Michigan; Kregel, 1997. *

Edmundson, George. *The Church of Roman in the First Century*. Oregon; Wipf & Stock, 2008 reprint. *

Evans, Craig, and Peter Flint (edits). *Eschatology, Messianism, and the Dead Sea Scrolls*. Michigan-Cambridge; Eerdmans, 1997.

Feldman, Louis H (transl). Josephus: *Jewish Antiquities, book XX*. Loeb Classic Library. Cambridge, Massachusetts-London, England: Harvard University Press, 1965.

Finegan, Jack. *Handbook of Biblical Chronology*. Massachusetts; Hendrickson, 1964, 1998.

Gentry Jr., Kenneth L. *Before Jerusalem Fell*. Atlanta; American Vision, 1988. *

Graves, Robert (transl)., Michael Grant, intro., *Suetonius: The Twelve Caesars*. London; Penguin Books, reprint 1987.

Green, Joel B., Scot McKnight, I Howard Marshall., edits. *Dictionary of Jesus and the Gospels*. Illinois-Leicester; Inter-Varsity Press, 1992. *

Green, Peter (transl). *Juvenal: The Sixteen Satires*. London; Penguin Books, reprint 1974.

Gregg, Steve (edit). *Revelation: Four Views; A Parallel Commentary*. Nashville; Thomas Nelson Publishers, 1997. *

Griffin, Miriam. *Nero: The End of a Dynasty*. New Haven-London; Yale University Press, 1984.*

Hawthorne, Gerald, Ralph P. Martin, Daniel G. Reid (edits). *Dictionary of Paul and his Letters*. Illinois-Leicester; Inter-Varsity Press, 1993.

Hays, Daniel, J. Scott Duvall, and C. Marvin Pate. *Dictionary of Biblical Prophecy and End Times*. Michigan; Zondervan, 2007.

Healy, John (transl). *Pliny the Elder: Natural History; a selection*. London; Penguin Books, 1991.

Hemer, Colin J. *Book of Acts in the Setting of Hellenistic History.* Indiana; Eisenbrauns, 1990. *

–*The Letters to the Seven Churches of Asia in their local setting.* Michigan-Cambridge; Sheffield Academic, 1986, 1989.

Henderson, Bernard *The Life and Principate of the Emperor Nero.* London; Methuen & CO.; Kessinger Publ. reprint of 1905 edition.

Hoehner, Harold W. *Chronological Aspects of the Life of Christ.* Michigan; Zondervan, 1977; Dallas Theological Seminary, 1975. *

Hoeing, Sidney. *The Great Sanhedrin.* New York; Bloch Publ. 1953. *

Howard, Kevin, and Marvin Rosenthal. *The Feasts of the Lord.* Nashville; Thomas Nelson, 1997. *

Keener, Craig. *The Gospel of John: A Commentary, Volume Two.* Massachusetts; Hendrickson, 2003.

–*Revelation: The NIV Application Commentary.* Michigan; Zondervan, 2000.

Le Glay, Marcel, Jean-Louis Voisin, and Yann Le Bohec. *A History of Rome.* Massachusetts- Oxford; Blackwell Publishers, 1996.

Leon, Harry J. *The Jews of Ancient Rome.* Massachusetts; Hendrickson Publ. 1960, 1995.

Lightfoot J. B, J.R. Harmer (transls), and Michael Holmes (edit). *The Apostolic Fathers* (Second Edition). Michigan; Baker Books, 1989. *

Longenecker, Richard. *Biblical Exegesis in the Apostolic Period.* Michigan-Vancouver; Eerdmans & Regent College, 1999.

Luttwak, Edward N. *The Grand Strategy of the Roman Empire from the First Century to the Third.* Baltimore-London; John Hopkins University Press, 1976, 1979.

MacDowall, David W. *The Western Coinages of Nero.* New York; The American Numismatic Society, 1979.

Malitz, Jurgen. *Nero.* Massachusetts; Blackwell Publishers 1999.

McBirnie, William Steuart. *The Search for the Twelve Apostles.* Illinois; Tyndale House, 1973.

Moore, Clifford H. and John Jackson (transl). *Tacitus: The Annals of Imperial Rome; books XIII-XVI.* Loeb Classic Library. Cambridge, Massachusetts-London, England: Harvard University Press, 1937, reprint 2006.*

Nadich, Judah. *The Legends of the Rabbis: Vol. Jewish legends of the Second Commonwealth.* New Jersey-London; Aronson Inc., 1994.

Ouaknin, Marc-Alain. *Symbols of Judaism.* Assouline Publishing, Barnes & Noble, 2000, 2003.

Pate, C Marvin. *Communities of the Last Days: The Dead Sea Scrolls, the New Testament & the Story of Israel.* Illinois; Inter-Varsity Press, 2000. *

Radice, Betty (transl). *The Letters of the Younger Pliny.* London; Penguin Books, 1969. *

Robinson John A.T. *Redating the New Testament.* Oregon; Wipf & Stock Publ. 2000 reprint. *

Ronning, John. *The Jewish Targums and John's Logos Theology.* Massachusetts; Hendrickson, 2010. *

Russ, Mike. *The Battle of Planet Earth: From Abraham to Armageddon.* California; Vision House, 1981. *

Russell, James. *The Parousia: The New Testament Doctrine of our Lord's Second Coming.* Michigan; Baker Books reprint 1983, 1999.

Schaff, Philip. *History of the Christian Church, Vol. I.* Massachusetts; Hendrickson reprint 2011.

Schauss, Hayyim. *The Jewish Festivals: A Guide to their History and Observance.* New York; Schocken, 1996.

Scullard, H.H. *From Gracchi to Nero: a History of Rome from 133BC to AD68.* (Fifth Edition) London-New York; Routledge, 1982.

Shepherd, W.G (transl). Betty Radice (intro). *Horace: The Complete Odes and Epodes.* London; Penguin Books, 1983.

Schurer, Emil. *A History of the Jewish People in Time of Jesus Christ.* (T.T Clark: Edinburgh, 1890) Massachusetts; Hendrickson reprint, 2008. *

Sproul, R.C. *The Last Days According to Jesus.* Michigan; Baker Books, 1998. *

Strong, James. *The New Strong's Exhaustive Concordance.* Nashville: Thomas Nelson Publishers, 1990.

Taylor, Lily Ross. *The Divinity of the Roman Emperor.* Connecticut; Scholars Press, 1931 reprint.

Thackeray, J (transl). *Josephus: The Life and Against Apion.* Loeb Classic Library. Cambridge, Massachusetts-London, England: Harvard University Press, 1926, reprint 2004.

Thackeray, J (transl). *Josephus: The Jewish War, books I-II.* Loeb Classic Library. Cambridge, Massachusetts-London, England: Harvard University Press, 1927, reprint 1997.

VanderKam, James C. *The Dead Sea Scrolls Today*. Michigan-London; Eerdmans-SPCK, 1994.*

Vermes, Geza. *The Complete Dead Sea Scrolls in English*. New York; Allen Lane-Penguin Press, 1997.

Walton, John H. *The Lost World of Genesis One* Illinois; Inter-Varsity Press, 2009.

Wenham, David. *Paul: Follower of Jesus or Founder of Christianity?* Michigan/Cambridge-; Eerdmans, 1993. *

Whiston, William (transl). *The Works of Josephus*. Massachusetts; Hendrickson, 2011.

White, Horace (transl). *Appian: Roman History; the Civil War, books 1-3.26*. Loeb Classic Library. Cambridge, Massachusetts-London, England: Harvard University Press, 1913

Witherington III, Ben. *Revelation*. Cambridge U.K.; Cambridge University Press, 2003.

Wohlberg Steve. *End Times Delusions: The Rapture, the Antichrist, and the End of the World*. Pennsylvania; Treasure House, 2004.

Wright, N.T. *The New Testament and the People of God*. Minneapolis; Fortress, 1992.

Yonge, C.D (transl). *The Works of Philo*. Massachusetts; Hendrickson, 1993.

Young, Brad H. *Jesus the Jewish Theologian*. Massachusetts; Hendrickson, 1995.

Online Sources

http://biblegateway.com/ *
http://biblestudytools.com/
http://bethlehemstar.com/
http://ccel.org/ *
http://penelope.uchicago.edu/Thayer/E/home.html *
http://livius.org
http://oll.libertyfund.org/ *
https://web.eecsutk.edu/~mclennan/BA/SNHIG.html
http://naturalesquaestiones.blogspot.com/
http://biblicalartifacts.org/caiaphas.html)

ENDNOTES

1   Eusebius, *History of the Church*, 7:25.1–3.

2   Kenneth Gentry, *Before Jerusalem Fell: Dating the Book of Revelation* (American Vision, 1988), pp. 3–10.

3   Such Futurist publications include the popular *Left Behind* series by Tim LaHay and Jerry Jenkins (Tyndale House, 1995). Also well known is the best seller *The Late Great Planet Earth* by Hal Lindsey (Zondervan, 1970).

4   In classical terms, the Second Coming often goes by the Greek word *Parousia* (parousia), meaning "presence, arrival". See Hays, Duvall, and Pate, *Dictionary of Biblical Prophecy and End Times* pg. 409–412.

5   James Stuart Russell, *The Parousia: The New Testament Doctrine of our Lord's Second Coming* (Baker Books, 1999 reprint) pg. 531–532.

6   For a modern defense of Historicism, see Steve Wohlberg, *End Times Delusions: The Rapture, the Antichrist, and the End of the World* (Treasure House, 2004).

7   Steve Gregg (Edit), *Revelation: Four Views; A Parallel Commentary* (Thomas Nelson Publishers, 1997), pp. 34, 276-306, 400–404.

8   Revelation 1:1–3. Emphasis added.

9   Versions that include, *King James Version*; *New International Version*; *English Standard Version*; *American Standard Version*; *Revised Standard Version*, to name a few. For a more comprehensive list of versions concerning Revelation 1:1–3, see chapter *Revelation 1: Patmos*.

10 Classic Preterists, such as James Russell, endorse the view that Revelation 19-20 only applies to the A.D. 70 Destruction (*The Parousia*, pg. 517–518). While not all modern Preterists share such a view, there seems to be a lack of consensus on what Revelation 19-20 represent. See Gregg, *Revelation: Four Views*, pp. 448-454.

11 Gregg, *Revelation: Four Views*, pp. 34–46. The fourth view of apocalyptic eschatology, known as *Idealism/Spiritualism*, will be addressed in its proper and valid place.

12 Matt. 13:31–32; Luke 13:18–19.

13 Matt. 19:30; Luke 13:30.

14 Matt. 23:1-28; Mark 12:38–40; Luke 20:45–47

15 Matt. 23:27–36; Luke 11: 47–51. See Alfred Edersheim, *The Life and Times of Jesus the Messiah*, (MacDonald Publishing, 1983 reprint) Vol. II pp. 413–414.

16 Matt. 23:37; Luke 13:34.

17 Matt. 24:1–2; Mark 13:1–2; Luke 21:6

18 While a 'generation' is usually defined as forty years (Num. 14:28–39; Ps. 95:10), a fifty-year (Lev. 25:1–55) or even seventy-year period (Ps. 90:9–10; Jer. 25:11) can also be argued.

19 Josephus, *Antiquities of the Jews* 18:85.

20 Ibid. 20:97.

21 Acts 21:38; Josephus, *Antiquities* 20:167–172; *Wars of the Jews* 2:261.

22 Josephus, *Wars*, 2:433–448.

23 Ibid. 6:312–313. While there is no direct evidence that any of the messianic imposters explicitly used the title "Messiah" or "Christ" in their verbal tirades, it is clear from their behaviors that they preyed on the messianic expectations of the day to draw audiences into believing they were divinely sanctioned deliverers

24 Josephus *Antiquities*, 18:109–119

25 Ibid, 18:120–124

26 Ibid. 18:261–309; Philo, *Embassy to Gaius* 42:330–337

27 Suetonius, *Caligula*, 26:1; Dio Cassius, *Roman History* (ca. A.D. 200) 60.9

28 Josephus, *Antiquities*, 19:326–349

29 Suetonius, *Claudius*, 17:1; *Vespasian,* 4:1–2

30 Tacitus, *Annals of Imperial Rome*, 6:36; 13:34–41; 15:1–29

31 Ibid. 14:31–37

32 Acts 11:28; Josephus, *Antiquities* 3:320–321;20:50–53; Tacitus, *Annals* 12:43; Suetonius, *Claudius,* 18:2

33 Tacitus, *The Histories*, 3:48; 4:52

34 Josephus, *Wars*, 6:1–3

35 Josephus, *Antiquities*, 18:373

36 Tacitus, *Annals*, 12:50

37 Ibid. 16:13; Suetonius, *Nero* 39:1. Flavius Philostratus (ca. A.D. 210) identifies the plague as Influenza (*The Life of Apollonius of Tyana*, 4:44).

38 Acts 4:31

39 Tacitus, *Annals*, 12:43

40 Ibid. 12:58

41 Acts 16:16–40

42 Tacitus, *Annals*, 14:27

43 Ibid. 15:22. Seneca provides the date for the Pompeii earthquake: February 5, A.D. 62 (*Questions Naturales* 6:1).

44 Josephus, *Wars*, 6:299–300

45 Pliny the Elder, *Natural History*, 2:199

46   Suetonius, *Galba*, 18:1

47   See also Mark 13:9, and Luke 21:12.

48   Josephus, *Wars*, 20:200.

49   Tacitus 15:44; *I Clement* 5:1–6:1

50   I Pet. 1:1–7, 6-7; 2:12–17; 3:14–16; 4:4, 12–16; 5:8–9.

51   Josephus, *Antiquities* 20:160–165; *Wars.* 5: 442–445, and 5:566.

52   Josephus, *Wars*, 4:128–129

53   Matt. 24:9–14; Mark 13:9–11; Luke 12:11–12; 21:12–15.

54   Romans 1:8; 15:19–23

55   N.T. Wright, *The New Testament and the People of God* (1992, Fortress Press), pg. 444.

56   Lev. 1:1–7:37

57   Daniel 8:26; 9:24; 12:4 and 9. Modern scholarship places the book to the time of Antiochus Epiphanes' oppression of the Jews (ca.167 B.C.), thereby precluding the six century B.C. Daniel as the author. However, the presence of canonical Daniel among the Dead Sea Scrolls, one manuscript 4QDanᶜ) dated to the late second century B.C., and the book's particular reverence among the writings at Qumran, disputes the late date scenario. Craig Evans and Peter Flint (edits.), *Eschatology, Messianism, and the Dead Sea Scrolls* (Eerdmans Publishing 1997), pp. 41–60.

58   Lev. 23:4–44; Deut. 16:16.

59   Matt. 24:32–33; Mark 13:28–29; Luke 21:29–31.

60   Matt. 24:34–35; Mark 13:30–31; Luke 21:32–33. The same word for "generation" (genea) is also found in Matt. 23:36; 24:34, Mark 13:30, Luke 11:29–32, 50-51; 17:25; 21:32, and Acts 2:40.

61   Gregg, *Revelation: Four Views*, pg. 38.

62   Ibid. 130–131.

63   Hays, Duvall, and Pate, *Dictionary of the Biblical Prophecy and End Times,* pp. 347–348.

64   Matt. 3:7–10; Luke 3:7–9; John 12:31, Acts 2:16–40; I Cor. 7:29–31; 10:11; I Thess. 2:14–16; II Tim. 3:1–5; Heb. 1:1–2; 9:26; 10:25, 37; Jam. 5:8–9; I Pet. 1:5–6, 20; 4:7, 17; I John 2:18.

65   C. Marvin Pate, *Communities of the Last Days: The Dead Sea Scrolls, the New Testament & the Story of Israel,* (InterVarsity Press, 2000), pp. 48–49; James C. VanderKam, *The Dead Sea Scrolls Today* (Eerdmans, 1994), pp. 176–184; Geza Vermes, *The Complete Dead Sea Scrolls in English,* (Allen Lane/Penguin Press, 1997) pp. 84–90.

66   Matt. 16:27; 24:30–31; 26:64; Mark 8:38; 13:26–27; 14:62; Luke 9:26; 18:8; 21:27–28; John 14:1–3; Acts 1:6–11; 3:19–21. See also I Cor. 11:26; I Thess. 4:15–5:11; I Pet. 1:13; I John 2:28.

67   Matt. 10:23; 21:43; 23:39; Luke 2:34; Rom. 10–11.

68 Kenneth Gentry, *Before Jerusalem Fell* (American Vision, 1988),, pp. 130–131; Gregg, *Revelation: Four Views*, pg. 38–39; James Russell, *The Parousia: The New Testament Doctrine of our Lord's Second Coming*, (Baker Books, reprint 1999) pp. 374–376.

69 John 2:19–22; 6:70–71; 7:37–39; 8:25–27; 12:32–33; 18:8–9; 19:28; 21:18–19,22–23.

70 The 'Second John' theory shall be addressed in its proper place.

71 Judg. 3:25; Is. 22:22; Matt. 16:19; Luke 11:52; Rev. 1:18; 3:7; 9:1; 20:1 (KJV). James Strong, *The New Strong's Exhaustive Concordance* (Thomas Nelson Publishers, 1990), pg. 581.

72 Eusebius, *History of the Church*, 7:25.4

73 Russell, *The Parousia*, pg. 431.

74 Deut. 29:29; Job 11:7; Matt. 24:36; Mark 13:32; Acts 1:7; Rom. 11:33; II Cor. 12:1–4.

75 Matthew 16:2–3. See also Luke 12:54–56.

76 Is. 28:1–4; Dan. 2:35; Amos 8:1–3; Micah 7:1–13; Zech. 7:3; Matt. 24:32; Mark 13:28; Luke 21:29–30. The warning to those on the roof tops to depart without coming down to take anything from the house, nor retrieve their clothes when working in the field (Matt. 24:17–18; Mark 13:15–16), strongly indicates summer time. During that season, whole families slept on the flat rooftops to enjoy the cooler night air, and field work required a degree of disrobing.

77 Is. 5:1–7; 63:1-6; Lam. 1:15; Joel 3:9-13; Zech 7:3; Matt. 21:33–44; Mark 12:1–11; Luke 20:9–18; Rev. 14:17–20. Kevin Howard and Marvin Rosenthal, *the Feasts of the Lord* (Thomas Nelson, 1997) pg. 202.

78 Hayyim Schauss, The *Jewish Festivals: A Guide to their History and Observance* (Schocken, 1996), pp. 143–144.

79 For an A.D. 33 dating for Christ's crucifixion, see Jack Finegan, *Handbook of Biblical Chronology* (Hendrickson, 1964; rev. edit. 1998), pp. 353–369; Harold W. Hoehner, *Chronological Aspects of the Life of Christ* (Zondervan, 1977; Dallas Theological Seminary 1973, 1974, 1975), pp. 95–114; and Joel B. Green, Scot McKnight, I Howard Marshall (Edits.), *Dictionary of Jesus and the Gospels* (InterVarsity Press, 1992), pp. 121–122.

80 Irenaeus of Lyon (ca. A.D.130-200), *Against Heresies,* book 5:30.1–3; Eusebius, *History of the Church*, 5.8.5

81 Rev. 3:14; 7:4–8, 12; 9:11; 16:16; 19:1, 3, 4, and 6. The Greek word *Hebraisti* (Ebraisti) in Revelation 9:11 and 16:16 can apply to either the Hebrew or Aramaic (John 5:2; 19:13, 17, and 20).

82 David Chilton, *The Days of Vengeance: An Exposition of the book of Revelation* (Dominion Press, 1987), pp. 142–145; Gentry, *Before Jerusalem Fell*, pp. 193–212; *The Beast of Revelation* (American Vision, 2002), pp. 37–47; Steve Gregg, *Revelation: Four Views*, pg. 302; Hays, Duvall, and Pate, *Dictionary of Biblical*

Prophecy and End Times, pg. 431; Bernard Henderson, *The Life and Principate of the Emperor Nero* (Kessinger Publishing re-print of 1905 edition), pg. 440; R.C. Sproul, *The Last Days According to Jesus* (Baker Books, 1998), pp. 182–189; Ben Witherington III, *Revelation* (Cambridge University Press, 2003), pp. 176–179.

[83] Andrea M. Berlin and Andrew Overman, *The First Jewish Revolt* Hanan Eshel, "Documents of the First Jewish Revolt from the Judean desert", pp. 157–163 (Routledge, 2002). See also Gentry, *Before Jerusalem Fell*, pp. 198–199, note 28.

[84] The Seven Hills: Palatine, Capitoline, Aventine, Caelian, Esquiline, Viminal, and Quirinal. The seven "mountains" imagery of Revelation 17:9 is generally accepted as the Seven Hills of Rome in nearly all eschatology quarters (Gentry, *Before Jerusalem Fell*, pp. 149–151; Gregg, *Revelation: Four Views*, pg. 408–409).

[85] Probable location was Esquiline Hill (Horace, *Odes* 3.29.10).

[86] While many modern historians amend or challenge *Quinquennium Neronis*, allegedly credited to Trajan Caesar (A.D. 53–117), the consensus stands that Nero inherited and initially ruled an Empire in very favorable condition. See H.H. Scullard, *From Gracchi to Nero: a History of Rome from 133BC to AD68*, (Routledge, Fifth Edition 1982), pg. 304.

[87] After the military disaster of Teutoberg Forest in A.D. 9, when German tribes annihilated three Roman legions, Germanicus, the older brother of Claudius Caesar, led a bludgeoning response campaign across the Rhine to the Elbe and the North Sea. Not only were these counter attacks well-earned victories for Rome, but they also re-established Roman reputation along the Rhine frontier. Had it not been for Tiberius sending Germanicus to Syria as administrator of the East, and withdrawing the legions back to the Rhine, a re-subjugation of interior Germany was likely.

[88] In anticipation to the marriage and to avoid national scandal, the Senate passed legislation to allow uncles marry their nieces; an act previously deemed incestuous. Tacitus, *Annals of Imperial Rome* 12:1–8; Suetonius, *Twelve Caesars: Claudius* 26:3

[89] Tacitus, *Annals* 12:26, 41–58; Suetonius, *Caesars: Nero* 7:1–2; Dio Cassius, *Roman History*, 60:31.8.

[90] In response to the assassination of Julius Caesar, Augustus created the Praetorian Guard as an elite bodyguard-army of nine cohorts of 1,000 men, totaling to 9000. The mission of the Praetorians was succinct: The bodily protection of the emperor and his family. The Guard would be stationed in the imperial palace, the city, and the surrounding towns, which, unlike the legionaries in the provinces, gave the Praetorians the benefit of close proximity to Rome. That, with the increase of pay and the prestige of being 'Caesar's own', the Praetorian Guard became the admiration, envy, and jealously of the military. See Matthew Bunson, *Dictionary of the Roman Empire*, (Oxford University Press 1991, 1995), pp. 340–343.

91 Tacitus, *Annals* 12:66–69; Suetonius, *Caesars: Claudius* 44–45.

92 II Thess. 2:2–9. If dating and Pauline authorship of II Thessalonians is correct (ca. A.D. 51–52), the epistle would roughly coincide with Claudius' adoption of Nero, making him heir-apparent, to be followed by his marriage to Octavia. Such could well indicate "the mystery of iniquity doth already work" as the beginning of Nero's rise to power. See Gerald Hawthorne, Ralph P. Martin, Daniel G. Reid (Edits.), *Dictionary of Paul and his Letters* (InterVarsity Press, 1993), pg. 937, and Russell, *The Parousia*, pp. 182–183.

93 Tacitus, *Annals* 13:1–5, 25; Suetonius, *Nero* 26:1–2; Dio Cassius, *Roman History* 61:3.2–4.

94 Tacitus, *Annals* 13:12–13.

95 Ibid. 13:14; Dio Cassius, *Roman History*, 61:7.1–3.

96 Tacitus, *Annals* 13:15–16; Suetonius, *Nero* 33:2–3; Dio Cassius, *Roman History* 61:7.4.

97 Tacitus, *Annals* 13:18; Suetonius, *Nero* 34:1.

98 Tacitus, *Annals* 13:19–21

99 Ibid. 13:45–46; Suetonius, *Caesars: Otho* 3:1–2.

100 Tacitus, *Annals* 14:1

101 Ibid. 14:4; Suetonius, *Nero*, 34:2–3; Dio Cassius *Roman History* 62:13.2

102 Tacitus, *Annals* 13:5–6.

103 Ibid. 14:8; Suetonius, *Nero* 34:2–3; Dio Cassius, *Roman History* 62:12:1–13:5.

104 Tacitus *Annals* 14:9.

105 Tacitus, *Annals* 14:10–12; Dio Cassius, *Roman History* 62:15.3–4

106 Suetonius, *Nero* 34:4

107 Ibid. 62:11.1; 62:14.1–15.6

108 Hawthorne, Martin, and Reid, *Dictionary of Paul and his Letters*, pp. 838–839. In his eight Oxford lectures (1913), George Edmundson makes an impressive case that the Church tradition crediting Peter as the founder of the Roman church is essentially correct (George Edmundson, *The Church of Roman in the First Century*, Wipf & Stock Publishers [1913] reprint 2008, pp. 30–58; lecture 2).

109 F.F. Bruce, *New Testament History* (Doubleday-Galilee, 1969, 1971), pg. 137; Harry J. Leon, *The Jews of Ancient Rome* (Hendrickson Publ. 1960, 1995), 1–5.

110 Acts 28:14–15; Rom. 1:16; 2:9–10; 3:9, 29; 9:24; 10:12.

111 I Cor. 1:2; Gal. 1:2; I Thess. 1:1. Paul does not greet the church of Philippi as a "church", though he does salute the bishops and deacons with the general community of Faithful, indicating a central authority (Phil. 1:1–2).

112 Bruce, *New Testament History*, pp. 393–394.

113 Rom. 1:2–7, 16; 2:9–11; 3:9, 29-30; 8:3–15; 9:24; 10:12.

114 Specifically, for bringing Gentiles into the inner precincts of the temple, which was accessible only to Jews; punishment for such an offense was the death

penalty (Acts 21:27–29; 24:1–9). Archaeological evidence of such a prohibition of Gentiles from entering the Temple's inner precincts was discovered in Jerusalem in 1871. Known as the *Clermont-Ganneau Tablet*, the Greek inscribed limestone warning tablet forbids Gentiles from entering the inner enclosures of the Temple on penalty of death.

[115] The term "Caesar's household" refers not only to members of the imperial family, but also slaves and freedmen who served the family in a considerable capacity. If Philippians was written from Rome in ca. A.D. 61 (alternative views offer Caesarea and Ephesus for the letter's place of origin), "Caesar household" likely included members of the imperial staff that embraced the Christian faith.

[116] Philo, *Embassy to Gaius* 157; 317–318

[117] According to Suetonius, Claudius' expulsion order was brought on by disturbances among the Jews "at the instigation of Chrestus": a probable variation of *Christ* (*Claudius* 25:4). Suetonius is generally corroborated by Luke where Paul met Aquila and Pricilla in Corinth, who recently came from Rome because of the Claudius expulsion, when Gallio was proconsul in Achaia (Acts 18:2, 11–12). Based on inscriptional evidence for Gallio's time as proconsul, the Corinth meeting can be dated to A.D. 50, thus placing the expulsion slightly earlier (A.D. 49); See Bruce, *New Testament History*, pp. 297–299.

[118] Matt. 13:10–15

[119] Because Nero refrained from presiding over cases (Tacitus, *Annals* 13:4), the designated judge of the court for Paul's appeal was probably the Praetorian Prefect, who in A.D. 62 was Burrus just prior to his death, or one of the succeeding duel Prefects: Rufus or Tigellinus. Further, Paul's letter to the Philippians seems to indicate the Praetorians were aware of the appeal case (Phil. 1:13), giving a degree of credence that a Praetorian officer would rule on the case

[120] To say that the two years ended with Paul's execution in A.D. 62 is forced, since Luke never mentions the appeal ruling at the close of Acts. From Philippians (1:23–26; 2:24) and Philemon (22), though he was aware of the death penalty, Paul was confident that such would not be his fate. See Colin J Hemer, *Book of Acts in the Setting of Hellenistic History* (Eisenbrauns, 1990), pp. 390–404.

[121] While on his deathbed, Burrus was convinced that Nero's servants administered poison to him in the guise of medicine (Tacitus, *Annals* 14:51; Suetonius, *Nero* 35:5; Dio Cassius, *History* 62:13.3)

[122] Tacitus, *Annals* 14:48

[123] Ibid. 14:52–56.

[124] Ibid. 14:57.

[125] Dio Cassius, *Roman History* 62:13.1

[126] Ibid. 14:60; Suetonius, *Nero* 35:1–2

[127] Tacitus, *Annals* 14:60–61.

128 Tacitus, *Annals* 14:61.

129 Tacitus, *Annals*. 14:61; Suetonius, *Nero* 35:2

130 Tacitus, *Annals*. 14:62; Suetonius, *Nero* 35:2

131 Tacitus, *Annals* 14:63–64

132 Ibid. 13:1; 14:22, 58–59; Suetonius, *Nero* 35:4; Pliny the Elder, *Natural History* 7:58. Poppaea was pregnant in A.D. 62, and gave birth to a daughter at about January of 63. Nero named his newborn daughter Claudia Augusta, but the child died some four months later. Soon after her death, the Senate motioned that she be declared a goddess (Tacitus, *Annals* 15:23; Suetonius, *Nero* 35:3).

133 Tacitus, *Annals* 15:38. See also Suetonius, *Nero* 38:1–3; Dio Cassius, *History* 62:16:1–18:5; Pliny the Elder, *Natural History* 17:1, 5.

134 Not only does Suetonius indicate that the granaries were destroyed, but that Nero ordered their stone housings broken down and the grain set afire. Suetonius, *Nero* 38:1.

135 Tacitus, *Annals*, 15:38.

136 Tacitus, *Annals* 15:39. Though Tacitus never cites the burning of the city granaries as found in Suetonius, Nero's order of food brought into the city, and the lowering of the grain price, indicates that Rome's immediate grain supply was unavailable.

137 Ibid. 15:40–41

138 Ibid. 15:39; Pliny, *Natural History* 17:5; Suetonius, *Nero* 38:1–3; Dio Cassius, *Roman History* 62:18.1.

139 Tacitus, *Annals* 15:40; Suetonius, *Nero* 55:1.

140 Tacitus, *Annals* 15:40

141 Henderson, *The Life and Principate of the Emperor Nero* pg. 251; Henderson cites Joseph Lightfoot, F.J.A Hort, and Ernest Renan effectively dating the Nero persecution to A.D. 64 "—and the summer of the year" (pg. 439). With the first fire associated with his harp-playing, to which Nero was highly sensitive (Suetonius, *Nero* 41:1), and the second blaze linked to Praetorian Prefect Tigellinus, thus Nero's inner circle, the young Caesar needed to quickly to find a scapegoat. In short order, Roman fires of July would be quenched by the Christian blood of August and September.

142 Tacitus, *Annals* 15:39.

143 Ibid. 15:42–44.

144 Ibid. 15:42; Suetonius, *Nero* 31:1–2.

145 Tacitus, *Annals* 15:44.

146 These equestrian events by Nero may very well have served as either a surrogate, or supplement, to the *Ludi Romani*, or Roman Games, the oldest series of games in the city that dated back to pre-Republic times (510 B.C). Running from September 4 to 19, the *Ludi Romani* was traditionally held in the Great Circus. By late summer of A.D. 64 however, the Great Circus was little more than an

empty burnt-out shell. With his arson charge against the Christians, and a chance to impress an audience, Nero could easily have used his private arena at Vatican hill as a substitute location to observe and celebrate the *Ludi Romani* (Bunson, Dictionary of the Roman Empire, pg. 246).

147 Tacitus, *Annals* 15:44; see also Juvenal (ca. A.D. 55–140), *Satire* 1:155; 8:236. Such was the regular method of capital punishment for arsonists.

148 Since Nero had a regiment for keeping his "divine" singing voice in the best of health (Suetonius, *Nero* 20:4), it is unlikely he would have scheduled a nocturnal equestrian event while driving an open chariot in a questionable charioteer's habit beyond late September. In Rome, at that time of the year, evening temperatures began dropping. Arguments have been offered to link this personal health feature of Nero's with his anti-Christian purge to the Piso Conspiracy in April of A.D. 65 (Edmundson, *Church of Rome* pg 141–142; Robinson, *Redating*, pp. 146). However, when considering Nero's character and vanity, it is virtually unthinkable he would have allowed allegations and rumors that he ordered the greatest fire disaster in Rome's history to prosper for a period of nine months. Instead, a time of one to two months, August–September of A.D. 64 seems more plausible when evening temperatures were temperate enough for Nero to allow himself to chariot ride without threatening his voice, and when said allegations and rumors were still early for him to stifle.

149 Tacitus, *Annals* 15:44. The term *panem et circuses*, or "bread and circuses", is from Juvenal's *Satire* 10:81), which describes the public being diverted from the troubles of the day with provided food and entertainment.

150 Tacitus, *Annals* 15:44.

151 I Pet. 1:1, 6–7; 2:12–17; 3:14–16; 4:4,12–16; 5:8–9; Rev. 2:8–10, 13; 3:10–11. See Henderson, *The Life and Principate of the Emperor Nero*, pg. 446.

152 The sensitive question on the precise nature of James' family relationship with Jesus shall remain open. Of the various views of the family relationship, the author of this work has opted (but will not demand) for Jesus and James to be half-brothers: the same mother but different fathers. Such a view best corresponds to Matt. 1:20–25 and Luke 2:7 in conjunction to Matt. 13:55–56 and Mark 6:3.

153 Eusebius, *Ecclesiastical History*, 2.23.6.

154 While James verbally proclaimed the Good News within the courts of the Jerusalem Temple, his general letter traveled across the Holy Land to the furthest reaches. Probably written early in his chief eldership (ca. A.D. 45; perhaps the earliest document in the New Testament Canon), and addressed to the Faithful dispersed across the tribal lands of Israel, the letter neither lacks reference to Scripture nor echoes to Jesus' teachings.

155 Matt. 22:37–40; Mark 12:29–34; Luke 10:25–37.

156 Dan. 9:27a; Matt. 27:51; Mark 15:38; Luke 23:45; Heb. 10:18–22

157 Eusebius, *Ecclesiastical History,* book 2.23.8

158 On the Apostolic pre-Pauline creed of I Cor. 15:3-4 (and possibly 5-7), and may date as early as the 30sAD, see David Wenham, *Paul: Follower of Jesus or Founder of Christianity?* (Eerdmans Publ. 1993), pg. 366-367, footnote #86. In a fragment of the so-called "Gospel of the Hebrews" (preserved by Jerome's *Lives of Illustrious Men,* chapter. 2), the Risen Christ appears to a fasting James and invites his "brother" eat and end his fast now that he has seen the Risen Messiah.

159 Eusebius, *History of the Church,* 2.23.9. In the prophetic spirit of Amos 9:11–12, James made his landmark ruling at the Jerusalem council meeting ("Wherefore my sentence is..."): Gentiles who come to the faith in Jesus are not required to convert to Judaism, but abide by the listed Noachian prohibitions (Acts 15:130–29; ca. A.D. 50).

160 Alfred Edersheim, *The Temple: Its ministry and services as they were at the time of Jesus Christ,* Kregel Publ., 1997; pp. 35–38.

161 Eusebius, *History of the Church,* book 2.23.10a

162 Josephus, *Antiquities* 18:85; 20:97–99, 169–172; *Wars* 2:261–263; Acts 21:38.

163 On the seeming historical discrepancy of Theudas in Gamaliel's statement in Acts 5:36, see Hemer, *The Book of Acts in the Setting of Hellenic History,* pp. 162–163. Possibly, Judas b. Ezekias, who raided the royal armory of Sepphoris and attempted to declare himself king in Galilee following the death of Herod 'the great' (Josephus, *Antiquities* 17.10. 271-272), could very well be the "Theudas" spoken in Acts 5:36 under an alias.

164 Josephus, *Antiquities.* 20:197, 202

165 Ibid 20:197–199

166 According to the Rabbis, the Sanhedrin re-located their original meeting place from the Chamber of Hewn Stone in the inner courts to 'the bazaars of the sons of Annas' (Edersheim, *The Life and Times of Jesus the Messiah,* Vol. I: 371-372). Although the location is in dispute, Acts 6:12-14 seems to suggest that the re-located court for Sanhedrin remained inside the Temple complex.

167 Josephus, *Antiquities* 20:200. See also Sidney Hoeing, *The Great Sanhedrin* (Bloch Publ. 1953), pp. 208–209.

168 Eusebius, *History of the Church,* 2.23.10–11.

169 Ibid. 2.23.12

170 Ibid. 2.23.13

171 Dan. 7:14; Matt. 26:64; Mark 14:62; Acts 7:55–56

172 Eusebius *History of the Church,* 2.23.14

173 Ibid. 2.23.16

174 Ibid. 2.23.17 While he wrote the account in his *Memoirs* over a hundred year after the event (ca. A.D. 170), Hegesippus' source was probably a family story that goes back to an eye-witness member from the priestly house of Rachab.

175 Eusebius *History of the Church,* 2.23.18a

176   One possible reason why Roman intervention for Paul wasn't repeated for James may have been a byproduct of Festus' death. After learning about the passing of that governor, either the ranking tribune of Caesarea or perhaps even the legate-governor of Syria, the fateful Gnaeus Domitius Corbulo, issued a general order to all garrisons and command posts in Judea, stipulating that until the new governor arrives in the province, no military action shall be initiated unless there is a clear and present threat to Roman interests. Such an order may have caused the senior officers of the Antonia to hesitate in deploying troops once a disturbance in the Temple was known. By the time a Roman detachment was finally on scene to investigate, the fracas was over and the body already removed.

177   Probably, it was from this high roof of the southern galleria, the Ancient Tempter offered Jesus to cast himself down into the Temple court and prematurely reveal himself as the Messiah to the on-looking and astonished crowds (Matt. 4:5–7; Luke 4:9–12). See Edersheim, *Temple*, pg. 38.

178   Eusebius, *History of the Church*, 2.1.5, 2.23.14–16. As to the closing line of Hegesippus' account to James' martyrdom "Immediately after this, Vespasian invaded and took Judea" (Eusebius, *History of the Church*, 2.23.18), and written some one hundred years after said events, should be taken in very loosely. Vespasian was commissioned by Nero to put down the Jewish revolt in the land of Israel in early A.D. 67, some five years after the death of James. That commission was the imperial prime mover leading up to the A.D. 70 destruction of Jerusalem and the Temple by Vespasian's elder son Titus.

179   Josephus, *Antiquities* 20:201–203

180   On the James ossuary box see, Uzi Dahari, *Final Report of the Examining Committees for the Yehoah Inscription and James Ossuary*, Israel Antiquities Authority, www.antiquities.org.il; retrieved 4/20/2015. See also Hershel Shanks of Biblical Archeology Review (*Brother of Jesus Inscription is Authentic!* Biblical Archeology Review, 38:04, July/August, 2012).

181   Josephus, *Wars* 2:14.273

182   Eusebius, *History of the Church*, 3.5.2

183   While Eusebius (likely based on Hegesippus) states the appointment of Symeon was done after the capture of Jerusalem (summer, A.D.70), he also asserts the appointment occurred immediately after the death of James, which took place near Passover of A.D. 62. (Eusebius, *History of the Church*, 3.11.1). More likely, a tentative appointment was made following James' death in A.D. 62, while a more official endorsement took place after the A.D. 70 Destruction.

184   Eusebius, *History of the Church*, 3.1.1–2; 5:10.3. The fates of James b. Alpheus, Simon the Zealot, Phillip, Thaddeus, and Matthias (Judas' replacement), are topics of legend and later on church tradition (see William Steuart McBirnie, *The Search for the Twelve Apostles*, Tyndale House, 1973). While Matthew b.

Alpheus is credited to composing the first Gospel account, what his particular apostolic activities involved remains largely unknown.

185   Eusebius, *History of the Church,* 3.1.1, 23.3–19. Although Irenaeus and Clement of Alexandria (writing ca.A.D.180–190) cite strong and widely held traditions that John was with the Asian churches, such assertions seemingly ring hallow at the silence of Ignatius and his seven letters (ca.A.D.108); three of which are addressed to Asian churches linked to the Revelation (Ephesians, Philadelphians, and Smyrnaeans), and one to Polycarp, bishop of Smyrna, and companion of John. On the other hand, Ignatius may have alluded to John in his letter to the Ephesians. Speaking specifically to the Christians of Ephesus, Ignatius credits them for always being "in agreement with the apostles" (*Ephesians* 11:2). Slightly further down, he mentions Paul in association with the Ephesians (12:2), leaving open the possibility that other of the *apostles* that the church of Ephesus was in personal agreement was indeed John (J.B. Lightfoot, J. R. Harmer [Transl.], and Michael Holmes [Edit], *The Apostolic Fathers*: Second Edition, Baker Books, 1989).

186   Acts 19:1–11; Rev. 2:13.

187   If John was arrested by the Roman provincial government and banished to Patmos, it was probably under the penalizing measure of *relegatio*: banishment for spreading superstitious beliefs. See Ben Witherington, *Revelation: The New Cambridge Bible Commentary* (Cambridge University Press, 2003), pg. 80.

188   The fourth century tradition that the John was banished to a slave mine on Patmos is faulty for two main reasons: **1)** there is no reference to mines in the Revelation. **2)** Archeological evidence for mining on Patmos is lacking - especially since the island was volcanic (Witherington, *Revelation*, pg. 79). Further, the tale of John being taken to Rome and cast into boiling oil, only to survive and be exiled to Patmos, is first recounted by Tertullian (*Exclusion of Heretics* 36; ca.A.D.200). The story is likely based on the fact that John avoided the fate of many Christians during the Nero persecution, where the victim was soaked in oil and set on fire (Tacitus, *Annals* 15:44). See Gentry, *Before Jerusalem Fell* pp. 96–97; Schaff, *History of the Christian Church* Vol. I. pg 428. Lastly, the obscure tradition that the Jews martyred John with James is likely a misread of Acts 12:2–3 (Gentry, *Before Jerusalem Fell*, pp. 92–93).

189   Today, and because of it is out-of-the-way location from the island's more frequent tourist/pilgrim centers, *Psili Ammos* is Patmos' secluded nudist beach (Rev. 16:15).

190   See also Col. 1:26–27; I Tim 3:16; I Pet. 1:9-12; Rev.10:7.

191   Gentry, *Before Jerusalem Fell*, pp. 134–139.

192   *New King Version* ("shortly"); *New Jerusalem Bible* ("very soon"); *New Living Translation* ("soon"), *American Standard Version* ("shortly"); *New Century Version* ("soon"); *Tyndale's New Testament* ("shortly"); *Today's New International Version*

("soon"); *Common English Bible* ("soon"); *J.B. Phillips New Testament* ("very soon"); *New American Standard* ("soon"); *New Revised Standard Version* ("soon"); *Complete* [Messianic] *Jewish Bible* ("very soon"); *Webster Bible* ("shortly"); *Good News Translation* ("very soon"); *God's Word Translation* ("soon"); *Third Millennium Bible* ("shortly"); *Weymouth New Testament* ("shortly"); *The Message* ("about to happen"); *New English Translation* ("very soon"); *Contemporary English Version* ("soon"). John R. Kohlenberger III (General Edit.), *The Evangelical Parallel New Testament* (Oxford, 2003), pp. 1614–1615. Gentry, *Before Jerusalem Fell*, pp. 133–140. See also BibleStudyTools.com, and BibleGateway.com.

[193] Mark 13:28–30; see also Matt. 24:32–34; Luke 21:29–32.

[194] The 'second John' theory was introduced by Dionysius of Alexandria (A.D. 250), endorsed by Eusebius (A.D. 325), and is held by many to this day. Prior to Dionysius, neither Tertullian (A.D. 200), Clement of Alexandria (ca. A.D. 150–ca.200), Justin Martyr (A.D. 100–165), the Muratorian Canon (ca. A.D. 170), or even Irenaeus (A.D. 130–202) ever cite of a second high-profile 'John' in Asia. The ambiguous passage from Papias (ca .A.D. 110; *History of the Church* 3:39.1–7) to justify a second 'John' is far more subjective bark than substantive bite. Instead of two men named John, it is more probable that Papias was speaking of one John, but at two different time periods: the Apostolic Period (A.D. 33–70) and Papias' own day (A.D. 90s). Most likely, the 'second John' theory is a contrived rationalization to insert authorship mileage between the Revelation and the Apostle John, from which the Revelation can arguably be de-canonized as Scripture.

[195] Ex. 33:20; John 1:18; 6:46; 17:5; I John 1:1–2.

[196] Acts 26:23; Rom. 6:4–5; I Cor. 15:20; Col. 1:18.

[197] Matt. 27:22; Mark 15:12–14; Luke 23:21–24; John 19:6, 15.

[198] John 1:1–5,10; Phil. 2:6–11; Heb. 1:1–6, 12:2, 13:8 I John 1:1. See Rev. 3:14.

[199] Gregg, *Four Views of Revelation*, pp. 58–59.

[200] I Pet. 1:6–7; 2:12–17; 3:14–16; 4:4, 12–16; 5:8–9. See Gentry, *Before Jerusalem Fell*, pg. 291; Henderson, *The Life and Principate of the Emperor Nero*, Appendix B, pp. 438–439.

[201] Acts 4:31; 8:17; 10:44; 19:6.

[202] "I am Alpha and Omega, the first and the last" of Rev. 1:11 is lacking in most manuscripts.

[203] There is a body of scholarly opinion that asserts John 21 as a later addition to the Fourth Gospel, and likely by a different author. Although contextual, thematic, linguistic, and vocabulary arguments for a separate author are notable, but not conclusive. On the other hand, textual evidence from manuscripts soundly places John 21 as a fixed and the concluding portion of the Fourth Gospel. See Craig L. Blomberg, *The Historical Reliability of John's Gospel: Issues and Commentary* (InterVarsity Press, 2001), pp. 272–273; D.A. Carson, *The*

Gospel According to John (Eerdmans Publishing, 1991) pp. 665–668; Craig S. Keener, *The Gospel of John: A Commentary, Volume Two* (Hendrickson, 2003), pp. 1219–1224.

204   Blomberg, *The Historical Reliability of John's Gospel*, pg. 279.

205   Matt. 17:2; Mark 9:3; Luke 9:28–29. Like the Olivet Discourse, the Fourth Gospel offers no narrative to the Transfiguration, save for a brief statement where the author declares "and we beheld his glory, the glory as of the only begotten of the Father, full of grace and truth." (John 1:14).

206   Ex. 25; 27:20; 30:8; Lev. 24:1–4; Num. 8:1–4; Edersheim, *The Temple*, pp. 72, 110–112.

207   Is. 49:1–2; Matt. 5:17–20; Eph. 6:17; Heb 4:12.

208   Is. 25; John 6:35-58; 11:25–26; Acts 2:24; Rom. 6; I Cor. 15:50–57.

209   Chilton takes a very interesting view that the seven stars in the hand of Christ could also represent the seven stars of the Pleiades in the Zodiac constellation of Taurus as the sun passed through during the 40-day period of Christ's resurrection on Earth (Acts 1:1–9), and concluded by his Ascension into Heaven (Chilton, *Days of Vengeance*, pg.42).

210   Throughout the Revelation's seven cover letters alone, the Risen Christ repeatedly cites or alludes to Old Testament Scripture (Rev. 2:7 = Gen. 2:9; Rev. 2:8 = Is. 41:4, 44:6, and 48:12; Rev. 2:14 = Num. 31:16; Rev. 2:20 = I Kings 18–21, II Kings 9:7,22; Rev. 2:26–27 = Ps. 2:9; Rev. 3:5 = Ex. 32:32 and Dan. 12:1; Rev. 3:7 = Is. 22–22; Rev. 3:18 = Job 23:10).

211   Gentry, *Before Jerusalem Fell*, pg. 209–212. See also Richard Longenecker, *Biblical Exegesis in the Apostolic Period* (Eerdmans Publishing & Regent College Publishing, 1999.) pg. 175–176.

212   Each of the seven letters have the same general format: Christ commands to write to the angel of said church; he gives a self-described introduction to the church; he commends them for their good works; then admonishes them of a particular sin; he gives exhortation and warning to repent of that sin; he calls on the church hear what the guiding Spirit says to them; Christ concludes with a charge to overcome with a promise of reward to those that do so. However, the format was not absolute. In the case with the letters of the churches of Smyrna and Philadelphia, no admonition of sin, and therefore no call repent, is made. In the grimmer situation with the Christians of Sardis and Laodicea, there was no commendation of good works, but go immediately to admonishment of sin and call to repent. See Hays, Duvall, and Plate, *Dictionary of Biblical Prophecy and End*, pp. 416–424.

213   Though the provincial capital was at Pergamum, the Treasury and Office of Public Records were in Ephesus.

214   In his own letter, Ignatius of Antioch made a similar compliment to the Ephesians some fifty years later (ca. A.D.108; *Ephesians* 7:1–9:1).

215 See also Rom. 14:17–18.

216 Irenaeus, *Against Heresies:* 1.26.3. Hippolytus of Rome (died A.D. 236) held a similar origin story (*Refutation of all Heresies,* 7:24).

217 Eusebius, *History of the Church* 3:29.1–4; Clement, *Miscellanies,* 3.4.25–26.

218 Acts 15:7–11, 13–20, 23–29.

219 Perhaps the Nicolaitans was the Gentile designation (and the religious forbears) for the Ebionites; a breakaway Jewish Christian sect that insisted on the observance of Torah. Eusebius speaks of a similar sect by the same name existing in his own time (A.D. 325; *The History of the Church,* 3:27.1–6).

220 Matt. 11:15; 13:9, 43; Mark 4:9, 23; Luke 8:8; 14:35.

221 Although the general region called *Smyrna* survived, reduced to village status, but the metropolis itself was destroyed and remained so for centuries. Gregg, *Revelation: Four Views,* pp. 66–67.

222 Tacitus, *Annals* 4:15, 55–56; Gregg, *Revelation: Four Views,* pg. 66.

223 Colin J. Hemer, *The Letters to the Seven Churches of Asia in their local setting* (Sheffield Academic, 1986, 1989; Eerdmans 2001), pp. 60–65.

224 Smyrna's other claim to Christian fame was that it was the home church of the Christian martyr Polycarp, who was burnt at the stake in c.A.D.155; *The Martyrdom of Polycarp* 9:1–18:3. On Polycarp's letter to the Philippians and the post-Pauline dating of the church of Smyrna, see Gentry, *Before Jerusalem Fell,* pp. 322–326.

225 Colin J. Hemer, *The Letters of the Seven Churches,* pg. 78, 84–85; Craig Keener, *Revelation: The NIV Application Commentary* (Zondervan, 2000), pg. 123; Witherington, *Revelation,* pg. 102

226 Or "shall be like God" according to *the New King James Version, the New International Version, and the English Standard Version.*

227 Luke 4:6–7 with emphasis added. See also Matt. 4:8–9.

228 Tacitus, *Annals* 4:37; Dio Cassius, *Roman History* 51:20:6–9

229 Hemer, *The Letters of the Seven Churches of Asia,* pg. 84.

230 Ben Witherington III, *Revelation,* pg. 102.

231 Craig Keener, *Revelation: The New Application Commentary* (Zondervan, 2000), pg. 123.

232 The description of "fornication" could apply to either literal sexual immorality, or spiritual indulgence to pagan practices (Craig Keener, *Revelation,* pg. 124).

233 Ex. 16:32–35; Heb. 9:4.

234 See also Matt. 27:51; Mark 15:38; Luke 23:45

235 Gregg, *Revelation: Four Views of Revelation,* pp. 68–70.

236 Rom. 3:23–29; 6:4; II Cor. 5:17; Gal. 6:15.

237 Of the few known historical gems of Thyatira, one of them is Lydia of Acts 16:14–15; a merchant of purple materials, accepted Christ through Paul's ministry during his stay in Philippi.

238 Gregg, *Revelation: Four Views*, pp. 70–71; Hemer, *The Letters to the Seven Churches*, pp. 108–109; Keener, *Revelation: The NIV Application Commentary*, pg. 133; Witherington, *Revelation*, pg. 104.

239 Matt. 22:37–40; Mark 12:29–31; Luke 10:25–28.

240 Although there is no historical reference of a particular calamity befalling Thyatira at the time in question (A.D.64–70), reference to Thyatira itself are very sparse (Hemer, *The Letters to the Seven Churches*, pg.106). Tacitus speaks of great disasters upon the Empire spanning from the death of Nero to Domitian (A.D.68–96; *The Histories*, 1:2). Such being the case, a divine judgment upon Thyatira, in the form of a local catastrophe, may have been historically obscured by the greater disaster striking the Empire. Further, a possible reason for such little reference to Thyatira is that the city may have been view as cursed.

241 Is. 60:1–3; Luke 1:78–79; John 1:5; Eph. 5:14; II Pet. 1:19.

242 See the *Excursus* at the end of *Revelation 13a: Pax Satanica*.

243 Ephesus: the Apostolic Church (A.D.33–70); Smyrna: the Roman persecutions (A.D.70–313); Pergamos: the Constantine State-Church (ca. A.D. 313–500); Thyatira: the Middle Ages (A.D.500–1517AD); Sardis: the Reformation (1517-1700); Philadelphia: the Missionary Church (1700-present); Laodicea: the Last Days (?).

244 Erasmus, More, Luther, Tyndale, Zwingli, Calvin, Henry VIII, Elisabeth I, Knox, Ignatius of Loyola, da Vinci, Xavier, Melanchthon, Michelangelo, Raphael, Copernicus, Galileo, Kepler, and Columbus. Gregg, *Four Views of Revelation*, pp. 62–63.

245 Hemer, *The Letters of the Seven Churches*, pp. 130 and 140.

246 Matt. 23:27. See Luke 11:44.

247 Matt.6:2,5,16; 15:7; 16:3; 22:18; 23:13–15, 23, 25, 27,29; 24:51; Mark 7:6; Luke 11:44; 12:56.

248 I Cor. 13:1–3; Gal. 5:2-6, 25–26; James 2:14–26

249 Herodotus, *The Histories* 1:84 and Polybius, *The Histories* 7:15–18.

250 Sardis' other claim to fame, its' red-dying garment industry, might be alluded to in verses 4 and 5.

251 Tacitus, *Annals* 2:47. Of the twelve Asian cities that were ruined from the 17AD earthquake, and while Sardis was the hardest hit, Philadelphia was among the heavily damaged cities whose tribute was remitted for five years so to finance reconstruction efforts.

252 II Kings 25 1–26; II Chron. 36:17–20; Jer. 52:1–30.

253 II Sam. 7:12–16; Ps. 89; Jer. 23:5–8; Amos 9:11–12; Luke 1:32–33; Rom.1:3–4.

254 In his letter to the Philadelphian church at about A.D. 108, Ignatius of Antioch repeatedly implores them to "flee" divisions, false teachings, and "the evil tricks" of this world (*Philadelphians* 2:1; 6:2; 7:2). While not explicit, these passages

might reflect a previous exodus from Philadelphia by the Faithful during the Nero persecution in the mid-60s.

255 Is. 45:14; 49:23; 60:14.

256 I Cor. 3:16; Eph. 2:19–22; I Pet 2:5.

257 According to manuscript evidence, "my God" is also found in the cover-letter to the church at Sardis (Rev. 3:2).

258 Tacitus, *Annals*, 14:27.

259 See Gregg, *Revelation: Four Views*, pp. 78-79.

260 Col. 1:15–17

261 John 1:1–3. In the New Testament, the Greek "Logos" is directly applied to Christ in John 1:1, 14; I John 1:1, 5:7 (though the textual integrity of this passage is highly questionable), and Rev. 19:13.

262 John Ronning, *The Jewish Targums and John's Logos Theology* (Hendrickson, 2010), pp. 13–24; Green, McKnight, and Marshall *Dictionary of Jesus and the Gospel*, pp. 482, 800–804; Alfred Edersheim, *Life and Times of Jesus the Messiah* (MacDonald Pub.), Vol. I, book 1, chapter 4, pp. 46–48. Though written centuries after the time of Christ, the repeated use of the *Memra* to God in Targums Onkelos (Torah) and Jonathan (Prophets) as reflected in Johannine passages (John 1:1–14;I John 1:1; Rev. 19:13) suggests an underlying theology going back to the First Century AD. See Ronning, *The Jewish Targums and John's Logos Theology*, pg. 51.

263 Hemer, *the Letter of the Seven Churches of Asia*, pg. 186–191.

264 Ibid. pp. 190–191.

265 Is. 60; 64:4; Jer. 31:31–34; Ezek.11:19–20; Dan. 9:24; Joel 2:28–32; Matt. 20:23; 25:34; John 17:2–3; Rom. 16:25–26; I Cor. 2:9 [Is. 64:4]; Eph. 3:3–10; Col. 1:26–27; I Tim 3:16; Heb. 11:16; I Pet. 1:10–12; Rev. 10:7.

266 See Matt. 19:4–6; Mark 10:6–9; Eph. 5:31–32.

267 Depending on geographic orientation, the river flowed "out" of the Garden, and "parted" into four rivers (Gen. 2:10–14). Although two of the four rivers remain unidentified, the remaining pair gives a general location of the Garden: the Tigris-Euphrates river valley of modern-day Iraq.

268 Ezek. 28:12–19; Jam. 3:14–15. On the rabbinical origin stories of Satan, see Alfred Edersheim, *The Life and Times of Jesus the Messiah*, Appendix 13, sec. 2.

269 Gen. 3:1; Matt. 13:18–19; Mark 4:13–15; Luke 8:11–12; John 8:44; II Cor. 11:3, 13–14; I Pet. 5:8.

270 Traditionally, there are two primary points of Scripture that are credited to describe the origins of Satan: Isaiah 14:12–17 and Ezekiel 28:11–19. Ezekiel speaks of Lucifer as the "anointed cherub", indicating an angelic nature, and was corrupted by his own high status and beauty among the Heavenly host (Ezek. 28:16–17a). Isaiah seems to make these the precursors of character to Lucifer's true corruption. Isaiah, speaking through the king of Babylon, states

that Lucifer entertained the desire to "be like the most high" (Is. 14:14), which could indicative to Man and his destiny to the closest to God.

271 In effect, the story of Noah and the Flood (Gen. 6:5–9:17) is God and Satan in dialogue: Satan insisting and proving that Man and his free will had failed God to be his closest and most loved creature, and therefore deserves genocide. God, grieving that Man had so greatly sinned against him, sent the Flood to destroy Man. Nevertheless, God will not revoke his destiny for Man as the creature closest and most loved by him; thus Noah's family, the ark, and the rainbow.

272 Marc-Alain Ouaknin, *Symbols of Judaism* (Assouline Publishing, Barnes & Noble, 2000, 2003), pp. 12–13. See also John H Walton, *The Lost World of Genesis One* (InterVarsity Press, 2009), 53–55.

273 Philo (20 B.C.–A.D.50), *On the Creation* 26, 55, and 60

274 See also David Chilton, *The Days of Vengeance;* Dominion Press, 1987, pg. 124–127, and Fredrick Larson's www.bethlehemstar.net

275 Gen. 12:2–3; 18:18; 22:18; 26:4; Acts 3:25–26; Gal. 3:8–14

276 Luke 4:5–6; John 12:31; 14:30; 16:11.

277 Greek rule over the Jews in the Holy Land, via Alexander, was comparatively brief; lasting some ten years (ca. 332–323 B.C). Following Alexander's death, the succeeding generals split his empire into the three kingdoms of the Ptolemy, Seleucid, Antigonid, plus the Greek province Hellas-Thrace.

278 Ex. 5:1–14:30.

279 II Kings 15:29.

280 II Kings 17:3–6. While Shalmaneser V began the conquest of the northern kingdom of Israel, he died before it was completed. His successor, Sargon II, finished the conquest and ordered the mass deportation of the northern tribes to Assyria (Hosea 1:6).

281 II Kings 18:13–19:37; II Chron. 32:1–22; Is. 36:1–37:38.

282 II Kings 24:10–16; 25:8–21; Jer. 39:1–10; Dan. 1:1.

283 I Macc. 1:10–64; Josephus, *Wars*, 1:31–40.

284 Matt. 2:1–20; Luke 1:5

285 Matt. 2:22; Josephus, *Wars*, 2:1–3

286 Acts 12:1–23.

287 Psalm 110:1; Mark 16:19; Luke 24:51; Acts 1:9–11; 2:33–35; 7:55–56; Heb. 1:1–3.

288 See also Gen 49:10, and Rev. 2:26–27.

289 Is. 61:1–2a; Amos 8:11; Matt. 11:4–6; Luke 4:14–21; 7:22–23; 9:1–2; 10:19–20; 11:28–30; John 3:1–21.

290 John 6:70–71;13:27;14:30

291 291 Isaiah 52:13-53–12; Rom. 5:12; 6:1–23; I John 1:7.

292 John Milton (1608-1674), *Paradise Lost*, book I, line 263.

293 Acts 2:22–24; Rom. 8:33–34; I Tim. 2:5; Heb. 2:9–18; I Pet. 1:9–23 I John 1:7; 2:1–2; 3:8.

294 John 12:31–32

295 John 16:7–12; Rom. 8:34, 14:17–18; I Tim 2:5; Heb. 7:22–28; I John 2:1.

296 John 17:1–5; Heb. 2:14–15; I John 3:8; Rev. 3:21

297 Alfred Edersheim, *The Life and Times of Jesus the Messiah*, Vol. 2, book 5, chapter 17: the closing line of the primary text.

298 Even in symbolic terms, it is highly unlikely that the Dragon-Satan would hope to destroy the Woman with a flood (Rev. 12:15) *after* she acquired eagles' wings to fly (Rev. 12:14). Therefore, the Woman attaining wings for flight (the Jewish Church quickly departing from Jerusalem) is re-sequenced after the earth swallowed the Satan-spawned flood (Rev. 12:16); Gospel message going out from Jerusalem, across the land of Israel and the Gentiles countries, despite lethal persecution.

299 Acts 9:23–25; 14:4–7, 19; 16:22–24; 19:23–41; I Cor. 4:10–14; II Cor. 11:23–33; I Thess. 2:2, 14–16.

300 Josephus, *Antiquities*, 20:200–201.

301 Acts 10:1–11:18, 15:13–35, 21:17–20, 25; Gal. 2:7–9.

302 Tacitus, *Annals* 15:44. Involving the powerful imagery of Jean-Leon Gerome's painting, *The Christian Martyrs' Last Prayer*, there is tenuous historical support to the notion that the Christians of Nero's Rome were fed to the lions. Both Clement and Tacitus are silent on the subject as is Suetonius. On the other hand, II Timothy 4:17, I Peter 5:8, and Revelation 13:2 may suggest a manner of Christian martyrdom involving lions. In connection, Ignatius' letter to the Romans (4:1–2; ca. A.D.108), while speaking of his approaching death, maybe alluding to lions, though the reference is not specific.

303 I Peter 4:17–18; 5:8–11.

304 As in the case with Pastoral Letters, even if the second epistle wasn't from Peter, it would still represent early church tradition on the final days of the Great Fisherman in concert with John 21:18–19.

305 As rendered in other versions (*New International Version, English Standard Version, American Standard Version,* and *New Century Version*), Rev. 13:1 describes "he", the Dragon, standing on the beach rather than John. See Gregg, *Revelation: Four Views*, pg. 276.

306 Interestingly, John discloses the prophetic animal features of the beast in reverse order from Daniel 7:3–7. After indicating the beast has ten horns (Rev 13:1 = Dan. 7:7), the beast was like a leopard (Rev. 13:2 = Dan. 7:6), with the feet of a bear (Rev. 13:2 = Dan. 7:5), and the mouth of a lion (Rev. 13:2 = Dan. 7:4). Evidently, when describing the beast, John begins from his own time and proceeded backwards into history, thereby making Rome as a world-empire heir to Babylon.

307 C. Marvin Pate, *Community of the Last Days* (Inter-Varsity Press, 2000), pg. 24–26. In those moments when Jewish independence or autonomy became a reality, it always came in the form of an anti-David usurper (Maccabees, Herods, and Bar-Kochba).

308 Although the murder of Galba in the Rome's Forum in January of A.D. 69 violently marked the start of a whole year of civil war for the Roman Empire (popularly called 'the Long Year' or 'The Year of the Four Emperors'), the assassination of Julius Caesar was the prime mover to set off twelve years of such political/military unrest.

309 Livy, *Roman History* 116; Plutarch, *Parallel Lives: Caesar* 66:4–14; Appian, *Roman History: Civil Wars* 2:16:117; Suetonius, *Twelve Caesars: Julius Caesar* 81:1–82:3; Dio Cassius, *Roman History* 44:19:1–5

310 Livy, *History of Rome* book 117; Appian, *Roman History: Civil Wars* 3:2:11; Suetonius, *Twelve Caesars: Augustus* 7:2; Dio Cassius, *Roman History* 45:3:2

311 Livy, *History of Rome* book 120; Plutarch, *Parallel Lives: Cicero* 46:2; Appian, *Roman History: The Civil Wars* 4:1:1–3; Suetonius, *The Twelve Caesars: Augustus* 8:3; Dio Cassius, *Roman History* 46:54:1–56:1. The first Triumvirate was in 60BC between Marcus Crassus, Pompey, and Julius Caesar.

312 Livy, *History of Rome* book 120; Plutarch, *Parallel Lives: Cicero* 46:2; Appian, *Roman History: The Civil Wars* 4:2:5–11

313 Dio Cassius, *Roman History* 51:17:1–3

314 Livy, *History of Rome* book 133; Suetonius, *Twelve Caesars: Augustus* 22:1; Dio Cassius, *Roman History* 51:21:1–9.

315 Livy, *History of Rome* book 134; Suetonius, *Twelve Caesars: Augustus* 7:2; Dio Cassius, *Roman History* 53:12:1–9

316 Livy, *Roman History* 116; Suetonius, *Twelve Caesars: Julius* 79:1–2; Plutarch, *Parallel Live: Caesars* 60:1–61:6; Appian, *Roman History: Civil Wars* 2:16:108–109; Dio Cassius, *Roman History* 44:11:1–3

317 In a story shared by Suetonius and echoed by Dio Cassius, just prior to Augustus' death in A.D.14, lightening struck one his statues in Rome and melted the "C" (the numerical equivalent for 100) in the name 'Caesar', leaving only the spelling 'aesar', which in ancient Etruscan was the word for "god". The prevailing interpretation to this perceived portent was that Augustus had only 100 days to live, and after be officially recognized as a god in Rome. Suetonius, *Twelve Caesars: Augustus* 97:2; Dio Cassius, *Roman History* 56:29:4.

318 Appian, *Roman History: Civil Wars* 2:16:106; Dio Cassius, *Roman History* 43:45:2–3; 44:4:4

319 Suetonius, *Twelve Caesars: Augustus* 52:1; Dio Cassius, *Roman History* 51:20:6– 9

320 Philo, *On the Embassy to Gaius* 149–150

In the Roman practice of Caesar-worship, devotionals were offered to the emperor in the capacity of his *genius;* the family or ancestral spirit of a man

170

who oversees his life, prosperity, and descendants. By offering homage to the 'genius' of Caesar meant that the emperor and the imperial family would endure and have a prosperous reign. However, the worship of Caesar's genius provided a ceremonial loop-hole for the worship of the emperor in Rome while he was alive. Lily Ross Taylor, *The Divinity of the Roman Emperor* (Scholars Press, 1931 reprint), pp. 181–204.

321 Tacitus, *Annals* 4:37; Dio Cassius, *Roman History* 51:20:6–9. Nearly all the cities in of Asia were home to the Imperial Cult via temple, altar, or priesthood. Of all the provinces, Asia was the most receptive for Caesar-worship See Hemer, *the Letters to the Seven Churches of Asia* pp. 84; Witherington, *Revelation* pg. 23–24; 184, footnote #305.

322 Josephus, *Wars of the Jews* 1:408–414; *Antiquities of the Jews* 15:331–339

323 Bunson, *Dictionary of the Roman Empire*, pp. 96–97; Edward N. Luttwak, *The Grand Strategy of the Roman Empire from the First Century to the Third* (John Hopkins University Press, 1976, 1979), pp. 20–40.

324 Josephus, *Wars* 3:68

325 Tacitus *Annals*, 13:7

326 Bunson, *Dictionary of the Roman Empire*, pg. 58; Luttwak, *The Grand Strategy of the Roman Empire*, pg. 20.

327 Ibid.

328 Josephus, *Antiquities* 19:276

329 While the Herodian kingdom of Agrippa II could be viewed as one of the many client states of Syria but for the fact that Herod Agrippa II had the power to appoint and remove the High Priest in Jerusalem (Josephus, *Antiquities* 20:179, 203–223). Such features an authority independent of the many vassal states and territories within the Syrian province.

330 Suetonius, *Nero* 18:1

331 Tacitus, *Annals* 13:7

332 Although officially a Roman province, Syria was also one large cache of client states and territories, including Emesa, Abilene, and the oasis city-state of Palmyra that bordered Parthia. Of the many vassal regions, Pliny the Elder counted 17 inside the province (*Natural History*, 5:81ff). See also Luttwak, *The Grand Strategy of the Roman Empire* pg. 20.

333 Ibid.

334 Bunson, *Dictionary of the Roman Empire*, pp. 58 and 116; Miriam Griffin, *Nero: The End of a Dynasty* (Yale University Press, 1985) pg. 228; Henderson, *The Life and Principate of the Emperor Nero*, pg. 226; pg. 480, note for pg. 226.

335 Suetonius, *Nero* 18:1. While Nero annexed the western kingdom of the Cottaen Alps in A.D. 58, the status of that kingdom was unique. Allowed to rule by Augustus sometime after 8BC, king Cottus also took on the Roman title of *Prefect*, meaning that Cottus was "king" to his own subjects, but to the Romans,

and for that matter everyone else, he was a Roman administrator ruling a prefecture. After Cottus' death and the reign of his son, Nero merely dropped the official titles declared the "kingdom" an outright Roman province (Marcel Le Glay, Jean-Louis Voisin, Yann Le Bohec, *A History of Rome*, [Blackwell Publishers, 1996] pp. 213–214); Luttwak, *The Grand Strategy of the Roman Empire*, pp. 39–40; Scullard, *From Gracchi to Nero*, pg. 255.

336 Josephus, *Wars*, books 3.110–4:439

337 Despite its' popularity in modern End-Times pop culture, the designation "Anti-Christ" is wholly absent in the book of Revelation. Though found in the letters of John (I John 2:18; 2:22; 4:3; II John 7), it may be represented in the Olivet Discourse under the term "false Christs" (Matt. 24:24; Mark 13:22).

338 One of the better historical snapshots of the Imperial Cult during the Nero years took place in the fall of A.D.63 at the Rhandeia truce ceremony between Rome and Parthia over the disputed kingdom of Armenia. During the formal procedures, prince Tiradates, king-designate of Armenia and younger brother of the Parthian king Vologases, approached a statue of Nero before a large contingent of Roman and Parthian troops. Before the image, he made the standard sacrifice offering, took off his crown, and place at the feet of the statue. As agreed by both sides, once placing it before the image, Tiradates vowed never to take it up again until Nero himself placed on his head at a grand coronation in the Roman forum; Nero crowing him as king of Armenia in front of the whole city. Tacitus, *Annals* 15:29.

339 Tacitus, *Annals*, 14:15; Suetonius, *Nero* 20:3 and 53:1; Dio Cassius, *Roman History*, book 61.20:1–5.

340 Tacitus, *Annals* 16:22; Suetonius, *Nero* 53:1; Dio Cassius *Roman History* 62:26:3

341 Acts 2:1–21; I Cor. 3:16–17; 6:19–20; II Cor. 6:16; Eph. 1:12–14; I John 4:15

342 Along with Caesarea, Herod also built temples to Rome-Augustus in Sabaste of Samaria, and Panium, later to be called Caesarea Philippi (Josephus, *Wars* 1:21.403–407; *Antiquities* 15:10.363–364).

343 Matt. 11:15; 13:9, 43; Mark 4:9; 23; 7:16; Luke 8:8; 14:35; Rev. 2:7, 11, 17, 29; 3:6, 13, 22

344 Suetonius, *Claudius* 2:1

345 Although Josephus' account of Herod Agrippa's death (*Antiquities* 19:8.343–350) generally matches with Luke's (Acts 12:19–23), there are independent details in each account that supplement the other. See Hemer, *Book of Acts in the Setting of Hellenistic History*, pp. 165–166.

346 Irenaeus, *Against Heresies* 5.30.1–3. From *Anti-Nicene Fathers* Vol. I by Philip Schaff (edit), provided by the Christian Classics Ethereal Library (ccel.org)

347 Eusebius, *History of the Church* 5:20:4–7

348 While Robinson regarded the linguistic argument "very dubious" (*Redating the New Testament*, pg. 221), Gentry deems it crucial in challenging validity for the

Irenaeus' passage (*Before Jerusalem Fell*, pp. 47–59). Nonetheless, both Robinson and Gentry note that Irenaeus describing those who saw John "face-to-face" could have learned of the correct number-name of the beast, thereby making for a contextual argument that John "was seen", not the Revelation, "towards the end of Domitian's reign" (*Redating the New Testament*, pp.. 221–222, note #5; *Before Jerusalem Fell*, pp. 51-52). In addition, when defending the number-name of the beast as being 666, Irenaeus cites "the most ancient" copies of Revelation validate the 666 sum. It is odd that Irenaeus would describe "the most ancient" copies of a document that originated almost in his own time.

349 Written at about A.D. 95 (the last full year of Domitian's reign) *I Clement* was addressed to the Corinthian church over certain issues arising in that congregation. That *I Clement* 1:1 and 7:1 should be linked to a Domitian-era persecution is both subjective and overrated. However, Clement was well aware of the martyrdoms of Peter and Paul, which Church tradition indisputably links to the Nero persecution (Eusebius *History of the Church*, 2:25:1-5), including "a vast multitude of the elect" who joined them in martyrdom (*I Clement* 5:1–6:1); such is generally corroborated by Tacitus' description of the Nero persecution (*Annals* 15:44). See Bruce, *New Testament History*, pg. 412.

350 In his letter to the *Romans*, written at about A.D.108, and though he speaks of his own coming martyrdom (and perhaps too proudly; *Romans* 4:1–5:3), Ignatius cites the apostle-martyrs of Peter and Paul during the Nero persecution forty years prior (*Romans* 4:3). Yet, the condemned bishop of Antioch never betray any knowledge of a more recent and deadly attack on the Church by Domitian, whose reign ended some twelve years earlier.

351 Pliny the Younger, *Letters* 10:96– 97. See Bruce, *New Testament History*, pg. 412

352 Pliny, *Letters* 58, 65, 66, and 72.

353 Eusebius, *History of the Church* 3:19:1–20.7. Also from Hegesippus (through Eusebius), a hunt for Davidic Jews was initiated by Vespasian after the A.D.70 Destruction (Eusebius, *History of the Church*, 3:12:1). Such continued under Domitian (3:19:1), and on into the Trajan years; specifically, the Judea governorship of Atticus in ca. A.D.104 (3:32:3–6). Since Jesus was a known Davidic Jew (Matt. 1:1–17; Luke 1:31–33, 67–69; Acts 2:22–32; Rom. 1:3; II Tim. 2:8; Rev. 22:16), such may have been probable cause for Domitian to start an aggressive investigation, which included the arrest, incarceration, and interrogation of Christians.

354 Tertullian, *Defense of the Faith* 5; Eusebius, *History of the Church* 3:20:7

355 Ibid. 4:26:9. From Melito's Asian perspective, such anti-Christian charges might have been the extent of direct imperial involvement against the churches in the senatorial province of Asia during the reigns of both Caesars In Nero's case, the charge against the Christians was arson; with Domitian, Christians worshipped a Davidic Jew as a king coming to defeat Rome.

356 Suetonius, *Domitian* 8:1

357 Robinson, *Redating the New Testament*, pg. 233; Chilton, *Days of Vengeance*, pg. 16. While Eusebius speaks of the exile of Flavia Domitilla, the niece of Flavius Clemens who was consul in A.D. 95 and both of whom were related to Domitian, on the charge of being a Christian (*History of the Church* 3:18:4) no such Christian detail is found in Suetonius' account, though he mentions the execution of Clemens Domitian (*Domitian* 15:1). According to Dio Cassius' account (*Roman History* 67:14:1–3), Clemens was executed and Domitilla exiled to Pandateria, but on the charge of "atheism", which could refer to an adherence to the Christian faith. However, Dio adds that such a charge referred persons who "drifted into Jewish ways". Whether this refers to Christianity is debatable, but it could also speak of those who converted to Judaism, but in secret in order to avoid the Roman tax on Jews (Suetonius, *Domitian* 12:2). If so, then the essential charge against Clemens and Domitilla was tax evasion. Add the fact they were relatives of Domitian, such would have been a public scandal.

358 Ibid. 16:1–17:3

359 Ibid. *Nero* 47:1–49:4

360 For documented arguments for a pre-A.D.70 composition of the book of Revelation, and to the alleged dating of the Revelation to the mid-90s by Irenaeus, see Kenneth L. Gentry Jr., *Before Jerusalem Fell*, and John A.T. Robinson, *Redating the New Testament*, pp. 221–253.

361 Josephus, *Against Apion* 2:76–77

362 Josephus, *Antiquities* 18:1.23

363 Unless a special courier was dispatched from Italy, news of Nero's persecution of the Christians likely came by way of Jewish pilgrims from Rome to Jerusalem for either the feast of Tabernacles (September, A.D. 64), or the Passover/feast of Unleavened Bread the following spring in A.D. 65.

364 364 The direct association of the Jerusalem temple to the Messianic Advent is illustrated in the Gospel accounts of the Temptation. Satan leads Jesus up to the Jerusalem Temple so to prematurely revel himself as the Messiah by descending into the sanctuary courts for all to see (Matt. 4:5–7; Luke 4:9–12). Further, Jewish expectation from rabbinical literature describes a scene where the Messiah is standing on the roof of the temple and declares to Israel that the time of redemption had arrived (Midrash: Pesikta Rabbati 36). If the oral tradition behind this passage dates back to the late Second Temple period, it further adds to an association of a standing Jerusalem temple with a general expectation of the coming Messiah. See Brad H. Young, *Jesus the Jewish Theologian*, Hendrickson, 1995, pp. 30–33.

365 According to Edersheim, these leased out zones in the Temple courts were the infamous "bazaars of the sons of Annas" as spoken by Talmud rabbis (*The Life and Times of Jesus the Messiah*, Vol. I: 371–372). However, the location of these

bazaars is in dispute; one other possibility being the Mount of Olives (Brown, *Death of the Messiah* Vol. I. pg. 348–350, Abrl-Doubleday, 1994). On the other hand, Jesus may have been employing a family themed pun in calling the Temple "my Father's house", and 'the bazaars of the sons of Annas' as the "house of merchandise" located in the Sanctuary courts (John 2:16). In addition, while citing Isaiah 56:7, that Jesus describes the temple as "of all nations the house of prayer" (Mark 11:17), then citing Jeremiah 7:11, he charges the Jerusalem establishment of turning the Sanctuary into a "den of thieves". Such suggests that Jesus was referring to the porches of the outer court of the Gentiles; most notably the grand galleria at the very southern end of that court.

[366] This *first* cleansing of the Temple is placed at A.D. 30AD during the first Passover pilgrimage of his ministry, and where Jesus declared to rebuild a destroyed temple in three days (John 2:13–17). Three years later, Jesus repeated the Temple cleansing at his final Passover prior to the Passion (Matt. 21:12–13; Mark 11:15–18; Luke 19:45–46), effectually bookending his Passover-to-Passover ministry with *two* cleansings of the Temple. See Jack Finegan, *Handbook of Biblical Chronology* (Hendrickson, 1964, 1999), pp. 346–349; *Dictionary of Jesus and the Gospels*, Editors Joel Green, Scot McKnight, I Howard Marshall (Inter-Varsity Press, 1992) pg. 119; Harold Hoehner, *Chronological Aspects of the Life of Christ* (Academie-Zondervan, 1977), pp. 38–43.

[367] Dated to the late first or early second century AD, and probably penned by a Jewish Christian, the so-called *Epistle of Barnabas* (16:1–5) seems to be preserving a memory of some kind of great apostasy, wide spread deception, involving the Jerusalem Temple that plagued Israel in the time leading up to the 70AD Destruction. See Lightfoot, Harmer, and Holmes, *The Apostolic Fathers* (Second Edit.), pg 183.

[368] See also Matt. 16:4; Mark 8:12; and Luke 11:29.

[369] Josephus, *Antiquities* 20:201–203.

[370] The whole episode at Mount Carmel with the prophet Elijah (I Kings 18:30–39) is generally consistent the symbolism of the second beast causing fire down from heaven to represent a burnt-offering. Hence making the profaned Jerusalem Temple of the Nero sacrilege the False Prophet antithesis to the Mount Carmel episode of Elijah; a true prophet of God.

[371] Suetonius, *Twelve Caesars: Nero*, 31:1; Pliny the Younger, *Natural History*, 34:45; Dio Cassius, *Roman History* 65:15:1.

[372] Philo, *On the Embassy to Gaius* 23:157; 40:317; Josephus, *Wars of the Jews* 2.10:197

[373] Josephus, *Against Apion* 2:76–77. One possible reason why payment for the imperial offering was transferred from the Romans to the Jews may have been a gesture of gratitude by the Jews toward Poppaea Sabina, Nero's second wife from A.D. 62 to 65, who was seeming sympathetic to the Jews and interceded

for them on certain occasions (Josephus, *Antiquities* 20.8:189–195; *Life* 13). Although Schurer is skeptical of Josephus' claim that the Nation paid for the daily Imperial offering, he does grant that the Nation did pay for other sacrifices on the emperor's behalf "on special occasions". Emil Schurer, *A History of the Jewish People in Time of Jesus Christ*, (T.T Clark: Edinburgh (1890); Hendrickson reprint (2008); second division, Vol. I pp. 303-304.

374   Matthew 24:24–25; Mark 13:22–23

375   Witherington, *Revelation*, pg. 184.

376   Miriam T. Griffin, *Nero: The End of a Dynasty*, pg. 120.

377   David W. MacDowall, *The Western Coinages of Nero* (The American Numismatic Society, 1979), coin plate # (A.D. 64-66; reverse side) 22, 23, (A.D. 63) 185, 186, 261 (A.D. 64), 200, 205, 207, 272, 276, 490, 493(1), 494, 496 (A.D. 65), 225, (A.D. 67) 238, 240, pp. 157–205, plates I–XV. Coins from Nero's reign are credited as the best in artistic quality, and that Nero may have taken a direct part in creating such quality (Griffin, *Nero*, pp.119–120). See also Scullard, *From Gracchi to Nero*, note # 21 to pg. 308; Jurgen Malitz, *Nero* (Blackwell Publishing Ltd., 1999), pg. 43.

378   The only other place in Scripture where six-hundred and sixty-six is found is the amount of gold talents king Solomon acquired in one year (I Kings 10:14–29), thereby setting an Old Testament foreshadow in attaching the number to money and commerce, and contemporary to a generation of Israel witnessing the construction of the Temple (I Kings 6:1; II Chron. 3:1).

379   The use of converting letters to numbers and adding them to create a number-name was quite known in the first century AD Roman world as evidenced in excavated graffiti-writing found at Pompeii and dated no later than 79AD. Further, a Greek-based number-name lampoon of Nero in reference to murdering his mother circulated during his reign (Suetonius, *Twelve Caesars: Nero*, 39:2. See also Gentry, *Before Jerusalem Fell*, pg. 194).

In some manuscripts of Revelation, and dating to the second century, the Beast's number is 616 rather than the more familiar 666. Irenaeus of Lyon was aware of this number variant, but still insisted that the "most ancient" and reliable manuscripts adhered to 666 sum as do the majority of manuscripts. Irenaeus offers no explanation on how this discrepancy arose (Irenaeus, *Against Heresies* 5:30.1–3). One plausible answer may be that second century Christian scribes switched the phonetic "Nero Caesar", which totaled to 666 in Hebrew/Aramaic *(Nrwn Qsr)*, to the Latin *(Nrw Qsr)*, thus dropping the final *nun*, which equaled 50. By doing so, the number was brought down to the sum of 616. Even so, this switch of the phonetic format from Semitic to Latin remains consistent that both 666 and 616 were keyed on the name *Nero Caesar* (Gentry, *Before Jerusalem Fell*, pp. 201–203).

INDEX

Printed in the United States
By Bookmasters